BIG MONEY CRIME

KITTY CALAVITA

HENRY N. PONTELL

ROBERT H. TILLMAN

UNIVERSITY OF CALIFORNIA PRESS

FRAUD AND POLITICS IN

THE SAVINGS AND

LOAN CRISIS

BERKELEY   LOS ANGELES   LONDON

The research reported here was funded by grants from
the University of California, Irvine, and the National
Institute of Justice, United States Department of Justice
(90-IJ-CX-0059). Points of view expressed in this book
are those of the authors and do not necessarily represent
the official position of the United States Department of
Justice.

University of California Press
Berkeley and Los Angeles, California

University of California Press, Ltd.
London, England

Library of Congress Cataloging-in-Publication Data

Calavita, Kitty.
Big money crime : fraud and politics in the savings and
loan crisis / Kitty Calavita, Henry N. Pontell, Robert H.
Tillman.
p.   cm.
Includes bibliographical references (p.) and index.
ISBN 0-520-20856-0 (cloth : alk.paper)
1. Savings and loan associations—Corrupt practices—
United States.   2. Savings and Loan Bailout, 1989–
3. Commercial crimes—United States.   I. Pontell,
Henry N., 1950–   .   II. Tillman, Robert.   III. Title.
HG2151.C35   1997
364.16'8—dc21   96-53295
                                            CIP

Printed in the United States of America
9 8 7 6 5 4 3 2 1

For our parents
and to the memory of Michelle Smith-Pontell

"We built thick vaults; we have cameras;
we have time clocks on the vaults; we
have dual control—all these controls
were to protect against somebody
stealing the cash. Well, you can steal
far more money, and take it out the
back door. *The best way to rob a
bank is to own one.*"

in U.S. Congress, House Committee
on Government Operations,
*Combatting Fraud, Abuse, and Misconduct
in the Nation's Financial Institutions*

CONTENTS

TABLES

ACKNOWLEDGMENTS

The research leading to this book would not have been possible without the interest and support of many people. We would like to thank the Committee on Research of the Academic Senate at the University of California, Irvine, without whose initial grant support this work might never have been accomplished. This award was followed by more substantial funding from the National Institute of Justice of the U.S. Department of Justice (Grant 90-IJ-CX-0059). We greatly appreciate the support and help of the institute's staff, especially Lois Mock, our grant manager, who assisted us in numerous ways during a particularly sensitive time in Washington, D.C. We also thank the various individuals in the Department of Justice (Executive Office of the U.S. Attorneys and the Criminal Division) who supplied us with information.

In our three years of fieldwork we had personal contacts with hundreds of people with special expertise on and inside experience with the S&L scandal. We gratefully acknowledge the many people, to whom we promised confidentiality, who granted us lengthy interviews and freely shared their time. A number of government agencies were particularly helpful. We especially want to thank officials and staff at the Resolution Trust Corporation in Washington, D.C., Tampa, Dallas, Houston, and Costa Mesa in Orange

County, California; the FBI in Washington, D.C., Los Angeles, Dallas, Houston, and Miami; the U.S. Attorneys in Fort Worth and Los Angeles; the Treasury Department; the U.S. General Accounting Office in Washington, D.C.; the Secret Service in Washington, D.C., Miami, Dallas, and Houston; the Office of Thrift Supervision in Washington, D.C., San Francisco, and Dallas; the Federal Reserve in Washington, D.C.; the Office of the Comptroller of the Currency; and the congressional staff of the House and Senate Banking committees. More often than not we found government officials who were interested in our research and eager to help us. We sincerely hope that we have done justice to their efforts on our behalf. Special thanks go to officials at the Resolution Trust Corporation and the Dallas Office of Thrift Supervision for providing us with invaluable statistical data.

Among those we wish to acknowledge by name, special recognition goes to William (Bill) Black, formerly of the San Francisco Office of Thrift Supervision and now a professor in the LBJ School of Public Affairs at the University of Texas. Professor Black assisted us in numerous ways, challenged many of our positions, and provided unique insights into the thrift debacle. He played a major historical role in bringing this dark chapter in American history to an end and shared with us his extensive insider knowledge. We greatly appreciate his support and value him as a close colleague and friend.

We thank our colleagues Gil Geis, Paul Jesilow, Bill Chambliss, Nancy Reichman, John Braithwaite, Neal Shover, Otto Reyer, and Rick Jerue for their special insights and support. Our graduate research assistant, Susan Will, was invaluable. Susan's organizational skills, scholarly attitude, and sheer endurance greatly facilitated the timely completion of this work, and we appreciate her devotion to the task. We are also grateful to our undergraduate assistants Kelly Lane, Steven Rennie, Niaz Kasravi, Shadi Sepehrband, Glenda Pimentel, Jade Wheatley, Sunny Lee, Betty Gonzalez, and Dave Sze-keres.

Finally, the staff of the School of Social Ecology at the University of California, Irvine, assisted us in many ways. We especially thank Judy Omiya of the Department of Criminology, Law, and Society for handling project matters, appointments, and clerical tasks in her usual efficient manner. We also thank Dianne Christianson, who assisted us with various word processing tasks and made up for our frequent lapses in technological know-how.

ABBREVIATIONS

ACC American Continental Corporation
ADC Acquisition, development, and construction
AP Associated Press
ARMs Adjustable rate mortgages
CDs Certificates of deposit
CDSL California Department of Savings and Loans
CPAs Certified public accountants
DCCC Democratic Congressional Campaign Committee
DIDMCA Depository Institutions Deregulation and Monetary Control Act
EOUSA Executive Office of the U.S. Attorneys
FBI Federal Bureau of Investigation
FDIC Federal Deposit Insurance Corporation
FHLB Federal Home Loan Bank
FHLBB Federal Home Loan Bank Board (Bank Board)
FIRREA Financial Institutions Reform, Recovery and Enforcement Act
FSLIC Federal Savings and Loan Insurance Corporation
GAAP Generally accepted accounting principles
GAO (U.S.) General Accounting Office
ICS Indictments, convictions, and sentences

LTOB   Loans to one borrower
LTV   Loan-to-value (ratio)
NCFIRRE   National Commission on Financial Institution
          Reform, Recovery and Enforcement
OLS   Ordinary least squares
OMB   Office of Management and Budget
ORA   Office of Regulatory Activities
OTS   Office of Thrift Supervision
PACS   Political action committees
RAP   Regulatory accounting principles
RTC   Resolution Trust Corporation
SEC   Securities and Exchange Commission
S&L   Savings and loan
TIMS   Thrift Information Management System

INTRODUCTION

The savings and loan crisis of the 1980s was one of the worst financial disasters of the twentieth century. The estimated cost to taxpayers, not counting the interest payments on government bonds sold to finance the industry's bailout, is $150 to $175 billion. If interest over the next thirty years is added to this tab, the cost approaches $500 billion.[1]

The savings and loan debacle involved a series of white-collar crimes unparalleled in American history. Numerous journalistic accounts and dozens of popular books, as well as authoritative pronouncements by economists and thrift industry consultants, have already appeared. One might wonder what more needs to be said. We believe a different approach is in order, as a number of myths have come to permeate popular understandings of the S&L scandal. Too often, for example, economists and financial experts have attributed the disaster to faulty business decisions or business risks gone awry. We argue instead that deliberate insider fraud was at the very center of the disaster. Furthermore, we contend that systematic political collusion—not just policy error—was a critical ingredient in this unprecedented series of frauds.

Following the tradition of research on white-collar crime by Edwin Sutherland and others, we examine not just the scope and scale of the fraud but also the government's response to these corporate offenders. The popular press, with its unwavering eye for the sensational, has covered the prosecution, imprisonment, and recent release of high-profile suspect Charles Keating. The reality, however, is that the vast majority of savings and loan wrongdoers will never be prosecuted, much less sent to prison.

Finally, we argue that the kind of financial crime evident in the S&L crisis differs substantially from the typical corporate crime in the industrial sector. Such traditional corporate crimes as price-fixing or occupational safety and health violations are committed on behalf of the corporation and enhance profits, at the expense of workers and consumers. In contrast, the savings and loan crimes decimated the industry itself and brought the American financial system to the brink of disaster. This victimization of thrift institutions by their own management for personal gain, the existence of networks of co-conspirators with influential political connections, and other aspects of thrift fraud suggest a greater similarity to organized crime than to traditional corporate crime.[2]

With the current transformation of the global financial system, the nature of white-collar crime is changing too. The French economist and Nobel Prize-winner Maurice Allais has called the new finance capitalism a "casino" economy.[3] Profits in this casino economy are made from speculative ventures designed to bring windfall profits from clever bets. In contrast to industrial capitalism, profits no longer depend on the production and sale of goods; instead, in finance capitalism, profits increasingly come from "fiddling with money."[4] Corporate takeovers, currency trading, loan swaps, land speculation, futures trading—these are the "means of production" of finance capitalism.

The proliferation of finance capitalism has created new opportunities for white-collar crime, as the amount that can be reaped from financial fraud is limited only by one's imagination. But there is another way in which the new economic structure encourages fraud, or at least fails to discourage it: unconstrained by long-term investments in the infrastructure of production (unlike their counterparts in manufacturing), perpetrators of financial fraud have little to lose by their reckless behavior. Their main concern is to make it big quickly, before the inevitable collapse. The repercussions of the rise of finance capitalism for both criminological theory and responsible policy making are substantial. We explore these repercussions and make modest—but no less urgent—recommendations for the prevention of future fraud-driven debacles.

THE SEARCH FOR RELIABLE DATA

In the late 1980s, as the savings and loan disaster was finally coming to public attention, members of Congress and the media urged more decisive action to bring the culprits to justice. Mounting evidence of massive frauds involving the loss of billions of dollars provoked an angry public to demand answers to tough questions: Who stole all the money? Why aren't they in prison? How much of the money can we get back? Government officials often pleaded ignorance, claiming they did not have adequate information to answer these questions.

This was not entirely an evasive tactic. While the federal government has spent billions of dollars developing sophisticated reporting systems to monitor street crime, there are virtually no comparable sets of data on far more costly suite crime. In the 1940s Edwin Sutherland explained that members of the lower class were overrepresented in official crime statistics because those statistics did not include economic crimes committed by high-status individuals in the course of doing business.[5] Some fifty years later we still lack systematic information on the nature of white-collar crime, as well as official reporting and tracking procedures designed to capture its incidence or the government's response.

To construct a reliable and detailed picture of S&L fraud and its prosecution, we were forced to start virtually from scratch. In addition to secondary sources such as government documents, regulators' reports, and other published accounts of the crisis, we gathered two sorts of primary data—interviews with key officials and statistical information on the government's prosecution effort. We interviewed 105 government officials involved in policy making, regulation, prosecution, and/or enforcement, both in Washington, D.C., and in field offices around the country, where investigation and prosecution take place. Our unstructured, open-ended conversations were a rich source of information about government procedure and practice. They also revealed a great deal about officials' perceptions of the crisis and the impact of these perceptions on decision making.[6]

Our statistical data proved indispensable for accurate estimates of the scale and scope of savings and loan crime and for deciphering the government's response. Although when we began this study there were no reliable data sources either to measure criminal activity in the industry or to track the many new criminal cases, this situation changed as public concern over the crisis and its price tag mounted. Pressures from many quarters, including Congress, forced federal agencies to develop computerized data systems to assess the dimensions of the problem and the government's response. We were able to gain access to this information, but only after extensive, and sometimes contentious, negotiations with officials at these agencies.

Some of the federal agency data sets were outdated, contained little information, or even failed to include important data, so that they were of no practical value. In the end we concentrated on data from three agencies: the Resolution Trust Corporation (RTC), the Office of Thrift Supervision (OTS), and the Executive Office of the U.S. Attorneys (EOUSA). These agencies had extensive computerized records on thrift fraud, but each focused on agency-specific interests—for example, regulators recorded criminal referrals, and prosecutors kept track of indictments, convictions, and sentences. By carefully reconciling and integrating these disparate data sets, we can now provide a more comprehensive picture of the response to thrift fraud.

Of course, the picture is far from complete, and the data are inevitably imperfect. We can never be sure how much crime went undetected, and there is no way to be certain that the cases that did come to light were representative. While this is a concern in all criminological research, the problem is particularly acute for white-collar crime, where fraud is often disguised within ordinary business transactions and elaborate paper trails cover offenders' tracks.

Further, unlike such immediately recognizable common crimes as armed robbery, white-collar crimes of the sort that plagued the thrift industry are often apparent only after careful investigation and detective work.[7] In a typical case of street crime, investigators start with a report that a crime has been committed, and the question they address is, Who did it? In contrast, white-collar crime investigators often start with a suspected con artist, and their question is, *What* did he or she do, and can we prove it? As one thrift investigator told us, "We pretty much know who the players are here, but we don't know exactly what they did."[8] Given the difficulties of detecting and prosecuting this kind of white-collar crime, much of it probably goes unrecorded.

Those of us who study white-collar crime are usually stuck with examining only cases that have found their way into the official process of arrest and prosecution. We have no information about offenders who "get away" undetected or who are not prosecuted even though there is some evidence of wrongdoing. One way to attack this problem is to use "criminal referrals"—that is, official reports of suspected misconduct—as a rough indicator of fraud. Although this is by no means a definitive measure of crime, it is the best available. Together with indictment and prosecution information, criminal referrals can provide us with some idea of how this front end compares to the indictment stage through which only a minority of offenders flow.

The filing of a criminal referral is the first official step in the process by which suspected thrift fraud is investigated and in some cases prosecuted. These referrals, usually filed by examiners from a regulatory agency or by individuals at the institution itself, describe the suspected crimes and the individuals who may have committed them; they also estimate the dollar loss to the institution. Referrals are generally sent to the regulatory agency's field office, where they are forwarded to the regional office and ultimately to the Federal Bureau of Investigation (FBI) and the U.S. Attorney's Office for investigation. In relatively few cases, this investigation results in an indictment by the U.S. Attorney, and the case proceeds to federal court.

In addition, a substantial number of indictments are initiated against persons never named in a criminal referral. For example, during an investigation the FBI or a U.S. Attorney may uncover evidence of crimes not mentioned in the referral and seek an indictment based on that evidence. In Texas, we discovered, more than a third of the individuals indicted in major S&L cases had not been cited in criminal referrals. Criminal referrals thus probably significantly underestimate the "crime rate" within the thrift industry.

In this regard, the data on criminal referrals at S&Ls are similar to official statistics on crimes known to the police. The accuracy of these official figures as measures of common crime, or street crime, is limited by the existence of a so-called dark figure of crime—that is, the significant number of crimes never reported to the police. Despite this problem, policy makers and social scientists routinely rely on the number of crimes known to the police to gain some sense of the incidence and distribution of common crime in the United States. Similarly, we use the criminal referral as an indicator of thrift crime with the understanding that referrals do not cover all instances of fraud.

It is true, of course, that criminal referrals are not held to the same evidentiary standards as convictions, and in some cases referrals may have been filed when there was no real criminal misconduct. Nonetheless, from our conversations with regulators and investigators and from our perusal of detailed criminal referrals, it is clear that these forms were not filed frivolously. Indeed, because of the amount of information required and because the credibility and reputation of the filing agency are at stake, only the most egregious cases of suspected misconduct are likely to be referred.[9]

So the primary problem with using referrals as an indicator is that they almost certainly underestimate thrift fraud.[10] Since one of our principal findings is that thrift crime was pervasive, but only a few of its perpetrators will ever be prosecuted, this bias works to understate our case. If there were a more inclusive indicator of thrift fraud, we would find that the percentage of those who are actually prosecuted and sentenced to prison is even lower.

The politics of our research and the implications for data quality are worth mentioning here. One reason we found it so difficult to obtain reliable data for this study was the highly politicized environment in which the S&L crisis unfolded. Many of the details of the S&L scandal were kept from the public until after the presidential election of 1988. Once the enormity of the problem became clear, politicians from both parties were eager to minimize the estimated costs of the thrift crisis as well as their own responsibility for creating the conditions that allowed the crisis to escalate. From the perspective of many of these politicians, the less the public knew, the better. Thus the obstacles we faced were unusually formidable.

One clear-cut example of these obstacles involved a senior federal official who almost succeeded in derailing our project. From the outset our negotiations with his office over access to key data on thrift fraud were unnecessarily contentious. Even though the data we requested were readily available in computerized form and could be easily downloaded onto floppy disks, this official refused to provide the disks. Instead, his staff gave us hard copy printouts for individual cases. We were then forced to laboriously re-create the original computerized format. At first we believed that the official's reluctance to give us the disks stemmed from simple ignorance; indeed, he and his staff seemed to believe that there might be some confidential information "hidden" somewhere on the disks. But the basis for his reluctance was not so simple, as later events revealed.

In an informal meeting we shared some of our preliminary findings (what we thought was noncontroversial descriptive information) with this official's staff. Soon after, we sat down with an advisory board, consisting of members of several federal agencies, to discuss the access we needed for our project. Before the meeting had even started, the senior official burst into the room. He proclaimed that he had ordered us not to pursue certain lines of inquiry with the data from his office and that we had disobeyed. We were "bean counters," he accused, and we were wasting taxpayers' money by duplicating work being done by his office. He then demanded that we not present our statistical data to the advisory board and abruptly left the room. Considerably taken aback by this unexpected turn of events, we were forced to adjourn the meeting.

We soon learned that this official had contacted our funding agency to insist that we stop analyzing the data that had led us to the "forbidden" lines of inquiry. He further stipulated that all future data analysis be submitted to his office "before they are made public or disseminated in any way." We recognize that government agencies may need to withhold confidential information if it jeopardizes ongoing civil and criminal investigations and prosecutions. Yet the data we requested simply involved information that had ostensibly been collected to keep Congress and the public abreast of the S&L cleanup. The problem was eventually resolved through delicate negotiations, but our project was put on hold for several months while this was sorted out.

More prosaically, although the federal government devoted hundreds of millions of dollars to the investigation and prosecution of S&L cases, few funds were earmarked for the routine collection of data on how those efforts were proceeding. In some cases individual prosecutors were forced to create their own small data bases, using whatever resources and expertise they could muster. Our ability to gain access to those decentralized files was critical to our project. But, once the files were obtained, we still faced the tedious and time-consuming tasks of cleaning, cross-checking, and reformatting the data. Official data on white-collar crime seems just as elusive as in Sutherland's day.

A SHORT HISTORY OF S&LS

To understand the S&L crisis, it is important first to know some history. The federally insured savings and loan system was established in the early 1930s to promote the construction of new homes during the Depression and to protect financial institutions against the kind of devastation that followed the panic of 1929. The Federal Home Loan Bank Act of 1932 established the Federal Home Loan Bank Board (FHLBB), whose purpose was to create a reserve credit system to ensure the availability of mortgage money for home financing and to oversee federally chartered savings and loans. The second principal building block of the modern savings and loan industry was put in place when the National Housing Act of 1934 created the Federal Savings and Loan Insurance Corporation (FSLIC) to insure S&L deposits.[11]

Until 1989 the FHLBB was the primary regulatory agency responsible for federally chartered savings and loans. This independent executive agency was made up of a chair and two members appointed by the president. It oversaw twelve regional Federal Home Loan Banks, which in turn served as the conduit to individual savings and loan institutions. The district banks provided a pool of funds—for disbursing loans and covering withdrawals—to their member institutions at below-market rates. In 1985 the FHLBB delegated to the district banks the task of examining and supervising the savings and loans within their regional jurisdictions.

The FSLIC, also under the jurisdiction of the FHLBB, provided federal insurance on savings and loan deposits. In exchange for this protection thrifts were regulated geographically and in terms of the kinds of loans they could make. Essentially, they were confined to issuing home loans within fifty miles of the home office. The 1960s brought a gradual loosening of these restraints—for example, the geographic area in which savings and loans could do business was extended and their lending powers were slowly expanded—but this did not significantly alter the protection/regulation formula.

A number of economic factors in the 1970s radically changed the fortunes of the savings and loan industry and ultimately its parameters. Thrifts had issued hundreds of billions of dollars of thirty-year fixed-rate loans (often at 6 percent), but they were prohibited from offering adjustable rate mortgages (ARMs). Thrift profitability thus declined rapidly as interest rates climbed. By the mid-1970s the industry was insolvent on a market-value basis (i.e., based on the current market value of its assets rather than on their reported book value). With inflation at 13.3 percent by 1979 and with thrifts constrained by regulation to pay no more than 5.5 percent interest on new deposits, the industry could not attract new money. When Paul Volcker, head of the Federal Reserve Board, tightened the money supply in 1979 in an effort to bring down inflation, interest rates soared to their highest level in the century and triggered a recession. Faced with defaults and foreclosures as a result of the recession and with increased competition from high-yield investments, given the hikes in the interest rate, S&Ls hemorrhaged losses. By 1982 the industry was insolvent by $150 billion on a market-value basis and the FSLIC had only $6 billion in reserves.[12]

Coinciding with these economic forces, a new ideological movement was gathering momentum. Since the early 1970s, policy makers had been discussing lifting the restrictions on savings and loans so that they could compete more equitably for new money and invest in more lucrative ventures. But it was not until the deregulatory fervor of the early Reagan administration that this strategy gained political acceptance as a solution to the rapidly escalating thrift crisis. Throwing caution to the wind and armed with the brashness born of overconfidence, policy makers undid most of the regulatory infrastructure that had kept the thrift industry together for half a century.

They believed that the free enterprise system works best if left alone, unhampered by perhaps well-meaning but ultimately counterproductive government regulations. The bind constraining the savings and loan industry seemed to confirm the theory that government regulations imposed an unfair handicap in the competitive process. The answer, policy makers insisted, was to turn the industry over to the self-regulating mechanisms of the free market. In 1980 the Depository Institutions Deregulation and Monetary Control Act (DIDMCA) began to do just that by phasing out restrictions on interest rates paid by savings and loans.[13] This move to the free market model, however, was accompanied by a decisive move in the *opposite* direction. At the same time that the law unleashed savings and loans to compete for new money, it bolstered the federal protection accorded these "free enterprise" institutions, increasing FSLIC insurance from a maximum of $40,000 to $100,000 per deposit. As we will see in chapter 3, this selective application of the principles of free enterprise—spearheaded in large part by members of Congress with ties to the thrift industry—laid the foundation for risk-free fraud.

When the industry did not rebound, Congress prescribed more deregulation. In 1982 the Garn–St. Germain Depository Institutions Act accelerated the phaseout of interest rate ceilings.[14] Probably more important, it dramatically expanded thrift investment powers, moving savings and loans farther and farther away from their traditional role as providers of home mortgages. They were now authorized to increase their consumer loans, up to a total of 30 percent of their assets; make commercial, corporate, or business loans; and invest in nonresidential real estate worth up to 40 percent of their total assets. The act also allowed thrifts to provide 100 percent financing, requiring no down payment from the borrower, apparently to attract new business to the desperate industry. On signing the fateful bill, President Reagan said, "I think we've hit a home run." The president later told an audience of savings and loan executives that the law was the "Emancipation Proclamation for America's savings institutions." [15]

The executive branch joined in the "emancipation." In 1980 the FHLBB removed the 5 percent limit on brokered deposits, allowing thrifts access to unprecedented amounts of cash. These deposits were placed by brokers who aggregated individual investments, which were then deposited as "jumbo" certificates of deposit (CDs). Since the maximum insured deposit was $100,000, brokered deposits were packaged as $100,000 CDs, on which the investors could command high interest rates. So attractive was this system to all concerned—to brokers who made hefty commissions, to investors who received high interest for their money, and to thrift operators who now had almost unlimited access to funds—that brokered deposits in S&Ls increased 400 percent between 1982 and 1984.[16]

In 1982 the FHLBB dropped the requirements that thrifts have at least four hundred stockholders and that no one stockholder could own more than 25 percent of the stock, opening the door for a single entrepreneur to own and operate a federally insured savings and loan. Furthermore, single investors could now start up thrifts using noncash assets such as land or real estate. Apparently hoping that innovative entrepreneurs would turn the industry around, zealous deregulators seemed unaware of the disastrous potential

of virtually unlimited new charters in the vulnerable industry.
Referring to this deregulatory mentality and the enthusiasm with
which deregulation was pursued, a senior thrift regulator told us,
"I always describe it as a freight train. I mean it was just the direction
and everybody got on board."

The deregulatory process was accelerated by the fact that federal
and state systems of regulation coexisted and often overlapped.
State-chartered thrifts were regulated by state agencies but could be
insured by the FSLIC if they paid the insurance premiums, which
most did. By 1986 the FSLIC insured 92.6 percent of the country's
savings and loans—holding over 98 percent of the industry's
assets.[17] The dual structure, which had operated smoothly for almost fifty years, had devastating consequences within the context
of federal deregulation. As the federal system deregulated, state
agencies were compelled to do the same, or risk their funding.
The experience of the California Department of Savings and Loans
(CDSL) is a good example of this domino effect of deregulation.

Beginning in 1975 the CDSL was staffed by tough regulators who
imposed strict rules and tolerated little deviation. California thrift
owners complained bitterly, and when federal regulations were re-
laxed in 1980, they switched en masse to federal charters.[18] With
the exodus, the CDSL lost more than half of its funding and staff. In
July 1978 the agency had 172 full-time examiners; by 1983 there
were just fifty-five.[19]

The California Department of Savings and Loans learned the hard
way that if it was to survive (and if state politicians were to continue
to have access to the industry's lobbying dollars), it had to loosen
up. On January 1, 1983, the Nolan Bill passed with only one dis-
senting vote, making it possible for almost anyone to charter a
savings and loan in California and virtually eliminating any limitations on investment powers.[20] As a savings and loan commissioner
for California later said of the deregulation, "All discipline for the
savings and loan industry was pretty well removed." Spurred on by

consultants and lawyers who held seminars for developers on how to buy their own "moneymaking machines," applications for thrift charters in California poured in.[21] By the end of 1984 the CDSL had received 235 applications for new charters, most of which were quickly approved.

Some states, such as Texas, already had thrift guidelines that were even more lax than the new federal regulations, but those that did not quickly enacted "me-too" legislation.[22] By 1984 thrift deregulation was complete, except, of course, that the industry was now more protected (by federal insurance) than ever before. Business Week pointed out the discrepancy: "In a system where the government both encourages risk taking and provides unconditional shelter from the adverse consequences, excess and hypocrisy can be expected to flourish in equal measure."[23]

Deregulation was heralded by its advocates as a free market solution to the competitive handicap placed on thrifts by restraints on their investment powers and interest rates. But the cure turned out to be worse than the disease. Deregulating interest rates triggered an escalating competition for deposits, as brokered deposits sought ever higher returns. One commentator attacked the logic of the deregulation frenzy: "[It can] be summed up by saying that, beginning in 1980, the thrift industry was turned loose to its own devices to find its own way out of its difficulties by taking in more high-priced deposits and lending them out at better than the historically high rates then prevailing. As an article of financial wisdom, this ranks with the notion, held by some, that it is possible to borrow one's way out of debt."[24]

It was worse than that. Deregulation not only sunk thrifts deeper into debt as they competed for "hot" brokered deposits, but more important, it opened the system up to pervasive and systemic fraud. With federally insured deposits flowing in, virtually all restrictions on thrift investment powers removed, and new owners flocking to the industry, deregulators had combined in one package the

opportunity for lucrative fraud and the irresistible force of temptation. L. William Seidman, former chair of the Resolution Trust
Corporation, which was responsible for managing the assets of
failed thrifts during the bailout, blamed the S&L crisis on the combination of deregulation and increased deposit insurance (which he
called "a credit card from the U.S. taxpayers"). He underlined the
possibilities for fraud that this combination opened up: "Crooks
and highflyers had found the perfect vehicle for self-enrichment.
Own your own money machine and use the product to make some
highodd bets. We provided them with such perverse incentives that
if I were asked to defend the S&L gang in court, I'd use the defense of entrapment." [25]

Business Week struck a warning note as early as 1985 with its
tongue-in-cheek description of the "Go-Go Thrift": "Start an S&L.
Offer a premium interest rate and watch the deposits roll in. Your
depositors are insured by Uncle Sam, so they don't care what you
do with their money. And in states like California, you can do almost
anything you want with it. Add enormous leverage—you can pile
$100 of assets on every $3 of capital—and you've built a speculator's dream machine." [26]

Losses piled up. In 1982 the FSLIC spent more than $2.4 billion
to close or merge insolvent savings and loans, and by 1986 the
agency itself was insolvent. [27] As the number of insolvent thrifts
climbed, the FSLIC was forced to slow the pace of closures. The
worse the industry got, the more likely its institutions would stay
open, as the FSLIC was now incapable of closing their doors and
paying off depositors. As the zombie thrifts churned out losses, the
price tag for the inevitable bailout mounted.

As we write this, Charles Keating has been released from prison,
his federal conviction thrown out on the grounds of jury misconduct. Although this judicial decision says nothing of the merits of
the case against Keating, it inevitably provokes speculation that the
role of criminal misconduct in the savings and loan crisis may have
been exaggerated by prosecutors and a scandal-hungry media:

If even this poster boy of the S&L crisis cannot be successfully prosecuted, perhaps thrift crime was not so rampant after all. In the face of such speculation, it becomes even more critical to reexamine the record of the thrift debacle and the role of fraud in the industry's collapse. It is critical not only for our understanding of the dynamics of this sort of white-collar crime, but to put in place policies that will prevent such financial disasters in the future.

"BAD GUYS" OR RISKY BUSINESS?

The American public was sent confusing and conflicting messages about the savings and loan debacle. In the early and mid-1980s, when the industry was already heavily in debt and its condition worsening every month, it received almost no political attention or news coverage. The message was: "Nothing is happening here." By 1987–88, with insolvencies multiplying and the FSLIC itself bankrupt, those paying close attention might have heard the Reagan administration admit discreetly that something potentially troublesome was brewing. "But don't worry, we can handle it," the government reassured.

Soon after the 1988 presidential election, the media dike broke and the S&L crisis was suddenly front-page news. In the hands of media prone to sensationalism, the thrift crisis became synonymous with a handful of con artists, with Charles Keating heading the list. In a frenzied effort to compensate for their neglect of this story while it was happening and ever sensitive to the sales value of a good scandal, the news media minced no words. The lead headline of the Los Angeles Times on September 20, 1990, announced in bold print "KEATING INDICTED FOR FRAUD, JAILED." [1] The next day, the front page of the business section featured a mugshot of Charles Keating being booked, with the headline "Keating Trades His

Business Suit for Prison Blues." [2] Overnight the names Keating, Don Dixon, and "Fast Eddie" Mcbirney became metaphors for evil. By 1990 the message to the American public was "You taxpayers have been ripped off by an assortment of high-profile, high-finance con men."

Media attention soon shifted, leaving the territory to academic economists and industry consultants. The public had been misled, these experts said, by journalistic accounts of massive fraud as a central cause of the thrift debacle. Instead, the crisis was brought on by structural economic forces, poor investments, and bad policies, with crime playing only a minor role. The economist and former Federal Home Loan Bank Board member Lawrence White warned that "any treatment of the S&L debacle that focuses largely . . . on . . . fraudulent and criminal activities is misguided and misleading." [3] The thrift consultant Bert Ely argued that it is "simply not true" that "crooks" were responsible for a large proportion of S&L losses.[4] Parlaying statistics purportedly showing crime to have cost "only" $5 billion, Ely blamed the bulk of the costs on bad government policies, a fall in real estate values, and misguided real estate lending.

Robert Litan, a Brookings Institution economist and a member of the National Commission on Financial Institution Reform, Recovery and Enforcement (NCFIRRE), also downplayed the role of "greedy wrongdoing." [5] Instead, he blamed excessive risk taking and abstract economic forces, such as the collapse of the Texas economy. The banker and lawyer Martin Lowy stated categorically that fraud did not sink the S&Ls; rather, "[inflation] and imprudent lending decisions caused all but a relative few of the failures." Lowy explained, "Some of the money—but not a large percentage of it— went to S&L executives and owners who committed fraud. Bad management cost a lot more money, but that's not fraud." [6] The economist Robert Samuelson joined the chorus, maintaining that it was not "sleaze" that caused the thrift debacle but inflation followed by deregulation and "reckless" investments.[7]

These financial experts even claimed that it would be a cover-up to blame crime. In Lowy's words, "The emphasis on fraud and criminal prosecutions is a cover-up that panders to the anger of the American people, who demand someone to blame. . . . The real causes of the S&L crisis weren't the bad guys. The real causes were *and are* far more fundamental and far more frightening. This wasn't a bank robbery; it was a fundamental economic failure of a substantial part of our financial system."[8] Counterintuitive as it may seem, Lowy contended that exposing individual culpability is a cover-up because it allows impersonal economic forces to go scot-free.

None of these conflicting scenarios for the thrift crisis is really accurate. We take issue with the economists' claim that deliberate wrongdoing was a negligible factor in the thrift industry's demise and the multibillion-dollar tab to taxpayers. There are many problems with their contention that bad government and a bad economy, not bad people, lay at the heart of the thrift crisis. For one thing, it is not necessary to frame the issue in either/or terms. As we will see, bad men and women took advantage of bad policies (which were bad in part *because* they opened up almost irresistible opportunities for fraud); bad men and women then made bad investments (often deliberately); and bad investments exacerbated a bad economy. There is no logical reason why these factors should be seen as discrete and mutually exclusive; empirically, there is every reason to recognize their reciprocal impact and overlap.

Ely's own calculations provide the best example of the fallacy of separating fraud from investment losses or bad government policies. In a table entitled "Where Did All the Money Go?" Ely divvies up losses into separate categories such as "losses on junk bonds," "real estate losses," and "crime," with no thought for any overlap— real estate losses due to fraudulent lending, to cite one obvious example.[9] Having precluded the possibility that crime and investment losses might be overlapping categories, Ely concludes that criminal activity was a relatively small part of the problem. He subtracts all other losses from the $147 billion "present value [1990] of cleaning up the S&L mess" and estimates that crime was responsible for only about $5 billion, or 3 percent of the tab. But, as of 1992, Justice Department calculations of the losses due to crimes that had already been indicted exceeded $11 billion.[10] That criminal convictions of these hard-to-detect white-collar crimes already surpass Ely's 1990 calculations of the *total* amount of crime by more than 200 percent attests to the inadequacy of his approach.[11]

Beyond this problem of distinguishing between government policies and economic forces, on the one hand, and individual wrongdoing, on the other, is the narrow definition of misconduct. "Sleaze," "bad guys," "bad men," "crooks," "greedy wrongdoing" —are loosely used as epithets in the experts' accounts,[12] but when calculating losses they define wrongdoing narrowly as prosecutable crimes only. Further, to the extent that crime is portrayed as distinct from business losses—as it is in Ely's analysis—only outright theft or siphoning off of funds is considered. Indeed, Ely uses the term *theft* when referring to thrift crime.[13]

The definition of crime is a long-standing problem for white-collar criminologists.[14] More than forty years ago Paul Tappan argued that criminologists must confine their study to those who have been "held guilty beyond a reasonable doubt." Otherwise, "the . . . criminologist reasons himself into a cul de sac" and the absence of objective yardsticks "invites individual systems of private values to run riot."[15] Sutherland responded to such criticism by pointing out that if we base our studies on the biases of the criminal justice system—in particular, the differential detection rate and treatment of white-collar offenders—we perpetuate those biases and lose all claims to science.[16] Gilbert Geis has observed that "Sutherland got much the better of th[e] debate by arguing that it was what the person actually had done . . . not . . . how the criminal justice system responded to what they had done, that was essential to whether they should be considered criminal offenders." [17]

This is particularly the case in the area of high finance, where criminal offenses can easily take on the appearance of ordinary business transactions and where it is sometimes impossible to unravel the complex paper trail designed to disguise the wrongdoing. The thrift industry in the 1980s was an ideal setting for what Jack Katz has called "pure" white-collar crimes. William Black, former deputy director of the Office of Thrift Supervision in San Francisco, explains, "Insiders [owners and officers] know when their bank is failing. If they took $10 million from the till at this point it would be an easily prosecutable crime. If instead they have the board of directors which they control pay them a large bonus and/or authorize large dividends at a time when the outside auditors are still blessing the . . . financials and no one writes or says out loud what is really happening one has . . . committed an unprosecutable crime." [18]

Black goes on: "There are a number of [other] perfect or near perfect crimes available to insiders who wish to loot their banks." For example, "the bank insider could have a [speculative] project of his own. He could mention this project to prospective borrowers from the bank without ever saying that the provision of the loan was dependent on the borrower purchasing an interest in his project. Soon, the major borrowers from the bank (all of whom would default) would buy interests in his project. Another perfect crime." Black describes the role of outside professionals in these loan frauds:

There was rarely any need to be so crude as to bribe an appraiser. The bank simply picked those who had a reputation for providing high values and then provided the appraiser with the value needed to support the loan [some of which could be funneled back to the insider's own project]. If the appraiser cooperated he would get the bank's business, if not, he would not get the bank's business and would be identified as overly conservative among like-minded banks. . . . [P]rosecution of the appraiser is impossible in the pattern just described, and prosecution of the insider is nearly impossible.[19]

Indicative of this alliance between appraisers and corrupt insiders and the difficulties of prosecution, in one major scandal in Ohio the cooperative bank appraiser (who was never indicted) was known by the nickname "How High Howie."[20]

Following the tradition of scholarship in white-collar crime and given the ready availability of such "pure" or "perfect" thrift crimes, we do not confine our discussion of wrongdoing to prosecuted, or even prosecutable, crimes. The issue here is not whether wrongdoing can be proven before a court of law but whether deliberate insider abuse occurred. Contrary to Tappan's fear, this expansion of the concept of wrongdoing does not take us into the realm of "private values" or subjective evaluations of social injury.[21] In the banking and thrift context a wide variety of misconduct is subject to criminal prosecution, because of federal deposit insurance and the opportunities and risks it opens up. Giving false financial information to a bank or thrift to obtain a loan is technically a crime and can be prosecuted as such; knowingly keeping false records and books is a crime; knowingly providing false information to a regulator is a crime; in fact, simple breaches of the fiduciary duty to the institution may be prosecuted as crimes. While prosecutorial distinctions are drawn between criminal bank fraud and civil fraud, their substantive elements are usually identical; only the burden of proof differs (the latter requires simply "a preponderance of the evidence").

All of the insider abuse we describe (Ponzi schemes, contingent loans, exorbitant bonuses, daisy chains, etc.) hinges on practices and conduct that are technically crimes and *could* be prosecuted criminally. Because the essence of insider abuse and fraud is deceit, it almost invariably requires false records and statements to regulators. Indeed, deliberate insider abuse of any kind by definition constitutes a breach of fiduciary duty to the institution. That such activities are rarely criminally prosecuted speaks to the burden of proof required and the difficulties of prosecution. For this reason, and to avoid reliance on the justice system's evaluation of what can be successfully prosecuted, our discussion focuses broadly on deliberate insider abuse for personal gain; indeed, we will use the terms *insider abuse, wrongdoing, fraud,* and *crime* interchangeably. This not only makes scientific and legal sense, it makes sense from the point of view of our debate with the experts. They have cast their argument in terms of what is to blame for the costly debacle: "bad people" or "bad investments," deliberate wrongdoing or impersonal economic forces. Our concern with deliberate insider abuse, broadly defined, fits well into this discussion of the assignment of responsibility.

In addition to these problems with the experts' either/or approach and their narrow definition of wrongdoing, their "minimal fraud" thesis is inconsistent with the extensive empirical accounts compiled by regulators and others who collectively have spent hundreds of thousands of hours investigating the corpses of insolvent institutions. We briefly describe several of the most notorious of these cases to give a sense of the strategies involved.

CRIMES OF THE RICH AND INFAMOUS

When Erwin "Erv" Hansen took over Centennial Savings and Loan in northern California at the end of 1980 it was a conservative, small-town thrift with a net worth of about $1.87 million. He immediately began one of the industry's most expensive shopping sprees. Hansen threw a Centennial-funded $148,000 Christmas party for five hundred friends and invited guests that included a ten-course sit-down dinner, roving minstrels, court jesters, and mimes. Hansen and his companion, Beverly Haines, a senior officer at Centennial, traveled around the world in the thrift's private airplanes, purchased antique furniture at the thrift's expense, and renovated an old house in the California countryside at a cost of over $1 million, equipping it with a gourmet chef at an annual salary of $48,000. A fleet of luxury cars was put at the disposal of Centennial personnel, and the thrift's offices were adorned with expensive art from around the world.[22]

To finance these extravagances, Hansen used "land flips," sales of land between associates for the purpose of artificially inflating the market value. Hansen and his high-financier friend Sid Shah regularly used this technique to mutual advantage. To cite one example, they bought and sold one property worth $50,000 back and forth in the early 1980s until it reached a market "value" of $487,000, whereupon they received a loan based on this inflated collateral.[23]

In 1983, several days after the Nolan Bill deregulated California thrifts, Centennial purchased Piombo Corporation, a California construction company, through exercising a stock option held by Shah. Overnight tiny Centennial became a development conglomerate. To maximize benefits, Hansen had to get around the prohibition against loaning money to one's own development company. Here some creative financing came in handy: Hansen was able to receive loans for Piombo development from his friends at other northern California thrifts, while he reciprocated with loans for their pet projects. As local journalists Stephen Pizzo, Mary Fricker, and Paul Muolo described it, "Immediately money began to flow like artesian spring water among the main players."[24]

Centennial's inevitable collapse in 1985 cost the FSLIC an estimated $160 million.[25] The day before Hansen was scheduled to appear before the Department of Justice to negotiate for his testimony against Sid Shah he was found dead, apparently of a cerebral aneurysm. Haines was convicted of embezzling $2.8 million and spent sixty-seven days of a five-year sentence in prison. Shah was not criminally prosecuted for his Centennial activities but was sentenced to seven years in prison for money laundering.

Don Dixon operated Vernon Savings and Loan in Texas using many of these same strategies. He and his wife, Dana, divided their time between a luxury ski resort in the Rocky Mountains and a $1 million beach house north of San Diego. They went on luxury vacations across Europe, including one adventure they called "Gastronomique Fantastique," a two-week culinary tour of France coordinated by Philippe Junot, former husband of Princess Caroline of Monaco, and paid for by Vernon.[26] Dixon purchased a 112-foot yacht for $2.6 million, with which he wooed members of Congress and regulators on extravagant boating parties. To pay for all this Dixon set up intricate networks of subsidiary companies for the express purpose of making illegal loans to himself.

A developer before buying his savings and loan, Dixon used Vernon largely as a way to provide funding for his commercial real estate projects. In 1980 deregulation had removed the 5 percent limit on brokered deposits, allowing thrifts access to unprecedented amounts of cash. Thrift owners like Dixon now had an almost unlimited source of cash—albeit at exorbitantly high interest rates—with which to fund their investment projects and finance their shopping sprees.[27] Officials later charged that Dixon used Vernon (which regulators nicknamed "Vermin") to funnel money from brokered deposits into his holding company, Dondi Financial Corporation. There Dixon could use federally insured deposit money to fund whatever venture he and his associates could conjure up, which usually involved adding commercial real estate to the already glutted Texas market. When Vernon was finally taken over in 1987, 96 percent of its loans were in default.[28] The resolution of Vernon cost taxpayers $1.3 billion. Vernon's chief executive officer, Woody Lemons, was sentenced to thirty years in prison for bank fraud. Dixon was sentenced to two consecutive five-year terms but was released in November 1994, after serving less than thirty-nine months.[29] The FSLIC filed a $500 million lawsuit against Dixon and his associates for having siphoned more than $540 million from Vernon.

Charles Keating, like Dixon, started out as a real estate developer and in 1984 purchased Lincoln Savings and Loan in Irvine, California, through his development company, American Continental Corporation (ACC).[30] He quickly transformed Lincoln from a thrift with 50 percent of its assets in traditional home mortgage loans into a giant conglomerate specializing in development and construction of commercial real estate ventures and other direct investments. In the first year Keating invested $18 million in a Saudi bank, $2.7 million in an oil company, $132 million in a takeover bid, $19.5 million in a hotel venture, and $5 million in junk bonds. Two years later 10 percent of Lincoln's assets—or $800 million—were tied up in junk bonds, most purchased from his associate Michael Milken at Drexel.[31] Much of this investment activity violated the 1985 limit on direct investments, a rule Keating circumvented by backdating and fabricating documents and records while fighting the FHLBB to have the rule rescinded.[32]

Loan swapping was also central to Keating's operations. As money came in the door from depositors, it went out in loans to Keating's associates in commercial real estate and junk bonds. Not only did this net him handsome upfront fees, points, and dividends, but the favor was returned in the form of loans for his own projects. To cite but one example, Keating associate Gene Phillips owned Southmark Corporation and its subsidiary, San Jacinto Savings and Loan, in Houston, Texas. Keating, who had met Phillips through Michael Milken, loaned $129 million to Southmark (vastly exceeding the loans-to-one-borrower [LTOB] limit) in late 1985 and early 1986. In January 1986 Southmark in turn loaned a Keating enterprise $35 million. At the same time, Keating and Phillips exchanged about $246 million in existing mortgages, booking $12 million in accounting profits from the swap.[33]

In 1987 and 1988 more than 23,000 investors purchased $230 million of ACC junk bonds from the offices of Lincoln Savings and Loan. Although the bonds were uninsured and inherently risky, these investors—many of whom were elderly and living on fixed incomes—were led to believe that since they were purchased in the lobby of an S&L, they were federally insured. As Pizzo, Fricker, and Muolo tell the story: "When a customer came in to renew a large certificate of deposit, he would be told he could earn more by investing in American Continental Corp.'s junk bonds. When he asked if his money would be safe, he was told that American Continental Corp. was as strong as its subsidiary Lincoln Savings, which was a federally insured institution. The subtleties of that reply were lost on many of the investors."[34] When ACC went bankrupt, the investments of these 23,000 Lincoln customers went up in smoke.

During the five-year period of Keating's control of Lincoln he and his family, all of whom were on the Lincoln payroll, took home more than $41.5 million in salaries and perks. When Lincoln was closed down by the federal government in 1989, it cost taxpayers more than $3 billion to resolve. Federal regulators sued Keating and his family, as well as some of his co-conspirators, for $1.25 billion, but the proceeds of the far-flung operation had long since evaporated or been taken offshore. Keating was released from prison in December 1996, after serving four and a half years of his twelve-year sentence. While his federal conviction was thrown out on the grounds that the jury improperly concealed knowledge of his earlier state conviction (also subsequently thrown out), federal prosecutors are now considering retrying Keating.

Keating, Dixon, and Hansen are among the best-known thrift highfliers, and indeed they were responsible for some of the costliest failures. But such activity was not confined to these high-profile cases. In its study of the twenty-six most costly thrift insolvencies by 1987, the U.S. General Accounting Office (GAO) found that "all of the 26 failed thrifts . . . violated laws and regulations and engaged in unsafe practices."[35] Eighty-five criminal referrals regarding these twenty-six thrifts had been forwarded to the Justice Department, alleging 179 violations of criminal law and implicating 182 people. The GAO concluded that criminal activity was a central ingredient in the collapse of each one of these institutions. Overall, the GAO estimated that 60 percent of the institutions it had taken over by 1990 had been plagued in some way by "serious criminal activity." [36] In a detailed empirical study of one district, the deputy regional director of the San Francisco Office of Thrift Supervision came to the same conclusion, finding evidence of fraud at 68 percent of the thrifts that failed between 1984 and 1988.[37] The National Commission on Financial Institution Reform, Recovery and Enforcement, appointed by President George Bush to examine the causes of the thrift crisis, issued its final report to Congress and the president in 1993. The report concluded that in "the typical large failure . . . [e]vidence of fraud was invariably present." [38]

Criminal referrals paint the same picture. In 1987 and 1988 alone, the FHLBB referred more than 11,000 savings and loan cases to the Justice Department for investigation and possible criminal prosecution.[39] According to statistical data on criminal referrals provided to us by the Resolution Trust Corporation, as of May 1992 criminal activity was suspected in two-thirds of all RTC-controlled institutions. Criminal referral data represent suspected criminal activity and in a few cases may include multiple referrals concerning only one offense. Yet, as we have noted, referrals are probably an underestimate of fraud since they do not include either those frauds that are never detected or those that are detected independent of a referral.

The number of criminal convictions—by any account the most conservative indicator of fraud—further points to the prevalence of wrongdoing. By the spring of 1992, in excess of one thousand defendants had been formally charged in major savings and loan cases, with a conviction rate of 91 percent (see chapter 5).[40] These convictions represent only a fraction of actual wrongdoing. As Marvin Collins, U.S. Attorney for the Northern District of Texas, has explained, "The fraud that we are prosecuting is what I would describe as outrageous, egregious criminal fraud."[41]

The precise extent to which criminal activities contributed to the downfall of these institutions is difficult to assess. Some early government reports suggested that criminal activity was a factor in 70 to 80 percent of thrift failures.[42] Based on a 1992 survey of its field offices, the Resolution Trust Corporation estimated that fraud and criminal conduct contributed significantly to the failure of 33 percent of its institutions.[43] The Dallas District of the OTS arrived at a similar estimate in its 1989 analysis of insolvent institutions in its district (which includes Texas, Arkansas, Louisiana, Mississippi, and New Mexico). It found that insider fraud had either a direct or an indirect effect on the failure of 44 percent of those institutions.[44]

George Akerloff and Paul Romer estimate that the resolution costs of all thrifts that the RTC suspected of criminal wrongdoing are approximately $54 billion. They point out this may be an overestimate as it may include losses carried over from the interest rate crisis of the 1970s; they believe, however, that it is probably an underestimate, since they "lack estimates for some of the thrifts on [their] list and because estimated resolution costs have typically been underestimates rather than overestimates." Akerloff and Romer conclude simply, "Evidence of looting abounds."[45]

The NCFIRRE reported to Congress, "We are convinced . . . that taxpayer losses due to fraud were large, probably amounting to 10 to 15 percent of total net losses." Members of the commission were strongly divided on this issue and appended "Additional Views" to the report specifically to address their disagreements. Commissioner Daniel Crippen, executive director of the Merrill Lynch International Advisory Council from 1985 to 1987 and assistant to President Bush from 1987 to 1989, voiced his concern: "I am afraid . . . that we leave the impression that 'fraud and abuse' was a major cause of the problem." Commissioner Elliott H. Levitas, a former professor at Emory University Law School and member of the U.S.

House of Representatives from 1975 to 1985, had just the opposite concern: "I believe the effect of fraud and abuse, or, more generally, misconduct is understated in the Report." [46] Clearly, this was a contentious issue and the "10 to 15 percent" estimate was something of a negotiated compromise. Despite the disagreement, the commission reported generally, "Fraud and misconduct were important elements in the S&L debacle." [47]

We were able to develop a partial indicator of the cost of fraud from our RTC referral data. As part of its mandate to take over insolvent S&Ls and manage and dispose of their assets, the RTC collects data on criminal referrals through its Thrift Information Management System (TIMS). This system records and tracks criminal referrals at all RTC institutions (i.e., institutions that have been declared insolvent and taken over by the RTC). These TIMS data on RTC institutions summarize the contents of "Category I" criminal referrals filed by RTC personnel or by other federal agencies, principally the OTS and its predecessor, the Federal Home Loan Bank Board.

Category I referrals are those in which the subject was (a) an officer, director, or shareholder; (b) a borrower and the estimated loss was $100,000 or more; (c) a borrower with more than one referral and/or a borrower who was a creditor to multiple institutions; (d) an employee of the institution or an affiliated outsider such as an attorney, accountant, appraiser, or broker and the suspected loss was $100,000 or greater. Category II referrals (which are more numerous) describe incidents involving unaffiliated parties or insiders below the officer level and include charges such as armed robbery, burglary, minor embezzlements, or check kiting. Generally, then, Category II referrals describe traditional crimes against S&Ls by lower-level employees or unassociated (e.g., not borrowers) outsiders. Our analysis focuses on Category I referrals, which comprise what we generally mean by white-collar thrift fraud—that is, those frauds carried out by owners, managers, or

Table 1
Institutions under RTC Supervision (May 19, 1992)

Institutions under RTC control	686
Institutions where criminal referral filed	455
	(66%)
Referrals	2,265
Individuals named in referrals	4,559
Mean loss due to fraud per institution	$12,420,652
Median loss due to fraud per institution	$1,010,247
Mean loss due to fraud per referral	$2,193,492
Median loss due to fraud per referral	$194,569
Total losses due to fraud	$4,968,260,619

Source: Data from Resolution Trust Corporation, TIMS data base.

shareholders, or by affiliated outsiders such as major borrowers, brokers, or other financial professionals who were employed by the institution.

As can be seen in table 1, the median estimated loss per referral was $194,569. Many referrals reported losses in the millions of dollars, so that the mean loss per referral reaches $2,193,492. Numerous referrals may be filed for a single institution, and when we sum the losses from all referrals for each institution we find that the median loss per institution was $1,010,247. Here again, the mean losses were much higher, reaching $12,420,652 per institution.

The losses reported for these institutions amount to almost $5 billion. We must point out that for several reasons this is not an estimate of the total amount of losses due to fraud in the S&L scandal. First, only frauds reported through criminal referrals are included here, even though in a significant proportion of thrift fraud cases fraud was discovered independent of a referral. Second, these are the losses reported at RTC institutions, that is, since late 1989, and therefore the numerous earlier insolvencies are excluded.

Third, these numbers refer only to officially insolvent institutions and therefore do not include cases of fraud at institutions that were not taken over. Further, as regulators indicated in our interviews, a significant amount of fraud is handled administratively or civilly, with no criminal referrals ever being filed. Finally, there is the dark figure of undetected crime, which by definition can never be precisely known. Nonetheless, this partial figure of $5 billion in losses suggests that fraud was a substantial ingredient in the S&L disaster, far beyond the $5 billion total estimated by Ely.[48]

THE DEDUCTIVE METHOD FOR ESTIMATING FRAUD

Beyond the empirical evidence, the contention that fraud played only a minor role in the thrift crisis is not logical.[49] Let us examine the argument more carefully. While a number of factors are often mentioned in the minimal fraud scenario, the argument typically boils down to this: The interest rate crisis of the late 1970s thrust the thrift industry into a tailspin, whereupon rational businesspeople "gambling for resurrection" through the risky investment vehicles provided by deregulation lost the gamble in an economic environment of falling real estate values, overvalued junk bonds, and so on. The central element here is gambling for resurrection, which minimal fraud proponents claim was both legal and eminently rational.

This gambling for resurrection theory is related to the key concept of moral hazard. Everyone now recognizes that the environment within which thrifts operated in the mid-1980s presented opportunities for "high-risk" investments at little risk for either depositors or thrift managers. Federal deposit insurance of up to $100,000 per deposit, in conjunction with the deregulation of interest rates, provided thrift managers with a steady stream of insured cash with which to invest in any endeavor they saw fit. If the investments turned a profit, the proceeds were privatized in the form of generous bonuses and dividends; if they failed, the losses were covered by the FSLIC (and once the FSLIC itself was bankrupt, by the U.S. taxpayer). Because so many thrifts were insolvent or close to insolvent by the early 1980s, the moral hazard was enhanced. With nothing to lose, thrift managers were given a perverse incentive to engage in ever-riskier behavior, much like a casino gambler going for broke. Within this context, the minimal fraud school argues, gambling for resurrection was the most rational behavior available to profit maximizers and accounts for the bulk of thrift losses in the mid-1980s.

But there are numerous logical problems with this "gambling for resurrection through excessive risk taking" explanation. First, to be consistent with the finance theory that its proponents claim underlies their analysis, the hypothesis would predict that virtually all rational thrifts faced with insolvency would gamble for resurrection. Instead, fewer than one-third (at a time when the whole industry was insolvent on a market-value basis) engaged in high-risk investment strategies. Second, while a rational risk taker gambling for resurrection would diversify his or her portfolio, the pattern prevalent among the worst thrift failures was just the opposite. Of the twenty-six failures studied by the GAO, twenty-three made "excessive loans to one borrower." [50] These LTOB violations are of unusual significance in the thrift context because the LTOB limit was generally 100 percent of capital. No rational gambler for resurrection, given the ample opportunities for diversification among the high-risk investments allowed by deregulation, would invest more than their entire capital in a single loan.

Third, the gambling for resurrection theory would predict that rational thrift operators not engaged in fraud would seek to optimize the underwriting and internal controls applied to the extraordinarily risky investments they made. In fact, however, these high-fliers were consistently lax in their underwriting and controls. [51] The FHLBB's review of S&L failures in 1988 found bad underwriting in 125 of the 147 cases for which they had adequate information. In Texas the pattern was even worse, with evidence of bad underwriting at 45 of 49 institutions.[52] The GAO reported that in the costliest failures it examined, all 26 had engaged in "inaccurate recordkeeping or inadequate controls" and 24 of the 26 routinely conducted "inadequate credit analysis" or "inadequate appraisals."[53] The market does not provide any reward for bad underwriting; rather, such practices increase risk substantially *without* increasing expected return.[54] The pattern found here is thus profoundly irrational for a profit maximizer who is gambling for resurrection through risky investments.

The fact that *every single thrift* that engaged in high-risk investments in this period failed, and failed catastrophically, is also inconsistent with this gambling for resurrection view. The failure of California highfliers investing primarily in California real estate—a market that was soaring—is particularly instructive. Every thrift that invested more than 10 percent of its assets in high-risk, direct investments prior to mid-1984 collapsed, piling up billions of dollars of losses.[55] It is inconceivable that well-intentioned entrepreneurs making even the riskiest investments would have experienced such a consistent record of abysmal failure in the booming California economy.

By the time Texas thrifts began to concentrate heavily on lending for commercial development, commercial real estate already had rapidly rising vacancy rates. By September 1983 the office vacancy rate was 28 percent in Dallas and 35 percent in Houston, but Texas thrifts continued to pour money into commercial development, guaranteeing failure.[56] As Ely himself points out, real estate lending in Texas continued to increase rapidly while the surrounding economy took a nosedive and vacancy rates skyrocketed.[57] There were myriad high-risk/high-expected-return investments available to highfliers in Texas; no rational businessperson would have continued to pump all of his or her capital into the saturated real estate

market. In contrast to the picture of a rational businessperson calculating the odds of survival, Business Week summed up the behavior of
thrift highfliers: "The flamboyant adventures of the go-go thrifts
have the desperate quality of a joyride by a terminally ill patient." [58]

Nor can mere incompetence explain this behavior. It is true that a
change in ownership was a principal "red flag" marking the worst
failures.[59] Of the twenty-six failures studied by the GAO, 62 percent
had experienced a change of control in the period preceding the
insolvency.[60] More generally, of the seventy-two thrifts placed in
government conservatorship between March 1985 and July 1987,
approximately one-half were managed or owned by individuals
who were new to the thrift industry.[61] In California, of the twenty-
six state-chartered institutions that failed and were turned over to
the FSLIC between 1985 and 1987, twenty-one were either new
institutions or had recently changed management. A report of the
Texas Savings and Loan League reveals that real estate developers
entered the Texas thrift industry en masse in the early 1980s and
that by 1987 they "owned 20 of the 24 most deeply insolvent thrifts
in Texas." [62]

Still, inexperience on the part of these new owners, most of
whom had never before been in banking, cannot explain their behavior over time. Some novices might have engaged in poor asset
diversification, but that all of these newcomers concentrated in only
a few investment areas, such as commercial real estate lending,
suggests something else was going on here. Similarly, poor credit
risks prevailed far beyond what even the most inexperienced thrift
managers might wreak. For example, the worst thrift failures consistently involved development loans to borrowers who were known
to be uncreditworthy.

Underwriting and internal controls were also far worse than simple incompetence could account for. We might expect novice managers to commit errors in the more difficult aspects of underwriting; however, at the worst failures managers were conspicuously

indifferent to underwriting, getting even the most basic aspects wrong and showing no improvement over time.[63] It was not unusual for the fastest-growing Texas thrifts in the mid-1980s to extend development and construction loans *before* a loan application had been completed and signed; appraisals and credit checks were often conducted *after* the loan had been disbursed.[64]

Managers of these troubled institutions were unresponsive to regulators' concerns about such unorthodox practices. In its study of twenty-six thrift failures the GAO found a persistent pattern of resistance to supervisory action. One-half of the twenty-two thrifts that signed administrative agreements with thrift regulators to alter their unsafe practices violated those agreements; others circumvented the agreements through subterfuge or technical loopholes.[65] By 1986 thrift lobbyists, led by the most insolvent Texas thrifts, were leading the campaign to neutralize thrift regulatory powers and end what the Texas Savings and Loan League referred to as the regulators' "antagonism" toward the industry.[66] Mere incompetence cannot explain why thrift managers failed to require, despite persistent regulatory warnings, that the most basic underwriting and internal control procedures be followed.

No "gambling for resurrection" or "excessive risk taking" theory—not even one that takes into consideration gross incompetence—can make sense of these patterns. In fact, the only explanation consistent with this behavior is widespread insider abuse. Let us follow the logic through.

If thrift highfliers were engaged in insider abuse and fraud, then it makes sense that losses would be concentrated in states with the highest degree of deregulation, allowing for the most nontraditional investments within which thrift fraud could easily be disguised. Texas, which in the early 1980s was considered a model for deregulation, incurred by far the most failures and the costliest insolvencies, followed by California, which by 1983 had enacted comparably permissive deregulation. Between 1985 and 1987 there

were 284 official thrift failures, with 46 located in Texas and 37 in
California (Illinois was third with 17). Of the 26 most costly failures
examined by the GAO, 10 were located in Texas and 8 in California.[67] The regional pattern remained constant for the rest of the
decade. Of the thrifts placed in RTC conservatorship in its first year
of operation in 1989, four times as many were located in Texas as
in any other state, followed by California.[68]

Our RTC data allow us to look more closely at the concentration
of thrift crime in Texas and California. Table 2 shows that together
these states accounted for less than one-third (29%) of all RTC
institutions, yet they accounted for 36 percent of referrals and 59
percent of losses due to fraud. By far the most extensive amount of
crime was reported at Texas thrifts, where 1,350 suspects were
cited in criminal referrals and estimated losses totaled nearly $2.7
billion—or 54 percent of reported losses due to fraud at RTC institutions nationwide. The median loss per referral was higher in Texas
($335,717) than in California ($240,491). Losses due to fraud
were much higher in Texas than in the rest of the country. Apparently, Texas S&L operators liked their criminal schemes big.

It makes sense too that losses would be disproportionate in thrifts
that experienced a change of ownership, since many individuals
would seek to enter the industry to commit fraud. Investment diversification would be minimal, since a manager committing deliberate insider abuse would be likely to collaborate with a network of
associates on the outside and would not be particularly interested
in moderating long-term risk. Following the same logic, it makes
sense that many loans would be at, or exceed, the LTOB limit.

Weak or nonexistent underwriting was also rational for insiders
intent on fraud, as proper underwriting would expose wrongdoing
to regulators subsequently examining the files. Further, managers
engaged in fraud had an incentive to undo any internal controls
that might obstruct their ability to perpetrate fraud. Fraudulent
managers would also be resistant to supervisory or regulatory

Table 2

Institutions under RTC Supervision in California and Texas

	Total	California	Texas
Institutions under RTC control	686	59 (8.6%)	137 (20.0%)
Institutions where a criminal referral was filed	455	42 (9.2%)	85 (18.7%)
Referrals	2,265	175 (7.7%)	631 (27.9%)
Individuals named in referrals	4,559	223 (4.9%)	1,350 (29.6%)
Mean loss due to fraud per institution	$12,420,652	$6,153,698	$40,203,200
Median loss due to fraud per institution	$1,101,247	$1,239,500	$1,824,596
Mean loss due to fraud per referral	$2,193,492	$1,371,607	$4,897,477
Median loss due to fraud per referral	$194,569	$240,491	$335,717
Total losses due to fraud	$4,968,260,619	$227,686,846 (4.6%)	$2,693,612,589 (54.2%)

Source: Data from Resolution Trust Corporation, TIMS data base.

action; indeed, they would attempt to deceive regulators, to cover up their fraud as well as the deteriorating financial health of their institutions. High-risk, heavily concentrated investments with grossly inadequate or nonexistent underwriting are highly irrational from the point of view of a profit maximizer not engaged in fraud (and unlikely even for the most inexperienced well-intentioned thrift managers). They are profoundly rational, however, from the viewpoint of a manager committing fraud. It may be useful here to illustrate this further by describing the mechanics of acquisition, development, and construction (ADC) loans.

An ADC loan is typically made to a real estate developer to buy land, develop it (grade, put in roads and sewers, etc.), and construct buildings. These loans are among the riskiest investments a financial institution can make. They combine construction risks (related to climate and weather conditions, as well as engineering, design, and planning glitches), market risks, and fraud risks associated with borrower integrity. ADC loans are known as direct investments. That is, if the project succeeds, the lender gets a share of the profit; if it fails, the lender absorbs the loss.

The risk factors inherent in ADC lending were compounded in most such loans in Texas and California after deregulation. No cash down payment was required, a 100 percent loan-to-value ratio (LTV; meaning that the lender fully funded the project from start to finish) was common, points and fees were self-funded through the loan (as were "soft costs" such as architects' and lawyers' fees), and the loan generally included an "interest reserve" from which interest payments for two years or more were drawn. There was no meaningful guarantee of repayment by the borrower, for example, no personal guarantee by a creditworthy builder, and developers frequently received an up-front fee funded by the thrift. The projects were usually speculative, or spec, projects, meaning that they were not preleased. As Lowy points out, this was a radical departure from previous practice. For example, in Dallas almost all new commercial construction was preleased in the early 1980s, but by 1984 two-thirds of such construction was speculative.[69]

The circumstances under which ADC loans were made ensured adverse selection of borrowers. Thrifts started the ADC lending process with two strikes against them. Banks had been making commercial ADC loans for many years and had good lending relationships with the best developers. Moreover, by the time thrifts began extensive ADC lending, commercial vacancy rates were high, especially in Texas where ADC lending was concentrated. By charging high interest rates and fees and taking a high percentage of future profits, thrifts attracted only the worst borrowers/developers—those who had such limited access to other lenders and such poor hopes of project profitability that committing a substantial portion of (unlikely) future profits to the thrift imposed no real cost.

The structure of such ADC loans creates moral hazard in the borrower. With a 100 percent LTV, any ADC project hangs by the thinnest of threads. If anything goes wrong, even slightly, the project is doomed. Given the poor quality of the borrowers involved and the ever-deepening glut of commercial real estate, it was highly probable that large numbers of ADC projects would go very wrong. When they did the developer had no financial stake in the project, no personal guarantee, and could convert loan funds to personal use. Not surprisingly, many simply walked away from troubled real estate projects, letting the thrift foreclose on the loans and suffer the loss.

These perverse aspects of the typical ADC loan in the 1980s—adverse selection and moral hazard—ensured losses and would seem to dictate against such investment strategies. If a rational, nonfraudulent thrift manager did decide to specialize in ADC lending, she or he would attempt to minimize risk through superb underwriting. In the context of ADC lending, underwriting would focus on the creditworthiness of the borrower and the viability of the project, maximizing the incentives of borrowers to repay loans and monitoring project progress.

The typical bad ADC loan in the 1980s deviated substantially from this course, with managers often sidestepping underwriting altogether or making a token effort after the loan had already been made. Despite the marked irrationality of this behavior from the standpoint of an honest lender, these loans were well suited to certain types of fraud. They generated unprecedented accounting income, providing huge salaries, bonuses, and dividends for managers and stockholders, and rewarded associated borrowers with large pools of cash. ADC lending was ideal for generating fee and interest income: not only were the borrowers often fronts in cooperative daisy chains with insiders, but points, fees, and interest were usually self-funded through the loan.[70]

ADC lending was also an ideal vehicle for avoiding loss recognition. Not only did the interest reserve guarantee that loans would be current until they came to term, but they could be "rolled over," or refinanced. Networks of thrifts frequently refinanced each other's bad loans to keep them current and to book new income, leading to the insider joke "A rolling loan gathers no loss." And as these speculative ventures had no readily ascertainable market value, insiders (with the aid of appraisers and accountants) could assure regulators that their value was adequate to repay the loan should the borrower default. Finally, selling a bad ADC loan to a straw buyer removed it from the books if necessary to enhance the institution's picture of health and postpone closure. These "sales" succeeded in turning a real loss into an accounting gain. Adverse selection of ADC borrowers was thus rational for thrifts engaged in fraud: Fraudulent borrowers would readily agree to the high interest rates and fees that provided phony accounting profits for the thrifts and would serve as "straw borrowers" when necessary.

A thrift that grew rapidly through ADC lending was thus *guaranteed* to report record income. It was a mathematical certainty. The more cash the thrift sent out the door, the more "income" it reported. It was the ideal paradox for the thrift manager intent on fraud: An extraordinarily risky asset would produce an extraordinarily risk-free *accounting* profit for several years, providing ample justification for generous bonuses and dividends. Growth, however, was not simply a means to maximize the fraudulent insiders' profits; rather, it was a necessity to postpone the collapse of the underlying Ponzi scheme. The only way for an ADC scheme to fund interest on deposits and cover withdrawals was to grow rapidly and pay the old depositors with the funds provided by new depositors, with federal insurance providing the ability to attract deposits in the necessary volume. It was for this reason that the most catastrophic thrift failures grew the fastest and consistently reported the highest profits throughout the mid-1980s.

The asset size of the fastest growers is astounding. In the first quarter of 1984, 724 thrifts grew at an annual rate of 25 percent or more and 336 grew at an annual rate of more than 50 percent. The fastest growers reported the highest profits, the highest net worth, and the most nontraditional assets. By the second quarter of 1984, California and Texas had respectively 74 and 62 thrifts growing at 50 percent annually, totaling over $75 billion in assets.[71] A study of the so-called Texas 40 (forty of the worst thrift failures in Texas) found that on average they had grown 300 percent between 1982 and 1986—more than three times the rate of other thrifts in Texas and more than five times the general industry average.[72] Some of the costliest failures occurred in institutions that had grown by as much as 1,000 percent in a single year.[73]

New York Review of Books essayist Michael Thomas rails against the impact of removing the downside of risk for such projects and accuses S&L operators of massive fraud: "There was . . . no limit to speculative effrontery, to disregard of law and public opinion, to contempt for history and economic truth. And why should there have been, when the notion of 'risk,' that vexing side of market capitalism, had been eliminated."[74] As we have seen, the problem is even worse than the elimination of risk. The moral hazard related to deposit insurance and the immunization to risk it provided investors was compounded many times over by the incentives for fraud provided by the risk-free accounting "income" guaranteed by these ADC Ponzis.

While pouring money into a glutted commercial real estate market through ADC lending makes no sense from the standpoint of a well-intentioned profit maximizer, it is perversely rational for those engaged in fraud. Following this logic, project viability is of no concern; what is important is growth and the fee income it generates. Tyrell Barker, owner and operator of State Savings and Loan in Texas, told developers in Dallas in the early 1980s, "You bring the dirt, I bring the money." When one Barker-financed developer was asked how he determined what property to buy, he replied, "Wherever my dog lifts his leg I buy that rock and all the acreage around it."[75] Such arrangements were so common that they were called "cash-for-dirt" loans. In a *Barron's* article on the collapse of commercial real estate in the 1980s, Maggie Mahar explains the symbiosis between thrift lenders and developers: "Developers didn't borrow in order to build; all too often they built in order to borrow—and borrow some more."[76] Laurie Holtz, a Florida regulator, concurs: "Money availability became more of a reason for real estate development than economics."[77] New commercial development thus undermined an already glutted market and compounded thrift insolvency.

Many of the highfliers who engaged in ADC loans entered the industry in the early 1980s by acquiring an insolvent thrift. It was cheaper and quicker to buy an existing thrift that was insolvent than to start one up de novo, which usually required $2 or $3 million in capital. Small thrifts could be purchased after the interest rate crisis of the late 1970s for $1 to $2 million, with the acquirer contributing grossly overvalued real estate in lieu of cash.[78] Some acquirers made money immediately through such inflated real estate contributions. For example, with the help of a cooperative appraiser an acquirer could claim that a $5 million property was worth $25 million, then exchange the real estate for $15 million in cash from the newly acquired S&L and "contribute" $10 million in capital to the thrift.

Phony profits could also be made from "goodwill" mergers. A thrift that was insolvent on a market-value basis could purchase a more deeply insolvent thrift and in the process receive accounting "goodwill." Presumably, the purpose of goodwill policies was to encourage entrepreneurs to bring new capital into the ailing industry and "resolve" defunct thrifts without incurring costs to the government. In practice, the acquirer received both goodwill (i.e., fictional accounting) capital to stave off inevitable collapse and regulatory goodwill that spelled forbearance for the acquirer who had cooperated in an unassisted "resolution." And *the more insolvent the S&L acquired, the larger the "goodwill" or "income"*: Those who acquired the most insolvent thrifts earned the most goodwill, accounting profits, and managerial dividends.

In the end, *every* thrift that concentrated on ADC loans and other direct investments, that experienced a change of ownership, and that grew rapidly in the 1980s failed catastrophically. Whether in Texas where the economy went from bad to worse in the mid-1980s or in California where the economy was booming, thrift highfliers crashed, leaving the taxpayers to pick up the pieces.

There is little disagreement about these facts. Experts, government officials, and academics from both sides of the fraud debate agree on the circumstances surrounding the worst thrift failures. What they disagree on is the issue of intent and the amount of deliberate fraud involved. But if we assume that thrift managers are rational economic actors, deliberate abuse is the only viable explanation for the behavior of insiders at the worst failures.

This is not to say that all failures were attributable to fraud. The

economic environment in Texas *was* stacked against real estate lenders, and the interest rate crisis of the late 1970s *had* brought the
industry to market-value insolvency.[79] No doubt some thrifts did
gamble unsuccessfully for resurrection. But such cases did not produce the catastrophic losses associated with the thrift debacle. Nor,
as we have seen, can they account for the *pattern of failures* that dominates the thrift disaster. It is hard to determine the precise cost of
fraud in the thrift debacle or the exact percentage of failures whose
primary cause was fraud. What we do know is that fraud and insider
abuse were central components of this financial disaster.

Referring to the major role of fraud in the thrift crisis and the
reluctance of many to admit to its importance, William Black, then
deputy chief counsel at the Office of Thrift Supervision in San
Francisco and a major protagonist in unraveling Charles Keating's
crimes, testified before Congress, "To steal another quotation from
folks I kind of like, Samuel Butler said this: 'It has been said that
though God cannot alter the past, historians can. It is perhaps because they are useful to him in this respect that he tolerates their
existence.' And there was a great deal of rewriting of history that
has been going on about the causes of the thrift problem." [80]

THRIFT CRIME DEMYSTIFIED

It has been said that one reason Americans lost interest in the thrift debacle was because it was too complex to follow. Compared to the simple "House bank scandal"[1] that soon eclipsed the thrift scandal as front-page news, the savings and loan crisis was—in the words of *Rolling Stone* reporter P. J. O'Rourke— "dictatorship by tedium." O'Rourke opined, "Government officials [in the S&L cleanup] can do anything they want, because any time regular people try to figure out what gives, the regular people get hopelessly bored and confused, as though they'd fallen a month behind in their high-school algebra class."[2]

While it is true that some of the transactions the highfliers engaged in were complex (often deliberately so), it does not take a Ph.D. in finance theory to understand what went on. There were a limited number of basic formulas for abusing thrifts, and many of the most complex strategies were a variation on these themes. Personal interviews with regulators and FBI investigators, journalistic accounts and congressional hearings, and the TIMS data provided to us by the RTC have allowed us to compile a classification of the major types of thrift fraud.

Before proceeding, it is important to reconfirm the importance of insider abuse, as compared to thrift victimization by outsiders. This issue is of both theoretical and practical importance. The position of offenders in relation to the organization in which they commit their crimes is important in the analysis of white-collar crime generally, a point recently made by David Weisburd and his colleagues: "The most consequential white-collar crimes—in terms of their scope, impact, and cost in dollars—appear to require for their commission that their perpetrators operate in an environment that provides access to both money and the organization through which money moves." [3]

Some representatives of the thrift industry have argued that many of the problems of failed thrifts in the 1980s were brought on by outsiders. Thrift officers, they claimed, unaccustomed to the complex financial transactions allowed by deregulation, were victimized by slick real estate developers, brokers, and speculators who lured them into high-risk ventures with fraudulent loan applications and inflated land appraisals. We will see that the complicated schemes at the heart of the scandal required the participation of thrift insiders and that much thrift fraud involved complex networks of insiders and outsiders who conspired to abuse their institutions. Our RTC data, which allow us to identify the positions of those cited in criminal referrals, confirm our argument that high-level insiders were the protagonists in the largest and costliest frauds.

We define "insiders" as directors, officers, shareholders, and employees of the thrift. "Outsiders" include agents, brokers, appraisers, account holders, and borrowers. In table 3, tabulated from the TIMS data on criminal referrals in insolvent institutions, we distinguish between those referrals in which one or more insiders were cited, with or without outsiders, and those in which outsiders alone were cited as suspects. Of the 2,051 referrals in which the suspect's position was identified, 63 percent involved insiders in some capacity and only 37 percent involved outsiders alone. Far from a case of naive insiders being victimized by slick con artists, the majority of suspected thrift fraud at RTC institutions was self-inflicted.

Table 3
Insiders/Outsiders Cited in Referrals

Position of Suspects	Number of Referrals
Insiders [a]	1,294 (63%)
Outsiders only [b]	757 (37%)
Total	2,051

Source: Data from Resolution Trust Corporation, TIMS data base.
[a] Insiders include directors, officers, employees, and shareholders.
[b] Outsiders include agents, brokers, appraisers, account holders, borrowers, and others.

Any classification scheme that pretends to be exhaustive is a risky undertaking; yet at the most general level we can identify three basic types of insider abuse: "hot deals," "looting," and "covering up." Within these categories there were a great variety of schemes, the most basic of which were repeated again and again as if someone had found the magic formula. This insider abuse involved practices that violated one or more federal bank fraud statutes, including prohibitions against "kickbacks and bribes"; "theft, embezzlement, or misapplication of funds"; "schemes or artifices to defraud federally insured institutions"; "knowingly or willfully falsifying or concealing material facts or making false statements"; "false entries in bank documents with intent to injure or defraud bank regulators [and] examiners"; and/or "aiding and abetting and conspiracy." [4]

HOT DEALS

Hot deals were the sine qua non of insider abuse, providing both the cash flow from which to siphon off funds and the transactional medium within which to disguise it. Without question this was the costliest category of thrift fraud; indeed, the other two forms are largely derivatives of it.

Four kinds of insider transactions were central elements in hot deals. As Senate Banking Committee staff members Konrad Alt and Kristen Siglin explain, these transactions include land flips, nominee loans, reciprocal lending, and linked financing. Alt and Siglin use the following example to explain the land flip strategy: "A sells a parcel of real estate to B for $1 million, its approximate market value. B finances the sale with a bank loan. . . . B sells the property back to A for $2 million. A finances the sale with a bank loan, with the bank relying on a fraudulent appraisal. B repays his original loan and takes $1 million in 'profit' off the table, which he shares with A. A defaults on the loan, leaving the bank with a $1 million loss." [5]

The scam requires at least three participants—two partners to "flip" the property and a corrupt appraiser. While the flip technically could be achieved without the lending institution's participation, the involvement of thrift insiders facilitated the transaction. For one thing, insiders were sometimes associates of the corrupt borrowers, who would at a future date exchange the favor. In addition, while the lending institution was left with an overpriced property, in the short term it made up-front points and fees from the huge loans, from which executive bonuses could be drawn.

It was not unusual in the mid-1980s for partners to sit down and in one afternoon flip a property until its price was double or triple its original market value, refinancing with each flip. The playful jargon for this was "cash for trash," and the loans were referred to as "drag-away loans," because the intention from the beginning was to default and drag away the proceeds. As we saw, Erv Hansen of Centennial Savings and Loan used land flips to increase the value of one property by almost 1,000 percent. In another case, loan broker J. William Oldenburg bought property in Richmond, California, in 1977 for $874,000. Two years later, after a number of flips, he had the land appraised for $83.5 million. He then bought a thrift—State Savings and Loan in Salt Lake City—for $10.5 million and sold his property to it for $55 million.[6] In 1985 State Savings and Loan went under, leaving the FSLIC responsible for $416 million in outstanding deposits, which made this the costliest failure yet in the rapidly escalating thrift crisis.

Don Dixon reportedly "flipped land deals [like] pancakes."[7] He and associates like (Fast Eddie) McBirney at Sunbelt Savings and Loan in Dallas (nicknamed "Gunbelt" by regulators) and Texas developer Danny Faulkner used land flips among other schemes to develop hundreds of miles of condominiums on I-30 northeast of Dallas. Officers at nearby Empire Savings and Loan financed the land flips so as to inflate the value of the land and provide the rationale for making the condo development loans despite an already glutted Dallas real estate market.[8] Faulkner and his partners hosted weekend brunches at Wise's Circle Grill in the I-30 corridor. Invited guests included officials from Empire Savings and Loan, investors, appraisers, and, increasingly, politicians, who drew huge campaign contributions from the events. Properties quickly changed hands over breakfast, and millions of dollars of phony profits were made in a few hours.[9]

A close associate of Faulkner's describes one occasion on which land flips were conducted in the hallway of an office building in Dallas: "The tables were lined all of the way down the hall, and the investors were lined up in front of the tables. The loan officers would close one sale and pass the papers to the next guy, who would close another sale at a higher price. It was unbelievable. It looked like kids registering for college. If an investor raised a question, someone would come over and tell them to get out of the line, they were out of the deal."[10]

In March 1984 Ed Gray, new chair of the FHLBB, received a videotape in the mail from the Federal Home Loan Bank (FHLB) in Dallas. He and two other Bank Board members inserted the tape in a VCR and watched what these land deals had wrought. A Dallas appraiser narrated the apparently homemade video, as a camera scanned mile after mile of empty, often unfinished condominiums left to rot, most of which had been financed by Empire. "The condominiums stretched as far as the eye could see, in two- and three-floor clusters, maybe 15 units per building. They were separated by stretches of arid, flat land. Many were half-finished shells. Most were abandoned, left to the ravages of the hot Texas sun."[11]

Ed Gray was, by all reports, appalled. When he sent some of his federal regulators to Texas to see the damage firsthand, they were shocked by the prevailing mentality. As one regulator tells it: "I went down there and this Texan showed me this piece of land and told me how this guy had sold it to that guy, and that guy had sold it again, until it had been sold about six times, and I said, 'Oh, my God. That's terrible,' and he said, 'Only if you're sixth.' " Empire or some other highflying thrift was usually "sixth," as they had to absorb the loss when the loans were defaulted on. American taxpayers of course were "seventh."

Empire was soon closed down, having grown from a $20 million thrift to one with a portfolio of $330 million two years later. Regulators determined that its participation in land flips and other forms of insider dealing was a major cause of its costly collapse. Beyond the expense of paying off Empire's depositors—most of whom had invested in high-interest brokered deposits—the frauds at Empire had powerful ripple effects, through their contribution to the already overbuilt Texas real estate market.[12] The Empire case—and the I-30 condominium fiasco in which it was involved—is a prime example of the folly of distinguishing deliberate insider abuse, on one hand, from investment practices and economic forces such as the real estate market, on the other.

Nominee loans were often used in conjunction with land flips. Nominee lending refers to the practice of using a straw borrower to act as a surrogate for another who does not wish to reveal his or her identity. The technique was used to circumvent loan-to-one-borrower regulations or restrictions on insider borrowing. One costly nominee loan partnership involved international real estate investor Franklin Winkler, Hawaii realtor Sam Daily, loan broker Mario Renda, and Indian Springs State Bank vice president Anthony Russo. According to Pizzo, Fricker, and Muolo, Renda advertised for brokered deposits at one percentage point above the going rate and placed the deposits at Indian Springs (for which he received a hefty "finder's fee"); straw borrowers, located by the partners and paid a kickback, then took out loans from the thrift, the proceeds of which they passed on to Renda, Daily, and Winkler.[13]

While the most straightforward nominee lending scheme involved this sort of straw borrower, a more complex variation entailed setting up holding companies or subsidiaries through which to make loans to oneself. The story of Ranbir Sahni, formerly a pilot for Air India, and his American Diversified Savings Bank in Lodi, California, is exemplary. Sahni bought American Diversified in 1983 and quickly turned the small-town thrift into a highflier. First he stopped writing home loans entirely, then closed the teller windows, and finally shut down the storefront bank, opening up instead ninth-floor office space for receiving brokered deposits and transacting his many investment schemes.[14]

Most of these investments were in two Sahni-owned subsidiaries—American Diversified Capital and American Diversified Investment—and a collection of tax-shelter partnerships. Through his ownership of American Diversified and its virtually endless source of high-interest brokered deposits (American Diversified paid the highest interest rates on deposits in the country during this time), Sahni had acquired a risk-free money machine for his development companies; looked at the other way round, these companies acted as straw borrowers for Sahni.

In one notorious transaction Sahni invested federally insured money in a giant windmill farm in the desert between San Bernardino and Palm Springs. Thousands of modern windmills with steel sails now sit idle in the central California desert. American Diversified also "invested" in a chicken farm purportedly designed to process chicken manure into methane energy, shopping centers and condominiums, and $300 million in worthless junk bonds. It was later revealed that Sahni was a partner in all of the real estate deals and alternative energy projects his thrift invested in.[15] The insider dealing and brokered deposits through which it was financed caused American Diversified to be the fastest-growing thrift in the United States, soon to collapse and leave almost a billion-dollar loss for the government. As one observer describes the life course of American Diversified: "With perhaps $500,000 in equity, it destroyed $800 million of insured deposits, a kill ratio of 1600 to 1. . . . This anecdote is tantamount to a news report that a drunken motorist has wiped out the entire city of Pittsburgh."[16] And this in the booming California economy of the mid-1980s.

In Santa Ana, California, Duayne Christensen and Janet McKinzie were busy constructing the same kind of complex nominee loan schemes. Christensen, a former dentist, opened North American Savings and Loan in Santa Ana in 1983. In partnership with McKinzie, Christensen used the thrift to make loans to his own real estate projects and to participate in multiple land flips, through a real estate company owned and controlled by McKinzie. In a typical scheme straw borrower David Morgan would purchase property brokered by McKinzie's company and financed by North American. He would then immediately resell the property at an inflated value to his own holding company. Fees and commissions poured into McKinzie's real estate brokerage. North American made up-front points and fees but apparently never saw the proceeds of any of the properties' resales.[17] North American was taken over by regulators in 1988, at a loss of $209 million. The day before the takeover, Christensen was killed in his Jaguar in a freak single-car accident.

In reciprocal lending, another way of circumventing restrictions against insider borrowing, instead of making a loan directly to oneself, which would have sounded the alarm among regulators, two or more insiders at different thrifts made loans to each other. Making loans to each other is not in itself illegal, but making loans solely or primarily on the basis of a reciprocal loan rather than underwriting is fraud.[18] These daisy chains often involved multiple participants, and unraveling them sometimes took investigators far afield of the original institution and exposed the complex conspiratorial quality of thrift fraud. One investigation in Wyoming in 1987 revealed a single daisy chain of reciprocal loans among four thrifts that by itself resulted in a $26 million loss to taxpayers.[19] A Texas network included at least seventy-four daisy chain participants and involved all the insolvent thrifts in the state.[20]

A macabre variation on reciprocal lending involved the trading not of loans but of bad assets. In this arrangement—the evocative jargon for which is trading "dead cows for dead horses"—savings and loans traded their nonperforming loans back and forth to each other, temporarily getting them off the books and artificially enhancing their pictures of financial health. These transactions were central to keeping zombie institutions open well after their insolvency so they could be further looted, increasing substantially the final cost of the bailout.[21] In one case nineteen of the largest thrifts in Texas sent representatives to a secret meeting in Houston in 1985 to exchange "dead cows and horses" for the explicit purpose of keeping regulators at bay.[22]

Similar in logic to reciprocal lending arrangements, linked financing involves depositing money in a thrift with the understanding that the depositor will receive a loan in return. Alt and Siglin provide an example: "Bank X, a weak institution facing a liquidity problem, badly needs $1 million in fresh deposits. A, a deposit broker, agrees to arrange a $1 million deposit, if Bank X will make a non-recourse loan of $250,000 so that ACorp, a concern in which A is an interested party, can purchase a parcel of real estate from B.

Bank X receives the deposit and makes the loan. ACorp's purchase from B turns out to be a land flip. Bank X forecloses and ends up holding worthless real estate, suffering a $250,000 loss." [23]

Don Dixon at Vernon was an expert at linked financing. For example, he and Vernon CEO Woody Lemons established the Moonlight Beach Joint Venture in Encinitas, California, north of San Diego, to develop a condominium project adjacent to an exclusive beach club. When the beach club decided to expand, it needed funding to acquire the Dixon/Lemons property. Dixon and Lemons came to the rescue, offering Vernon depositors as a source of new members—and hence revenue. O'Shea explains how it worked: "Pretty soon, big customers seeking loans at Vernon Savings started hearing about this great beach club near San Diego. . . . No one said a $10-million loan request for a shopping center would be denied if the developer didn't join the beach club. But everyone got the message." [24] Regulator William Black calls Dixon's beach club scam a "perfect crime." [25] As in many of the deals discussed here, transactions were accomplished according to implicit agreements, leaving little incriminating evidence.

Loan broker Mario Renda specialized in setting up linked financing deals. So adept was he at these "special deals" [26] and so brazen did he become that he advertised in the Wall Street Journal, the New York Times, and the Los Angeles Times: "MONEY FOR RENT: BORROWING OBSTACLES NEUTRALIZED BY HAVING US DEPOSIT FUNDS WITH YOUR LOCAL BANK: NEW TURNSTYLE APPROACH TO FINANC-ING." [27] The scam went like this: Renda placed large brokered deposits in a thrift, for which he received the usual finder's fee, in return for which borrowers with credit "obstacles" automatically received a generous loan from the thrift. Response to Renda's ads was overwhelming. According to his own court testimony, Renda brokered the deposits for hundreds of linked financing schemes. When investigators examined the files at his First United Fund, they found two sets of lyrics written by Renda employees. One entitled

"The Twelve Days of Bilking" was to be sung to the tune of "The
Twelve Days of Christmas"; the other was "Bilkers in the Night,"
sung to the tune of "Strangers in the Night."

Renda has been called the "Typhoid Mary" of the thrift industry.
His firm placed more deposits in thrifts and banks that subsequently
failed than any other brokerage house in the country. But the expression "Typhoid Mary" suggests that the thrifts themselves were inno-
cent victims of Renda's abuse. Some no doubt were. Apparently,
Renda increasingly dealt with savings and loans rather than banks
because he believed they were easier targets. One observer explained, "Renda used to tell his troops at First United Fund that as
stupid and sheeplike as bankers were, savings and loan officials were
on an even lower grade of intelligence." [28]

It should be pointed out that it is an offense to offer loans contingent on receipt of deposits, whatever the naïveté of thrift insiders
regarding the likelihood of repayment. Furthermore, in addition to
many Midwest thrifts with perhaps unsophisticated management,
Renda did much of his business with highfliers in California and
Texas who knew exactly what they were doing. Not just Erv Hansen
at Centennial but many other thrift insiders who have been charged
with major insider abuse did business with Mario Renda. [29]

Investigators and regulators report finding variations of land flips,
nominee loans, linked financing, and reciprocal lending arrangements over and over in their autopsies of seized thrifts. One regulator told us the pattern was repeated so often "it was as if someone
had found a cookie cutter." [30] Many hot deals used elements of these
four transaction frauds in combination. ADC lending is a good
example. As the National Commission on Financial Institution Reform, Recovery and Enforcement put it, "ADC loans were an attractive vehicle for abuse. They bound up in one instrument many of
the opportunities available." [31] A land flip might provide inflated
collateral for a generous ADC loan; the loan then might be made
to a straw borrower who shared the proceeds with thrift insiders

(nominee lending); thrift managers might provide the loan in return for a deposit or other investment (linked financing); and/or
thrift insiders might exchange loans to finance development projects with each other (reciprocal lending arrangements). ADC lending thus not only had the advantage of providing huge up-front fees
from which bonuses could be drawn, but it was often the vehicle
for lucrative insider dealing.

Inventive accounting practices were central to this kind of lending.
In the early 1980s thrifts were encouraged by the FHLBB to take
advantage of the fact that generally accepted accounting principles
(GAAP) contained extensive gray areas. To stave off closing insolvent thrifts, which by the early 1980s was beyond the financial
capacity of the FSLIC, the Bank Board allowed them to report loan
fees and future interest as current income and to underreport bad
debts. In addition, GAAP provided no clear rules for distinguishing
direct investments from traditional loans. This was an important
distinction, because self-funded fees and interest on direct investments could not be reported as income, but such fees and interest
on loans could be reported as income. William Black describes the
consequence of this gray area in GAAP: "This allowed unscrupulous
insiders to use competitive pressures of accountant shopping to
seek out auditors who would permit almost any ADC transaction to
be treated as a true loan." [32]

Instead of curbing such abuses, the FHLBB introduced further
flexibility through regulatory accounting principles (RAP). These
increased the level of up-front loan fees that could be counted as
income and allowed thrifts to sell assets at a loss while continuing
to report them as assets. [33] Together these accounting practices provided an incentive for ADC lending that was in essence a Ponzi
scheme (see chapter 1). The thrift fully funded the loan including
up-front fees and interest for the first few years; with each new loan
made, the thrift reported more income through self-funded fees
and interest payments from a reserve provided by the loan itself; as

in any Ponzi, this scheme required a continual flow of new money, provided by new deposits at interest rates of up to 22 percent.

When the house of cards collapsed, as it inevitably did, the loss to taxpayers often went far beyond what insiders had made on the fraud. As explained by the NCFIRRE, "In order to manufacture $14 of loan fees and interest, it was necessary to grant a $114 loan. If the loan proved to be worth only 50 percent of its face value, taxpayers were stuck with a $57 loss, even though the S&L operators only enriched themselves by $14." [34] Of course, when insiders were involved with straw borrowers or had other reciprocal arrangements with borrowers, they benefited directly as well, beyond the bonuses they derived from loan points and fees.

LOOTING

"Looting" refers to the more direct siphoning off of funds by thrift insiders and is thus more like traditional forms of crime than are the business transactions involved in hot deals. In its report on fraud in financial institutions the House Committee on Government Operations expressed frustration with management looting: "Usual internal controls do not work in this instance." The committee went on to quote the commissioner of the California Department of Savings and Loans: "*The best way to rob a bank is to own one.*" [35]

Because thrift management was doing the robbing—or looting—it took different forms from a typical bank robbery or embezzlement by a lower-level employee. The most straightforward, but probably least common, way to loot was simply to remove deposits from the thrift and stash them away. Former rug salesman John Molinaro and associate Donald Mangano looted their small Ramona Savings and Loan in this way. When the FBI arrested Molinaro on his way to the Cayman Islands after the collapse of Ramona, they found his memos to himself: "consider storing gold in Cayman deposit box . . . write out a plan for depositing Cayman cash and bringing some back thru Canada." Diamonds, gold, and millions of dollars in cash were found at First Cayman Bank. Molinaro and Mangano were charged with taking more than $24 million out of the small thrift.[36]

Subtler, and probably more common, forms of looting were shopping sprees with thrift funds and excessive bonuses or other forms of compensation. Examples of the former abound. Thomas Spiegel, director and chief executive officer of Columbia Savings and Loan Association in Beverly Hills, was charged with multiple counts of bank fraud including the use of Columbia funds to finance his lavish lifestyle. Spiegel and his family made at least four trips to Europe and innumerable domestic trips; purchased guns, ammunition, and accessories totaling $91,000; bought several condominiums and resort villas; and purchased a jet aircraft for $5.6 million—all paid for by federally insured Columbia deposits. The notice of charges against Spiegel listed other "miscellaneous personal expenses" funded by Columbia deposits: "approximately $1,953 for silverware and table linens . . . $8,600 for towels . . . $19,775 for 16 cashmere throws and 3 comforters selected by Helene Spiegel . . . $6,830 for Christmas gifts, including $1,660 for champagne and $3,778 for televisions and clocks . . . $2,000 for a French wine tasting course . . . $11,840 for music concerts . . . [and] $1,800 for the installation of a stereo into a Mercedes Benz 560 SEL."[37]

Janet McKinzie and Duayne Christensen similarly used North American Savings and Loan as their own personal piggy bank, or "cash cow."[38] Each had a Rolls Royce; McKinzie charged hundreds of thousands of dollars of clothes from Neiman Marcus to North American; and they spent $125,000 for a gold eagle statue, $18,500 for a letter opener, and $500 for a solid gold paper clip. On McKinzie's birthday they hosted a five-course dinner party for several hundred guests, with Sammy Davis, Jr., providing the entertainment.[39]

Ed McBirney at Sunbelt Savings and Loan threw parties on an even grander scale. According to regulators, in 1984 and 1985 McBirney spent over $1 million of Sunbelt funds on Halloween and Christmas parties, including a $32,000 payment to his wife for planning the extravaganzas.[40] At his 1984 Halloween party McBirney went as a king, and the dinner featured broiled lion, antelope, and pheasant to fit the medieval theme. The next year the theme was an African safari, complete with a "jungle" and real elephants. McBirney specialized in parties and entertainment. Besides his seven airplanes on which he shuttled business partners and political allies to resorts and hunting trips and his notorious $1,000 bar tabs for himself and guests at the latest Dallas clubs, McBirney "produced prostitutes for his customers the same way an ordinary businessman might spring for lunch."[41] As one reporter put it, "McBirney . . . ran an Animal House version of a savings and loan."[42]

David Paul bought CenTrust Savings Bank in Miami in 1983 and quickly turned it into a megathrift with $9.8 billion in assets, $1.35 billion of it in junk bonds purchased from Milken at Drexel.[43] The massive thrift provided for his every need. Arguing later that his personal and home life were integral to his business, Paul spent over $40 million of CenTrust money for a yacht, a Rubens painting (for $12 million), a sailboat, Limoges china, and Baccarat crystal.[44] In addition, Paul built a monument to himself—the forty-seven-floor CenTrust tower. The tower, with a gold-inlay ceiling in Paul's private office, cost $170 million to build.[45] When CenTrust collapsed, it was the largest S&L failure in the Southeast, costing taxpayers $1.7 billion. For his part in the insolvency David Paul was convicted of ninety-seven counts of racketeering and fraud and sentenced to eleven years in prison.[46]

Excessive compensation schemes often went hand in hand with profligate spending. The General Accounting Office defines "compensation" as "salaries as well as bonuses, dividend payments, and perquisites for executives."[47] A federal regulation limits permissible compensation for thrift personnel to that which is "reasonable and commensurate with their duties and responsibilities." The GAO found flagrant violations of this regulation in 17 of the 26 failed thrifts it studied.[48]

At one thrift the chairman of the board of directors resigned his formal position and arranged a "services agreement" through which he would be paid $326,000 a year plus a percentage of profits. Six months later the thrift paid him a bonus of $500,000 in "special employee compensation," even though it reported a loss of $23 million that year.[49] Spiegel at Columbia Savings and Loan received $22 million in compensation from 1985 to 1989. In 1990 he was charged with excessive compensation for taking a bonus of $3 million in 1988, when Columbia reported a net income loss of $240 million.[50]

Don Dixon at Vernon declared $22.9 million in dividends between 1982 and 1986, almost all of it going to Dixon-owned Dondi Financial Corp. At the same time Dixon and his top executives took more than $15 million in bonuses, even though subsequent investigations would show that the thrift was already deeply in debt.[51] During the six years that David Paul was driving CenTrust into the ground, he paid himself $16 million in salary and bonuses, $5 million of it coming in 1988 and 1989 when the thrift was piling up losses from its junk bond investments.[52]

Charles Keating ranked among the worst offenders in taking excessive compensation from his thrift, which he referred to as a "merchant bank" with which to finance his investments and lifestyle.[53] But not all looters were as high-profile as Dixon, McBirney, and Keating. Lesser-known Jeffrey and Karol Levitt plundered their Old Court Savings and Loan in Maryland, taking out $2 million a year in salary and using Old Court to buy $500,000 in jewelry, purchasing art, and financing gambling excursions to nearby Atlantic City. The couple also charged to their thrift two beach condominiums, three racehorses, an apartment in Baltimore and one in New York City, and an interest in a Florida country club.[54] Michael

Binstein says the Levitts "bought whatever got in their way: cars, crystal, silver, china, art, pastries." On his way to prison for the misappropriation of $14.5 million of thrift funds, Levitt said simply, "I got carried away."[55]

It is difficult to know precisely what proportion of the thrift debacle is due to looting, or siphoning off of thrift funds for personal use. Of the twenty-six thrifts studied by the GAO in 1989, shopping sprees and excessive compensation had occurred in the vast majority.[56] Compared to hot deals, a large number of lootings have been prosecuted, but this is probably because of the relative ease of building a convincing body of evidence for these more straightforward frauds compared to the complex business transactions surrounding hot deals.[57] In any case, hot deals and insider looting went hand in hand: the deals provided the cash flow and reported income with which to finance shopping sprees and excessive compensation. Indeed, the ability to siphon off "profits" often provided the incentive for hot deals and the rapid growth they fueled.

HOT DEALS AND LOOTING AS COLLECTIVE EMBEZZLEMENT

In discussing different forms of white-collar crime, Sutherland described embezzlement: "The ordinary case of embezzlement is a crime by a single individual in a subordinate position against a strong corporation."[58] Donald Cressey, in his landmark study, *Other People's Money*, focused on the behavior of the lone white-collar embezzler stealing from his or her employer.[59] Traditionally, then, embezzlement is thought of as an isolated act of an individual employee who steals from the corporation for personal gain.

Criminologists have typically drawn a sharp distinction between this "embezzlement" by individuals against the corporation and "corporate crime," in which fraud is perpetrated by the corporation on behalf of the corporation. Stanton Wheeler and Mitchell Lewis

Rothman speak of two distinct types of white-collar crime: "Either the individual gains at the organization's expense, as in embezzlement, or the organization profits regardless of individual advantage, as in price-fixing."[60] And James Coleman argues, "The distinction between organizational crimes committed with support from an organization that is, at least in part, furthering its own ends, and occupational crimes committed for the benefit of individual criminals without organizational support, provides an especially powerful way of classifying different kinds of white-collar crime."[61]

Neglected in this distinction is the possibility of organizational crime in which the organization or corporation is a vehicle for perpetrating crime *against itself*, as in hot deals and looting. This form of white-collar crime is a hybrid between traditional corporate crime and embezzlement—crime *by* the corporation *against* the corporation—and might be thought of as "collective embezzlement." Unlike the embezzlers described by Sutherland and Cressey, these "collective embezzlers" were not lone, lower-level employees but thrift owners and managers, acting within networks of co-conspirators inside and outside the institution. Indeed, this embezzlement was company policy.

In some cases it was the very purpose of the organization to provide a vehicle for fraud against itself. Wheeler and Rothman have pointed to "the organization as weapon" in white-collar crime: "The organization . . . is for white-collar criminals what the gun or knife is for the common criminal—a tool to obtain money from victims."[62] In the collective embezzlement in the thrift industry the organization was both weapon *and* victim. As we will see in a moment, this hybrid form of white-collar crime in some important ways more closely resembles organized crime than it does traditional forms of corporate crime on which the criminological literature has tended to focus.

The structure of the thrift industry—and finance capitalism more generally—provides a particularly opportune environment for collective embezzlement. Unlike the manufacturing sector, in which consumers receive products or services for their money, thrift managers need not actually produce anything in exchange for the cash flow of their customers. And because deposits are insured, opportunities for embezzlement can be expanded almost indefinitely through raising the interest paid for deposits. Furthermore, with no long-term investment in the infrastructure of production such as constrains industrial capitalists, the main concern of those intent on financial fraud is to make as much money as fast as possible, without concern for the impact of their crimes on the health of the institution.

Indeed, collective embezzlement may be integrally related to late twentieth-century finance capitalism. In this casino economy the largest profits are made from placing a good bet, not making a better mousetrap.[63] Maurice Allais underscores the shift from an economy based on the circulation of goods to one circulating money itself, pointing out that "more than $400 billion is exchanged every day on the foreign exchange markets, while the flow of commercial transactions is only about $12 billion."[64] Nothing epitomizes the new financial era like the junk bond. The irony of its name should not be lost. This device transforms debt into wealth and "junk" into "one of the greatest fortunes in Wall Street history."[65]

Finance capitalism spawns vast new opportunities for fraud, as we have seen. This economic structure may actually encourage fraud, or at least fail to inhibit it. There are of course numerous incentives and opportunities for serious crime in industrial capitalism as well, as several generations of white-collar crime scholars have documented. But corporate criminals in the industrial sector generally commit crime to *advance* corporate interests and are constrained by a vested interest in their corporation's long-term survival. By contrast, perpetrators of financial fraud in the casino economy have little to lose. The effect of their crimes on the health of the casino or even its survival is unimportant to these financial highfliers. *Business Week* describes "all the games the casino society plays": "The object . . . is to get rich today, come what may."[66] Collective embezzlement, in which highly placed insiders loot their own institutions, may be the prototypical form of white-collar crime in this context, much as violations of fair labor standards or consumer protections are to the industrial production process.

COVERING UP

As savings and loans teetered on the brink of insolvency, broken by hot deals and looting, their operators struggled to hide both the insolvency and the fraud through manipulating their books and records. Of the 179 violations of criminal fraud reported in the twenty-six failed thrifts studied by the GAO, 42 were for such cover-up activities, making it the largest single category of crime.[67] Furthermore, every one of the twenty-six thrifts had been cited by examiners for "deficiencies in accounting."[68]

In some cases the cover-up came in the form of deals like those discussed above, where the primary purpose of the transaction was to produce a misleading picture of the institution's state of health. U.S. Attorney Anton R. Valukas describes a number of cover-up deals: "In the prosecuted cases of Manning Savings and Loan, American Heritage Savings and Loan of Bloomingdale and First Suburban Bank of Maywood, when the loans [nominee loans] became nonperforming the assets were taken back into the institution, again sold at inflated prices to straw purchasers, financed by the institution, in order to inflate the net worth of the bank or savings and loan. The clear purpose was to keep the federal regulatory agencies . . . at bay by maintaining a net worth above the trigger point for forced reorganization or liquidation."[69] In another instance, when Molinaro and his partner Mangano of Ramona S&L suffered substantial losses on a fraudulent real estate project, they sold the project at an inflated price to straw borrowers, posting a significant profit. Having recorded the profit, they then repurchased the project through their affiliated service corporation.[70]

Insiders also could simply doctor their books to shield their thrift from regulatory action. At one S&L studied by the GAO, three sets of books were kept—two on different computer systems and one manually. At another, $21 million of income was reported in the last few days of 1985 in transactions that were either fabricated or fraudulent, allowing the thrift to report a net worth of $9 million rather than its actual negative worth of $12 million.[71] McKinzie and Christensen at North American S&L had a policy of preparing bogus documents when challenged by regulators. When the thrift was finally taken over, examiners found evidence of fake certificates of deposit, forged bank confirmation letters, and other cover-up paraphernalia. They even found a memo from McKinzie to her secretary telling her to "be sure to sign good" and to prepare "sealed envelopes so that it looks professional" when forging bank confirmation letters.[72]

It was sometimes necessary to doctor the minutes of board meetings as well. When Don Dixon received a "supervisory agreement" from regulators in 1984, his first instinct was to ignore its restrictions on Vernon. But when examiners notified Dixon of their intention to inspect Vernon's records, he told his secretary to rewrite the minutes of meetings to be consistent with the supervisory agreement he had signed. On other occasions Dixon's secretary was instructed to add things to the minutes that had never been discussed at the board meetings.[73]

Keating was the king of cover-up. When examiners studied Lincoln's records after it was taken over, they discovered thousands of forged documents. In one instance Keating's employees were flown from Phoenix to Irvine to doctor more than a thousand pages of board meeting minutes extending over a two-year period. At Keating's instructions they forged signatures, fabricated information, and shredded the original documents. Keating and his partners would later claim that they were only tidying up in preparation for the examiners.[74]

Having perpetrated fraud and brought their institutions to ruin, thrift operators had to cover their tracks, both to protect themselves from prosecution and to keep their money machines running. Ironically, they were aided in their efforts by the same agencies from which they were presumably hiding. The FHLBB set in place bookkeeping strategies during the deregulatory period in the early 1980s—such as the revised GAAP and RAP policies—that provided the industry with the tools to juggle their books to present themselves in the best light and relayed the message that, in trying to stay open, anything goes.

EXAMPLES FROM THE DALLAS OTS FILES

A subsample of Category I criminal referrals in one state, Texas, offers a more detailed picture of the part these types of insider fraud played in the thrift crisis. Here we rely on data from the Dallas Office of Thrift Supervision, which maintains computer files on all criminal referrals in the state. We selected a 20 percent sample from the list of 1,210 Category I criminal referrals filed between January 1985 and March 1993 by choosing every fifth referral. We then examined closely the actual referral forms for each of the 241 cases in our sample. The files we had access to consisted of the original referrals as well as numerous supporting documents describing suspect transactions. From these referrals and documents we coded the type of suspected violation, whether insiders were alleged to have been involved, the dollar amount of loss from the suspected crime, and information regarding the impact of the suspected crime on the institution.

Our main objective was to obtain a better sense of the nature of the crimes being reported at thrift institutions. To do this we had to create a coding scheme that was more naturalistic than legalistic. All of the suspected violations could be described in vague terms such as "bank fraud" or "misrepresentation." But these legal categories tell us little about how the frauds were actually accomplished and what they consisted of. For this we needed a set of categories that were closer to the actual events. Based on a careful perusal of the original referrals to which we had access, we developed eleven specific categories of fraud that described insider abuse at these institutions and two categories for outsider fraud. While many of these categories overlap in practice, particularly since these frauds were generally complex and often contained several layers of deception, we made these distinctions according to what was the primary offense or central ingredient of the suspected misconduct.

Let us look first at our descriptive scheme for insider fraud, which is our primary focus. Although we have already discussed a number of these types of fraudulent transactions, for purposes of clarity we will define them again here. *Insider loans* refer to loans granted by an institution to insiders themselves, or to their associates, or to entities in which insiders had a stake. Often these transactions involved the use of straw borrowers to disguise the identity of the actual loan recipient. The second category, *self-dealing*, is similarly an illegal transfer of funds to institutional insiders. This could involve, for example, direct investments by the institution in subsidiaries or limited partnerships in which institutional insiders had a stake.

Cash for trash involves the sale of bad loans to an associate in order to remove them from the books and thereby artificially enhance an institution's financial profile. *Daisy chains* are comprised of a network (or chain) of associates who accommodate each other's phony transactions; they are essentially Ponzi schemes in which the participants are co-conspirators. *Land flips* involve selling a property back and forth among two or more partners until its "value" has increased many times over (the property may then be used as collateral for a large loan).

Misuse of funds covers a variety of improper uses of an institution's funds. In one instance the thrift's president used $390,000 of the S&L's money to pay for a company Christmas party. In another an S&L owner used thrift funds to purchase a $2 million yacht and dock it in Washington, D.C., where it was used to host lavish parties for highly placed politicians. *Siphoning off of funds* refers to the diversion of thrift funds for the personal use of highly placed insiders. Under the category *misconduct*, we include potentially criminal behavior by insiders who indirectly divert the thrift's funds for personal gain (unlike siphoning or misuse of funds, in which direct diversions take place). In one such case, for example, a thrift president purchased a car from the institution at below-market value. *Kickbacks* typically involved thrift insiders requiring cash payments from borrowers to whom they had made loans.

Institutional insiders also collaborated with outsiders to file *false documents*—for example, in connection with loans (but since the investigator presumably had no specific knowledge of the actual loans, the charge was simply "false documents"). *Misrepresentation* refers to the altering of thrift records, often to give regulators a false impression of the financial health of the institution.[75]

As we can see from table 4, all but three of the 193 insider cases in our sample involved one of these types of fraud. Further, if we look at these frauds through the lens of the classificatory scheme we developed, we can see that they all constitute some form of hot deal, looting, or covering up: insider loans, self-dealing, cash for trash, daisy chains, and land flips are hot deals; misuse of funds, siphoning off of funds, misconduct, and kickbacks are specific forms of looting; and misrepresentation and the filing of false documents are cover-ups.

Four forms of looting and two forms of covering up made up approximately 20 percent and 11 percent, respectively, of these cases of insider fraud. By far the most common forms of fraud were hot deals, with insider loans and self-dealing constituting 44

Table 4
Crime Types and Losses
(Texas Criminal Referrals, 1985–1993)

Crimes	Number		Mean Losses
Involving Insiders			
Insider loans	56		$5,664,864
Self-dealing	50		$3,784,440
Cash for trash	7		$21,552,796
Daisy chains	2		$11,500,000
Land flips	16		$20,540,788
Misuse of funds	11		$15,755,454
Misconduct	6		$12,728
Siphoning funds	14		$310,267
Kickbacks	7		$195,972
False documents	10		$5,111,348
Misrepresentation	11		$32,664,458
Miscellaneous	3		$4,572,176
Subtotal	193	(80%)	$8,353,459
Involving Outsiders Only			
Diversion of loan proceeds	9		$1,070,946
False documents	27		$4,935,615
Miscellaneous	12		$118,611
Subtotal	48	(20%)	$3,006,738
Total	241	(100%)	$7,288,552

Source: Data from Office of Thrift Supervision, Dallas.

percent of all the cases in this sample and land flips constituting 7 percent—a distant third place. Together, the different forms of hot deals made up almost 68 percent of these suspected frauds and contributed by far the highest price tag. As these deals often involved multiple institutions and the swapping of many loans and/or properties, the resulting losses could be staggering. Not surprisingly, the average cost of these conspiracies far outstripped the lone embezzler who, on average, siphoned a "mere" $310,267.

These OTS data confirm several more general points as well about the prevalence of insider fraud and the repercussions of these crimes. As table 4 shows, approximately 80 percent of our sample cases involved insider fraud and only 20 percent involved outsiders acting alone. This is consistent with our contention, which is supported by the RTC/TIMS data, that insider fraud was a central ingredient in the crisis.

The OTS referral forms also contain coded responses to several general questions about the nature of the suspected crimes. One of these asks, "Was the suspected crime an isolated incident?" And another, "Did the suspected crime have an impact on the financial soundness of the institution?" As we see in table 5, in 71 percent of the referrals where the question was answered, the suspected crime was not an isolated incident but part of a broader pattern of crime and abuse. As to the consequences of these crimes, in 129 of the referrals the offense was described as having an impact on the "financial soundness" of the institution where it occurred.

These data suggest that, in Texas at least, thrift crimes in the 1980s did not consist primarily of the petty embezzlement and defalcations that made up the bulk of white-collar crimes at lending institutions in the past. Rather, these thrift crimes involved enormously expensive hot deals and looting—crimes by the organization against the organization, or collective embezzlement. While less serious offenses by lone perpetrators continued to occur, they were dwarfed in frequency and scale by these complex, multiparty

Table 5

Criminal Networking and Impact on "Financial Soundness"
(Texas Criminal Referrals, 1985–1993)

Suspected Crime	Yes	No	Unknown	Total
Isolated incident	55	133	53	241
	(23%)	(55%)	(22%)	(100%)
Had impact on	129	66	46	241
"financial	(54%)	(27%)	(19%)	(100%)
soundness"				
of institution				

Source: Data from Office of Thrift Supervision, Dallas.

schemes, often orchestrated by thrift owners and officers to defraud
their own institutions and ultimately the U.S. taxpayer.

THE HIRED GUNS

As thrift crimes were facilitated by their resemblance to ordinary
business activity, it was critical to secure the support of professionals—appraisers, lawyers, and accountants—who provided their official stamp of approval and thereby conferred on the transactions
their "ordinariness." Perhaps most important was the role of accountants, whose favorable audits of S&L records allowed many
scam transactions to go unnoticed. Professional accounting firms
were highly paid for their services and dependent on repeat business and referrals, creating the temptation to ignore evidence of
their clients' wrongdoing. By 1990 twenty-one certified public accountants (CPAs) had been sued by the federal government for their
role in the thrift debacle, fourteen of which involved the Big Six
companies that dominate the industry. So prevalent was the partici-

pation of these large CPA firms (only Price-Waterhouse was not implicated) that the Federal Deposit Insurance Corporation (FDIC) had to abandon its rule against hiring as consultants those who had contributed to the disaster.

In one GAO study of eleven failed thrifts in Texas, six involved such negligence on the part of accountants that investigators referred them for formal action.[76] Among the firms referred were Arthur Young and Company, Ernst & Whinney, and Deloitte, Haskins and Sells—three of the largest accounting firms in the United States. Arthur Andersen endorsed the bookkeeping of Charlie Knapp, head of Financial Corporation of America with $30 billion in assets, before the institution was taken over, costing taxpayers $2 billion, and he is said to have later helped Keating stuff his files with appropriate documentation.[77] Deloitte, Haskins and Sells approved David Paul's records at CenTrust in Florida at a time when Paul and Keating were artificially enhancing the financial health of their respective institutions through "a series of round robin stock trades."[78] At the same time Paul was paying himself several million dollars in salary and bonuses and running up millions of dollars in costs for artwork, limousines, and sailboats, while the thrift was experiencing heavy losses on its investments.[79] Touche Ross confirmed the viability of Beverly Hills Savings and Loan before its failure cost taxpayers an estimated $900 million and the House Committee on Energy and Commerce revealed evidence of criminal misconduct. Arthur Young and Company had audited the books of Don Dixon's Vernon Savings and Loan and reported no irregularities only a few months before it was taken over by federal regulators who found that virtually all of the thrift's loans were in default. Arthur Young had also provided a favorable audit to Western Savings and Loan, which was subsequently bankrupt by fraudulent land flip transactions. William Black was so outraged by the accommodating behavior of the Arthur Young accountants in Dallas that he called their services "the K-Mart blue-light special."[80]

Although they have denied any wrongdoing, a number of the largest accounting firms have settled with the federal government, paying a total of more than $1.4 billion in fines.[81] Ernst & Young (Arthur Young merged with Ernst & Whinney) agreed to pay $400 million, and Deloitte & Touche (Deloitte, Haskins and Sells merged with Touche Ross) contributed the second largest settlement at $312 million.[82] KPMG Peat Marwick, which claims to have audited the books of almost half the thrift industry in the 1980s, making it the nation's biggest thrift auditor, settled for $186.5 million in a blanket agreement involving its audits of twenty-two insolvent banks and thrifts.[83]

Lawyers were also on hand to provide legitimacy to thrift schemes. In a series of lawsuits by the federal government, some of the largest law firms are being brought to task for advising their thrift clients on loans that violated federal regulations. In one case the Philadelphia firm of Blank, Rome, Comisky and McCauley agreed to pay the FSLIC $50 million for its part in the demise of Sunrise Savings and Loan in Fort Lauderdale, Florida. The thrift's top management was convicted of conspiracy in 1989, and the prosecutor dubbed a partner and associate at Blank, Rome, Comisky and McCauley "unindicted co-conspirators" for their role in putting together bogus loan transactions.[84] The firm was later charged with negligence and aiding and abetting Sunrise management in the violation of state and federal laws.

In a similar case the New York law firm of Paul, Weiss, Rifkind, Wharton & Garrison settled for $45 million for its part in the collapse of CenTrust. In the Lincoln debacle three accounting firms and three law firms have paid a total of $146.2 million in private lawsuits brought by Lincoln investors.[85] In Lincoln-related lawsuits brought by the federal government, the Cleveland law firm of Jones, Day, Reavis & Pogue was fined $51 million, and the New York–based Kaye, Scholer, Fierman, Hays & Handler paid fines of $41 million.[86]

These large cases often involved allegations of professional malpractice against lawyers for neglecting to inform regulators of the
wrongdoing of their clients and thus brought to light the tension
within professional codes of ethics concerning lawyer-client privilege. In other instances the professional misconduct was more blatant. In one case Michael Gardner, a partner in the Washington,
D.C., law firm of Akin, Gump, Stauss, Hauer and Feld, accepted
from Charles Keating a "gift" of seven payments totaling $1.5 mil-
lion while representing Lincoln S&L. The irregular arrangement is
described in the formal complaint filed against Gardner by the
Resolution Trust Corporation: "Gardner accepted these payments without providing any legitimate service to Lincoln. . . .
[T]hese payments amounted to an unnecessary and improper gift
of a federally insured institution's funds. . . . No written agreement governed the payment of these substantial fees. No tangible
service was performed in exchange. . . . The arrangement was
not disclosed to Lincoln. Likewise, it appears that Gardner concealed his acceptance of these payments from his partners at Akin
Gump."[87] The formal complaint against Gardner cites three
grounds on which these "side payments" were improper: "unjust
enrichment, breach of his [Gardner's] fiduciary duties to Lincoln,
and aiding and abetting Keating's breach of fiduciary duties to
Lincoln."[88] Although the improprieties enumerated are limited
to Gardner's enrichment at the expense of Lincoln, one is left to
speculate about what informal "services" were expected in return.

Appraisers were central players as well. As assessors of property
values, appraisers are essential to the real estate and banking systems. In the context of ADC lending in the 1980s, appraisers were
absolutely critical. Deregulation had made it possible for thrifts to
lend up to 100 percent of a construction project's appraised value,
or what is called in the industry a 100 percent "loan-to-value," or
LTV. As Lowy points out,

The . . . problem with construction lending based on LTVs is that the appraiser is guessing. . . . The key to the appraisal will be the rent that the appraiser projects can be earned from the property. It will be a projection about a building that does not exist and about a market that also may not yet exist. . . . As part of the process, he or she will look at the optimistic market studies and projections prepared by the developer, which may be quite persuasive. . . . Obviously, the problem with the resulting appraisal is that it is only as good as the developer's carefully prepared brief on why the market will be wonderful. Often the problem is worse because the appraiser knows what value is needed in order to sustain the loan; the real estate community is pretty tight-knit, and even if an appraiser is not dishonest, it is tempting to shade an appraisal in the direction of getting the deal done, because business breeds business.[89]

Needless to say, a conservative appraisal does not "breed business."

Inflated appraisals were at the heart of ADC lending in Texas, essential as they were to continued lending—and related paper profits—in a commercial real estate glut. Accommodating appraisers were also central to the land flips that artificially inflated property values that could be used as collateral for generous loans. In both cases, "the bigger the appraisal, the bigger the loan. The bigger the loan, the bigger the loan fee."[90] With the cooperation of a willing appraiser, developers got not only 100 percent financing but also generous "walking around money," and thrift officials reported hefty (self-funded) loan fees, through which extravagant bonuses and salaries could be justified.

Despite the central role of appraisers in this process and the ample opportunity for conflict of interest, the appraisal system in Texas was completely unregulated.[91] Not surprisingly, thrift regulators report finding inaccurate and inflated appraisals in the wreckage of failed thrifts throughout Texas and around the country.[92] William Crawford, savings and loan commissioner in California, testified before Congress that of the state-chartered thrifts that his office had

examined after insolvency, "nearly all 29 contained some form of
. . . fraudulent appraisals."[93]

One limited measure of the extent of misconduct among these
hired guns is the substantial amount of legal damages they have
incurred. In addition to the amounts paid through legal settlements
with the accounting firms, appraisers, lawyers, and other professionals who collaborated with thrift insiders in disguising their
misconduct, the government has collected on a number of large
professional liability claims. As of 1996, $2.4 billion has been re-
covered from insurance companies to pay for the malpractice of
professionals involved in the S&L crisis.[94]

NETWORKS AND SUPPORT GROUPS

The conspiratorial quality of these frauds is striking. The hot deals
described above—which made up 68 percent of our sample of OTS
cases—all require a network of participants, including insiders,
outside borrowers, associates at other thrifts, and an assortment of
professionals. Arthur Leiser, a longtime examiner in Texas, kept a
diary noting the partnerships involved in thrift fraud. Ultimately,
Leiser linked virtually all the insolvent thrifts in Texas in a massive
daisy chain of reciprocal lending, or what he called "back-
scratching" transactions.[95]

The pattern of criminal referrals paints the same picture of intrigue. Formal referrals against McBirney's Sunbelt S&L named a
total of 155 individuals who had variously conspired to commit
fraud against this one institution.[96] In the twenty-six insolvent
thrifts studied by the GAO, 85 criminal referrals were filed, naming
182 suspects and citing 179 violations of criminal law.[97] The organized nature of thrift crime was particularly apparent in the
I-30 scandal, involving the development of condominiums along
Interstate 30 just east of Dallas. The Empire Task Force (named for
the S&L at the hub of the scheme) was organized in 1987 out of the

U.S. Attorney's Office in the Northern District of Texas to investigate
the scandal. By 1992 more than 108 individuals had been convicted
in this wide-ranging conspiracy that drew hundreds of millions of
dollars from insured thrift deposits to line the pockets of fraudulent
developers and affiliated insiders.[98]

The Dallas Bank Fraud Task Force, a separate interagency unit
investigating criminal fraud outside of the I-30 corridor, by 1992
had also charged 135 individuals and secured 107 convictions.
Since 1985, in the Northern District of Texas alone, a total of 550
people have been convicted of bank and savings and loan fraud.[99]
In the single biggest network of thrift fraud, criminal referrals were
filed against 155 individuals involved with Sunbelt Savings in
Texas.[100] A senior Justice Department official based in Dallas com-
mented on the interlocking nature of thrift crimes and the extensive
circle of participants: "You cannot look at various cases as discrete
events. These S&Ls were networking." [101]

Our TIMS data similarly underscore the importance of networks
of co-conspirators. Table 1 shows that the average number of individuals cited per institution is 10. That is, a total of 4,559 individuals
were cited in criminal referrals naming 455 RTC institutions. As
we saw from table 2, the average number of individuals cited per
institution is substantially higher in Texas (15) than in California
(5), a finding consistent with the observation of regulators in Texas
that large "old boy networks" were central ingredients of the S&L
debacle in that state.[102]

The importance of networks was not confined to the Southwest.
In a speech to the American Bar Association in 1987, Assistant
Attorney General William Weld told his audience, "We now have
evidence to suggest a nationwide scheme linking numerous failures
of banks and savings and loan institutions throughout the country." [103] Nor were these networks confined to the private sector.
As we will see in the next chapter, their success often depended on
the participation of regulators and key political figures who were

in a position to grease the wheels of fraud and to shield it from prosecution.

COLLECTIVE EMBEZZLEMENT AS ORGANIZED CRIME

The nature of collective embezzlement, the importance of organized networks of participants, and the central role of official complicity suggest that the fraud that permeated the thrift industry was similar in important ways to organized crime. Given this similarity, perhaps we need to reconsider the distinction between corporate crime and organized crime and replace the traditional distinctions—based largely on the social status and ethnicity of the offenders—with more analytic ones.

Edwin Sutherland's formal definition of white-collar crime included crimes committed by anyone of high social respectability in the course of his or her occupation. In fact, however, the bulk of Sutherland's research dealt with *corporate* crime, or crime committed by corporate executives on behalf of their companies. In a recent essay on white-collar crime, Gilbert Geis notes that Sutherland's conceptualization was vague and shifted from one context to another. Geis concludes, however, that "Sutherland was most concerned with the illegal abuse of power by upper-echelon businessmen in the service of their corporations." [104] Thus, in his landmark book *White Collar Crime*, Sutherland focused on price-fixing, false advertising, and other statutory and regulatory violations aimed at enhancing corporate profits through curtailing competition, cutting costs, or expanding the market.

Subsequent research on corporate crime has generally followed Sutherland's example, examining the myriad ways that corporate managers violate and otherwise circumvent laws that stand in the way of corporate profits. In his overview of corporate crime research, Coleman concludes that the "demand for profit is one of the most important economic influences on the opportunity structure for organizational crime."[105] Geis's study of the electrical company price-fixing conspiracy reveals the central role played by the emphasis on profit maximization and the related corporate subculture that is conducive to—or at least tolerant of—illegal behavior in the interest of profits.[106] Harvey A. Farberman argues that the necessity to maximize profits despite intense competition has produced a "criminogenic market structure" in the automobile industry.[107] Francis T. Cullen, William J. Maakestad, and Gray Cavender and Mark Dowie link the corporate mandate to reduce costs and increase profits to the fatal decision of Ford Motor Company managers in the 1970s to build the Pinto with a defective rear assembly despite their knowledge that it would lead to serious injury and death.[108]

Much of the corporate crime literature examines the characteristics of firms and market structures that trigger differing amounts and types of crime in the search for reduced costs and increased profits. Wheeler and Rothman, summarizing the literature, note that "illegal behavior is found more often in newer, smaller, and less profitable organizations on the margins of more central business networks."[109] Others document the ways in which a high degree of concentration facilitates price-fixing and other illegal conspiracies to maximize and stabilize profits.[110]

While a heuristically useful definition of "white-collar crime" remains elusive and debates continue to rage regarding its causal structure,[111] there is at least an implicit consensus about the narrower category "corporate crime." The vast literature on corporate crime, a small portion of which is cited above, focuses on crimes committed by corporate owners and managers on behalf of their corporations or companies. While top managers may themselves stand to benefit financially from these crimes, the driving force and principal goal is to advance corporate profits (and indeed, it is generally only through increasing corporate profits that individual employees may indirectly accrue benefits from the illegal activity). Thus Marshall Clinard and Richard Quinney distinguish between "occupational crimes" in which employees violate the law on their own behalf and "corporate crimes" in which executives violate the law on behalf of their corporations.[112] As Wheeler and Rothman put it, in contrast to the victimization of organizations by outsiders or individual insiders, the organization is used as a weapon in corporate crime to advance organizational goals.[113] "Corporate crime" is thus consistently treated in the literature as *an illegal act perpetrated by corporate employees on behalf of the corporation.* It is "corporate" not simply because corporate actors are involved but because the driving force and primary goal is to advance *corporate* interests.

Just as a growing body of literature grapples with the definition of white-collar crime handed down by Sutherland, criminologists have increasingly drawn attention to the inadequacies of the traditional depiction of organized crime—a depiction that was fashioned originally by policy makers and law enforcers. In 1951 Senator Estes Kefauver's Special Committee to Investigate Organized Crime in Interstate Commerce held a series of hearings, launching more than thirty years of research into organized crime by academics and law enforcement agencies.

Kefauver's committee concluded that organized crime in the United States was perpetrated by a syndicate known as the "Mafia," which was a transplant of the Italian operation.[114] The President's Commission on Law Enforcement and Administration of Justice reiterated this definition of organized crime as an Italian-American phenomenon: "The core of organized crime activity is the supplying of illegal goods and services. . . . And to carry on its many activities secure from government interference, organized crime corrupts public officials. . . . Their membership is exclusively men of Italian descent."[115] Other authorities agreed: "The fact is that the Italian gangs—Cosa Nostra—do make up the center of organized crime."[116]

Donald Cressey, who had been a consultant to the President's Commission in 1967, laid out the scholarly basis for much subsequent organized crime research in his *Theft of the Nation*. Highlighting the Italian composition of organized crime in the United States, he wrote, "the Cosa Nostra organization is so extensive, so powerful, and so central that precise description and control of it would be description of all but a tiny part of all organized crime."[117] A number of major criminological texts and case studies have perpetuated this view of organized crime as synonymous with "the syndicate" or the "Mafia," and thus as largely based on ethnicity and kinship.[118]

A few scholars have challenged the traditional conspiratorial view of organized crime, pointing to evidence of a far less organized and monopolistic structure than is suggested by the Mafia stereotype.[119] Thus Alan A. Block defines organized crime simply as crime that depends on a "relationship binding members of the underworld to upperworld institutions and individuals," and contends that these relationships are by no means confined to a Mafia syndicate with far-ranging influence and a fixed hierarchy.[120] While these critics advance beyond a single-syndicate definition of organized crime, they continue implicitly or explicitly to define organized crime according to the participation of "members of the underworld."[121]

There have been a number of recent attempts to demonstrate the parallels between and interactions among organized criminals and "legitimate" entrepreneurs. Jay S. Albanese, in comparing the Lockheed scandal and the Cosa Nostra, stresses the role of entrepreneurs and the facilitating function of political corruption in each.[122] Others point out that the line between organized crime and legitimate business is increasingly blurred as organized crime groups "diversify," entering legitimate businesses and joining the ranks of white-collar executives.[123] These studies, however, generally do not replace the traditional definitions of organized and white-collar crime and continue to assume largely ad hominem distinctions between the two.

A few studies extend and reconstitute the definition of organized crime, focusing on the nature of the activity rather than on the ethnicity or social respectability of its perpetrators. Dwight C. Smith, Jr., for example, suggests eliminating altogether the notion of organized crime as a distinct phenomenon and replacing it with a "spectrum" of entrepreneurial activities ranging from criminal enterprises to legitimate businesses.[124] Michael D. Maltz treats white-collar crime as a subset of the broader category of organized crime, which he defines as "crime committed by two or more offenders who are or intend to remain associated for the purpose of committing crimes."[125]

This definition, which includes the dimensions of premeditation, organization, and continuity, avoids the traditional focus on offender characteristics, but it may be overly broad, as it does not distinguish organized crime from *any* ongoing criminal conspiracy. In fact, Maltz has omitted an important component of the modus operandi of organized crime: it is facilitated by direct or indirect links to politicians or law enforcement agents. The "organization," in other words, is not just between the offenders themselves, but also involves a network of offenders and local police, city hall, and state officials, or anyone else in a position to minimize the risk of detection and prosecution. It is precisely this quality of organized crime that historically has hindered its prosecution relative to other types of criminal conspiracies.

Drawing from these studies, a good working definition of organized crime can be put together. In contrast to corporate crime, in which the primary goal is the pursuit of corporate interests, in *organized crime the purpose is personal gain. In pursuit of this goal organized crime is premeditated, organized, continuous, and facilitated by relationships between its perpetrators and public officials.*

At first glance, it may seem that there is overlap between the methods of organized crime and those used by traditional corporate criminals. Sutherland and others have discussed the organized nature of much corporate crime.[126] No doubt most corporate crime is also premeditated in that it is based on a rational calculation of costs and benefits. Finally, we know that some corporate crime is facilitated by captured regulatory agencies, campaign contributions to influential policy makers, or other forms of direct or indirect collusion by public officials.[127]

These operative qualities, however, take on a distinctive meaning within the context of the overriding purpose of organized crime. Organized crime is "premeditated" not only in that the illegal activity is rationally calculated in advance but also in that it is company policy to use the organization as a vehicle for committing illegal transactions for personal gain. Similarly, it is "organized" in the sense that networks inside and outside the organization are the conduit for illegal activity and are put in place for that purpose. Illegal activity by these networks is "continuous" rather than sporadic, because that is their primary purpose. Finally, while corporate criminals may develop connections to public officials to facilitate a "favorable business climate" that periodically includes illegal activity, in organized crime the raison d'être of these relationships is to protect them from prosecution.

Collective embezzlement quite clearly fits this definition of organized crime. In the cases we described, not only was it company policy to victimize the organization for personal gain, but it required networks of co-conspirators, was continuous, and was facilitated by complicity with key officials over time. Of course, not all thrift fraud fits this organized crime model. Some illegal behavior by thrift executives no doubt involved efforts—albeit ill-conceived ones—to rescue their institutions through illegal risk taking. Nor were all thrift executives in the 1980s engaged in misconduct. Despite the overwhelmingly criminogenic environment, a significant portion of thrift operators refrained from fraud altogether. The point here is that much of the extensive fraud that *was* committed more closely resembles organized crime than traditional corporate crime, despite the corporate status of its perpetrators.

Speaking of the collapse of thrifts in Texas, a staff member of the Senate Banking Committee told us, "What you are going to find in these thrifts is sort of a mafia behind them. I don't mean Italians, but I'm using it in a generic sense: a fraudulent mutual support." [128] This mutual support included not only thrift insiders (owners and operators) and outsiders (executives at other thrifts, accountants, appraisers, lawyers, brokers, developers, and others) but government officials as well. In the next chapter, we explore in more detail the nature of this government complicity and its contribution to the collapse of the thrift industry.

THE POLITICAL CONNECTION

 Evidence suggests that political corruption was at the very heart of the thrift debacle. Sometimes the evidence is direct and incontrovertible; sometimes the line between politics-as-usual and outright corruption is blurred. But in the aggregate the evidence points to the central role that blatant or implicit political collusion played in the S&L debacle and confirms the insight of the former FHLBB chairman, Edwin Gray: "As bad as the financial crisis—that is to say, the 'thrift crisis'—is . . . the real issues are far less 'financial' than they are 'political.' The thrift crisis is, and has been from the beginning, a political crisis." [1]

W. Michael Reisman, in his book on political bribery evocatively entitled Folded Lies, explains the "operational code" associated with accepting campaign contributions and the implicit, unspoken nature of most official favors: "Although bribery is prevalent, it is conducted in an atmosphere of understandable secrecy. Part of the reason for this secrecy stems from fear of prosecution and sanctions, not for violation of the laws against bribery but rather for violation of the operational code that some types of bribery are acceptable but are not to be talked about." [2]

Amitai Etzioni similarly argues that the technical legality of exchanges of money for political favors does not alter the fact that such exchanges are intrinsically bribery: "During the Keating hearings, a senator stated that no one approached him and offered money for a particular service. It is a statement often repeated; it hoodwinks not only members of the electorate at large but even some who study Congress professionally. The point is a legal technicality. The law, as widely interpreted, defines corruption as occurring when there is a clear payoff. . . . Even a third-rate politico and a rather inexperienced lobbyist can and do find ways to observe the letter of the law." [3]

Such implicit bribery was central to the evolution of the savings and loan scandal. In the critical period between 1983 and 1988, more than 160 political action committees (PACs) representing savings and loans poured almost $4.5 million into House and Senate campaigns, with over $1 million going to members of the banking committees. [4] Ironically, as thrifts fell deeper and deeper into debt, they sent larger and larger amounts of cash to Washington, D.C., increasing their contributions 42 percent in the two years preceding the bailout. [5] According to a study by Common Cause, in the 1980s savings and loan interests spent $12 million in PAC and individual contributions to congressional candidates and political parties—a conservative estimate, since only those who listed themselves on disclosure forms as associated with a thrift were included in the study. [6] The Federal Elections Commission reports that 333 representatives and 61 senators received contributions from the thrift industry in 1988. The House and Senate Banking committees—sometimes referred to as the "cash-and-carry" committees—were by far the greatest beneficiaries of this largesse.

In addition to campaign contributions, which by law must go toward reelection campaigns, members of Congress receive lucrative "honoraria" for speeches, which are considered personal earnings. In the 1980s the financial industry was the leading sponsor of such honoraria, and Senator Jake Garn, chair of the Senate Banking Committee, was the primary recipient. One observer calls this "a substantial special-interest salary" and adds, "The practice comes so close to legalized bribery that it was dubbed 'dishonoraria' by Representative Andy Jacobs (D-IN) and is widely condemned by the public." [7]

Key members of Congress reciprocated with legislation and intervention with regulators that favored their thrift benefactors and ultimately cost American taxpayers billions of dollars. A number of the most well-connected thrift executives were engaged in flagrantly illegal activity. As one senior official expressed it, "It was always the worst S&Ls in America that were able to get dramatically more political intervention. The good guys could never get political muscle like this. Some of it makes sense, of course, because you have a bigger incentive [to make contributions] if you are a sleaze. . . . If you know you are engaged in fraud, what better return is there than a political contribution?" [8]

This "political fraud"—which paralleled and made possible the financial fraud of the industry—was manifest in the deregulatory policies that set the stage for the debacle; in the shielding of thrift benefactors from prosecution; and in the political cover-up that prolonged and enhanced the crisis. Let us examine each in turn.

DEREGULATION: SETTING THE STAGE

The thrift interest rate crisis of the late 1970s came at a particularly bad time for the new Reagan administration, which had been carried into power on its promise of budget reductions and tax cuts—an impossibility even without a major thrift bailout. A senior thrift regulator reports that the administration responded strategically by papering over the disaster with accounting gimmicks and forbearance for insolvent thrifts.[9] Most important, a decision was made by the administration, the FHLBB, and Congress to encourage the industry to "grow out of its problems" through deregulation. After all, the prohibition against adjustable rate mortgages had played an important role in the interest rate crisis. With "overregulation" thus discredited, a financial crisis under way, and political reluctance to expose the scale of that crisis, the ground was ripe for substantial deregulation.

The political influence of the savings and loan industry was instrumental in the form that deregulation was to take. First, a little history. As chair of the House Banking Committee, Congressman Fernand St. Germain had for years been at the forefront of thrift policy making and had been exposed to the vast potential for insider fraud. In 1976, almost a decade before the heyday of thrift high-fliers, he led an investigation into the failure of Citizens State Bank in Texas, which had been run into the ground by fraudulent insiders and affiliated outsiders. At those hearings, St. Germain had observed, "There has been a growing feeling in recent years of the need for greater uniformity in statutes and regulations relating to self-dealing loans, conflict of interest, duties and responsibilities of boards of directors, and loan limitations for directors and stockholders."[10] Congressman Henry Gonzalez concurred: "We have found regulation that is forgetful, benign, and on some levels pitiful. Inadequate regulation is what has made possible the kind of outlandish sordid conduct we have discovered. We have lifted only a corner of the rock. What we have seen is enough to disgust anyone. Corrective action is needed both at the state and federal level. Administrative regulation can be—and must be—strengthened. State statutes need to be strengthened. Federal statutes probably need updating."[11]

Despite these strong words in support of statutory restrictions and regulation in 1976 and St. Germain's firsthand knowledge of the potential for insider abuse of financial institutions, by 1980 St. Germain was a major congressional proponent of deregulation.[12] After sponsoring the Depository Institutions Deregulation and Monetary Control Act of 1980 that increased the flow of thrift deposits by relaxing the restrictions on interest rates, in 1982 the Garn–St. Germain Depository Institutions Act completed the mission, accelerating the phaseout of the ceiling on interest rates and dramatically expanding the investment powers of federally chartered savings and loans.[13]

St. Germain's promotion of deregulation, despite his earlier call for "greater uniformity in statutes and regulations" relating to insider fraud, coincided with his increasingly cozy relationship with lobbyists for the U.S. League of Savings Institutions (the League). The League was at the time one of the most powerful lobbying groups in Washington, D.C. The former chair of the FHLBB, Ed Gray, summarized its power in those days: "When it came to thrift matters in the U.S. Congress, the U.S. League and many of its affiliates were the *de facto* government. . . . What the League wanted, it got. What it did not want from Congress, it got killed." [14] Congressman Gonzalez, then a key senior member of the House Banking Committee, said during congressional hearings, "I have sat here on this committee for 26 years. I have seen committee after committee do everything the industry has asked us to do. Everything the industry has wanted the Congress has rolled over and given it to them . . . and the results are plain." [15] The League's chair, William O'Connell, was not shy about the clout enjoyed by his association, bragging "everything we tried to do we were successful at." [16]

St. Germain was a regular recipient of the League's largesse in the early 1980s as thrift deregulation was being considered. In fact, one of the League's main lobbyists, James "Snake" Freeman, was assigned the task of taking the House Banking Committee chair out on the town on a regular basis. Having been observed frequently dining out in Washington on the League's expense account and in the company of the League lobbyist, St. Germain was investigated by the U.S. Department of Justice for conflict of interest violations. The Justice Department concluded that there was "substantial evidence of serious and sustained misconduct" by St. Germain in his connections with the thrift industry.[17] A House Ethics Committee investigation came to the same conclusion. However, no formal prosecution was initiated, and St. Germain was voted out of office in 1988.[18]

Congress was not alone in deregulating thrifts. As we saw in the introduction, the FHLBB followed suit during this period, beginning by lifting the limit on brokered deposits in 1980. When Richard Pratt, an educator and businessman from Utah, was appointed FHLBB chair in 1981, he quickly set about "freeing" the industry from regulatory restraint. In his first year he reduced the net worth requirement for thrifts to 3 percent (the outgoing chair had already reduced the requirement from 5 to 4 percent in 1980) and further liberalized the accounting principles according to which this requirement could be satisfied, with the anticipated result that actual net worth was substantially overstated. Soon afterward he dropped the long-standing requirement that thrifts have at least four hundred stockholders with no one controlling more than 25 percent of the stock, thus allowing for a single entrepreneur to own and operate a federally insured thrift. This combination of lowering net worth requirements and opening up thrift charters to individual owners was key to the epidemic of new thrift charters granted to real estate developers and others who entered the industry to take advantage of deregulation.

While Pratt was busy dismantling regulations, he was also lobbying hard for the Garn–St. Germain bill. So central was his role in the legislative process that when the bill was first introduced, it was known colloquially as "the Pratt Bill." One author calls Pratt "the angel of death for the thrift industry."[19] All evidence points to Pratt's

unflinching ideological support for deregulation and his sincere—
if ill-placed—faith in the salutary effect of his policies. But he was
generously rewarded for his convictions. When he left the FHLBB
in 1983 he took a senior position with Merrill Lynch, where he
reaped substantial benefits from his own deregulatory policies. By
1989 Merrill Lynch investors had almost $1 billion in Gibraltar Sav-
ings of Beverly Hills and approximately $500 million in Lincoln
Savings of Irvine and Imperial Savings of San Diego. All three institutions were in turn heavily invested in Merrill Lynch mortgage-
backed securities (the division that Pratt headed) and junk bonds,
and all three were deeply insolvent.[20]

Perhaps the most persuasive evidence that the policy shifts of the
early 1980s were motivated by more than ideological fervor is
the fact that the deregulation was decidedly selective. The 1980
deregulatory act had phased out restrictions on thrift interest rates
but at the same time had moved *away* from the free market model on
which deregulation is usually based, by increasing FSLIC insurance
from $40,000 to $100,000 per deposit.[21] This increase in deposit
insurance was arranged without congressional debate, and behind
closed doors. The Senate bill had called for an increase to $50,000
per deposit; the House bill had included no increase at all. During
the conference proceedings to reconcile the two bills, conferees
interrupted the session late at night and reconvened in a private
back room. When the backroom session was over, the cap on insurance had been raised to $100,000 per deposit—twice the amount
even the Senate bill had provided. For the thrift industry—which
fought hard for the increase through League lobbyists—it spelled
greater access to funds with which to invest in the new markets
made available through deregulation; for taxpayers, it meant vastly
increased liability. Senator Alan Cranston, one of the "Keating 5"
discussed below, was reported to be a major force promoting the
change in the backroom session.[22] Also spearheading the deposit

insurance increase was House Banking Committee chair Fernand St. Germain.

Three points are important here. First, deregulation exacerbated the savings and loan crisis and multiplied its costs many times over. The NCFIRRE estimates that had the interest rate crisis of the late 1970s and early 1980s been resolved by closing insolvent institutions rather than encouraging them to grow through deregulation, the costs would have been less than $25 billion.[23] The skyrocketing costs associated with deregulation were related to expanded opportunities for high-risk investments, the rapid growth these opportunities triggered, and deliberate insider abuse.[24]

Second, deregulation was at least in part the product of political decisions made by individuals with personal and career interests at stake. Not only was there a general interest in the early Reagan administration not to expose the magnitude of the crisis or pay for its resolution, but some of those who launched deregulation had direct connections to the thrift industry. Of course, the deregulation movement enjoyed an ideological advantage in the early 1980s, but the ideological impetus dovetailed well with these more immediate political and financial incentives.

Third, that a deposit insurance increase of over 150 percent was incorporated into the 1980 deregulation legislation—a protectionist move starkly at odds with the free market rhetoric of deregulation—reveals the inadequacy of ideological motives alone as an explanation for the policy shifts affecting thrifts in the early 1980s. And the backroom decision-making process surrounding these shifts together with the well-documented connections between the chair of the House Banking Committee and the League suggest that private financial interests were at least as important to that process as the frequently remarked on ideological "freight train" of deregulation.[25]

William Proxmire, after thirty-one years on the Senate Banking

Committee and eight years as its chair, tried to be kind to his Senate colleagues in describing the system that inevitably corrupts:

> I recently suggested to a group of Members of Congress that they re-
> fuse campaign contributions that come from the special interests over
> which their committees have jurisdiction. Now, keep in mind that be-
> cause of their committee membership, these legislators have unique
> power to push legislation through Congress that will bring, for exam-
> ple, millions of dollars of benefits to banks, savings and loans, real es-
> tate firms, and housing developers. These legislators are not evil. They
> are not crooks. They are among the most ethical and honorable people
> in public life. . . . *I am also convinced they are sincerely, honestly hypnotized by a sys-*
> *tem of thinly concealed bribery that not only buys their attention but frequently buys*
> *their vote.*

Proxmire went on to compare the system of campaign contributions to a rigged baseball game:

> Imagine that you are watching a World Series baseball game. The
> pitcher walks over to the umpire before the game begins. The pitcher
> pulls a wad of $100 bills out of his pocket and counts out 100 of
> them, $10,000, and hands the whole fat wad to the plate umpire. The
> umpire jams the bills into his pocket, warmly thanks the pitcher and
> settles down to call that same pitcher's balls and strikes. What would
> be the reaction of the other team? Of the fans? The media? All would
> be furious. The game had obviously been fixed. Far fetched? Not a
> bit. . . . Yes, the game is fixed.[26]

SHIELDING THRIFT BENEFACTORS FROM SCRUTINY: THE ATTACK ON REGULATORS

At their annual convention in New Orleans in November 1982, the
incoming chair of the League told Edwin Gray that he was their
choice to be the new director of the FHLBB. A longtime Californian,

Gray had been a close friend of and press secretary to Ronald Reagan when he was still governor of California, had later served briefly as President Reagan's director of domestic policy, and had recently returned to San Diego as public relations officer for Great American First Savings Bank. As a thrift executive, Gray had lobbied hard for the Garn–St. Germain bill, and was known as a staunch advocate of deregulation with close ties to the White House. As one of the most influential lobbying groups in Washington, D.C., at the time, the League played a key role in selecting FHLBB chairs as well as the board's two other members, although nominally these three positions were presidential appointments.

Gray was sworn in as FHLBB chair in May 1983, to serve a four-year term. As he remembers his first day on the job, Gray was telephoned by then Secretary of the Treasury Don Regan, who asked, "You're going to be a team player, I take it?" Gray's response was "Sure."[27] But Gray soon began to have trepidations about the state of the industry. He was particularly concerned about the inflationary impact that brokered jumbo deposits had on deposit interest rates and their contribution to explosive growth, high-risk investments, and the opportunity for fraud and abuse.

In January 1984 Gray and FDIC chair Bill Isaac proposed new regulations that would limit to $100,000 the insured deposits that any one broker could place in a given bank or thrift.[28] During the ensuing public comment period, angry responses poured in. Most important, Don Regan—who before coming to Washington had headed up Merrill Lynch, which since thrift deregulation was enjoying a lucrative business brokering thrift deposits[29]—derisively labeled Gray "the Great Reregulator" and told Treasury Deputy Secretary Tim McNamar, "Gray has got to go."[30] Merrill Lynch submitted a report to the press that was highly critical of the job Gray was doing and lambasted the proposed limitations on brokered deposits.

Several days later Gray had what has been called his "Road to

Damascus experience," as he watched a homemade videotape of miles of abandoned condominiums in the I-30 corridor east of Dallas financed by the insured deposits of Empire Savings and Loan.[31] Gray describes the experience: "I was so sickened by what I saw that I couldn't watch it. It was so bad that I closed my eyes. I was so ashamed. . . . I don't even like to talk about it now."[32] Convinced of the dangers of unlimited growth, excessive risk taking, and unregulated speculation with federally insured funds, Gray spent the rest of his tenure as FHLBB chair fighting the industry, Wall Street, and Don Regan and others in the administration who now declared him "off the reservation" (no longer a "team player").[33]

Indicative of the anger that Gray's conversion unleashed in the thrift industry and its repercussions in the political establishment is the vitriolic letter the former California savings and loan commissioner sent to Don Regan, then chief of staff at the White House. In this letter Lawrence Taggart—at the time of the letter writing a consultant and lobbyist for Don Dixon and other thrift highfliers—launched an unrestrained attack on Gray's regulatory policies and warned Regan of the political effect of Gray's activities: "These actions being done to the industry by the current chief regulator of the Federal Home Loan Bank Board are likely to have a very adverse impact on the ability of our [Republican] Party to raise needed campaign funds in the upcoming elections."[34]

As one senior regulator and close associate of Gray's interprets what happened:

Gray's transformation is all the more remarkable because he was chosen by the Administration and the League precisely because he was thought unlikely to buck the political currents. Ultimately, Gray took on, simultaneously, Speaker [Jim] Wright (the second most powerful politician in America), the "Keating 5" and much of the rest of Congress, the most powerful unelected official in America (President Reagan's

Chief of Staff, Don Regan, and his copious Administration minions, including OMB), the League, the top state regulators of Texas and California, and much of the Bank Board staff, to insist on reregulating and supervising S&Ls.[35]

One investigative reporter who gained access to the Bank Board in
1987 and spent six months studying inside memos, secret reports,
and other correspondence and documents described the concerted
attack on Gray: "If Gray's reign as the bank board's chairman had
been a fight . . . they would have stopped it. . . . Gray was never a
very nimble counterpuncher. He stood in the center of the ring like
a slow-footed heavyweight, taking repeated blows. But he never fell
to the canvas."[36]

In quick succession Gray raised the net worth requirement for
new thrifts; implemented the limitation on brokered deposits;[37]
adopted a limitation on growth rates that reduced the industry's
explosive growth by half; instituted limitations on the nature and
quantity of direct investments (such as ADC loans); barred any
new thrift charters in Texas and California; and in July 1985—in
response to the hopelessly inadequate budget provided by the federal Office of Management and Budget (OMB)[38]—transferred all
thrift examination functions to the regional Federal Home Loan
Banks, with the result that examination personnel doubled in two
years and thrift supervision was significantly tightened.[39]

Most important here, Gray campaigned aggressively for a recapitalization of the FSLIC, without which these regulatory reforms
would remain toothless and the thrift crisis continue to escalate.
For without funds the FSLIC was incapable of closing down insolvent and fraudulent institutions, since such closures demanded
that insured depositors be reimbursed; and without the ability to
take over these institutions, zombie thrifts would continue to hemorrhage losses and abusive insiders could continue to loot their
lucrative money machines. It was within the context of this FSLIC

recapitalization effort that Gray confronted most unambiguously the links between thrift highfliers and their political patrons—links that comprised what one senior official has called "one of the most powerful political coalitions ever assembled."[40]

By 1985 the FSLIC insurance fund had only $4.6 billion in reserves while insolvent thrifts held over $300 billion in assets.[41] A 1986 GAO report estimated that it would cost the FSLIC at least $20 billion to resolve the thrift crisis.[42] In retrospect this is a gross underestimate of what it would have cost at that early date, but Congress failed to take even this conservative estimate seriously.

The Reagan administration submitted an FSLIC recapitalization bill to Congress in April 1986, which was to provide the insurance fund with only $15 billion to resolve insolvent thrifts. Because the FSLIC was supposed to be self-supporting and because the administration wanted to keep this expense off-budget, the money was to be raised from the sale of bonds through a newly created Financial Corporation, the interest and principal of which were to come from assessments on the thrift industry and the regional Federal Home Loan Banks. The Subcommittee on Financial Institutions of the House Banking Committee quickly passed the bill by voice vote and without major change, a sign that at this point it was considered uncontroversial.[43]

But the League was adamantly opposed to a substantial recapitalization of the FSLIC, and it made its views known at private meetings, at its annual convention in 1986, in congressional testimony, and in private communication with administration officials.[44] Solvent thrifts were reluctant to pay assessments to bail out their unhealthy counterparts, and insolvent thrifts wished to stave off recapitalization so as to postpone their closure.[45] Beyond this, Gray has testified that the League did not want an FSLIC recapitalization because it wanted the insolvencies to get so big that the industry could not bail itself out and the taxpayers would have to foot the bill. Gray told Congress, "The folks at the League told me this was the strategy. Not once, but on a number of occasions." [46] Gray was not the only one to expose this strategy. The staff director of the Senate Banking Committee, Kenneth McLean, told reporter William Greider, "The good ol' boy crowd . . . deliberately wanted to keep the money low so they wouldn't be shut down. So the message [to Congress] was: Let's let the problem build up and dump it on the taxpayers." [47] California congressman Tony Coelho, chair of the Democratic Congressional Campaign Committee (DCCC) whose job it was to solicit critical "soft money" for Democratic campaigns, later reported that he went to a meeting of S&L executives and was told, "Don't give Gray his $15 billion to keep harassing us." Coelho assured them he would not, and "the place went wild, it went absolutely wild." [48]

In the letter that Lawrence Taggart, former California S&L commissioner and thrift consultant, sent Don Regan in August 1986 complaining that Gray was responsible for "the serious and irreparable harm that is being done to savings and loan associations across this land," he specifically warned Regan against recapitalization. He urged,

It is felt by many in the industry that the 250 extra Federal examiners on temporary duty in Texas are poised awaiting passage of the Recapitalization Bill pending approval in the Senate and House. If approved, sufficient funds will then be available to the FSLIC to proceed quickly to take-over or close down associations, many of which are now being closely monitored and under Cease and Desist Orders or Supervisory Agreements. It is then anticipated that a substantial number of these "loaned" examiners will be transferred to California to begin a pattern of strict examinations and additional closures. . . . Passage of the proposed Recapitalization Bill will provide Chairman Gray the necessary resources to proceed ahead in his pattern of eradicating those individuals and associations he has targeted for removal. [49]

Copies of the letter were sent to Jake Garn, chair of the Senate Banking Committee, and Doug Barnard, chair of the Subcommittee on Commerce, Consumer, and Monetary Affairs of the House Committee on Government Operations.[50]

In the face of this opposition from the thrift industry, no recapitalization bill was enacted for more than a year, despite its apparently uncontroversial introduction in the House. Eventually Treasury Secretary Jim Baker became alarmed at the congressional postponement of FSLIC recapitalization (recap). He met with Jim Wright and promised him that if a recap bill was passed, M. Danny Wall— former staff director of the Senate Banking Committee who had spearheaded the Garn–St. Germain bill, protégé of Senator Garn, and quintessential team player—would replace Edwin Gray as FHLBB chair. Danny Wall had been an urban planner until he was taken on by Garn as his staff director (he had worked for Garn in Salt Lake City government and his wife had been Garn's secretary). A Senate Banking Committee aide remembers that Wall had no previous experience in banking matters, and "everything that Danny Wall knew about banking, he learned over a fancy lunch from a banking lobbyist."[51]

Wall had many a "fancy lunch." It is alleged that during his stint on the Hill, Wall was hosted by private interests on ninety-five trips around the country, outdoing any other congressional staffer. Wall has called himself a "lab assistant" in putting together the Garn bill. Wall and Richard Hohlt, the chief League lobbyist in Washington, reportedly spoke several times a day during the time the Garn bill was being drafted and debated. They became fast friends, and it is said that Wall soon programmed his touch-tone phone so that Hohlt was #1 on the dial. Hohlt reportedly led "an intense campaign" to replace Gray with Wall as FHLBB chair, a move that Treasury Secretary Baker now dangled tantalizingly before Speaker Wright.[52]

Wright promised Baker he would push for an ample FSLIC recap. On the day of the House vote, Wright stood before his House colleagues and argued passionately for a $15 billion recapitalization. However, according to several independent reports, during Wright's speech Coelho did as he had been instructed and spread the word among Democratic members that Wright's speech was merely a political performance, that he did not really mean it.[53] As one observer remembers it, "And sure enough, the House 'repudiated' its Speaker by a record margin. The hypocrisy was incredible."[54]

The final House bill provided for only $5 billion for the FSLIC; the Senate bill authorized $7.5 billion. After substantial negotiation with the White House and the Treasury Department, Congress passed the Competitive Equality Banking Act of 1987, authorizing $10.8 billion in recapitalization. The act included a stipulation that no more than $3.75 billion be provided in any given year and contained a generous forbearance clause precluding regulators from too "hastily" closing insolvent institutions.

Perhaps no other public policy in this period better represents the power of the thrift industry. As regulator William Black describes it, "The triumph of the League in the May 5 House vote was complete. . . . [I]n the face of a crisis of epic proportions that was growing at a frightening rate . . . the House voted 258 to 153 against a $15 billion FSLIC recap plan—effectively in favor of the League's $5 billion plus forbearance. A majority of *Republicans*, including the whip, Trent Lott, and Rep. Gingrich voted against their president. Fewer than 80 Democrats voted to support a $15 billion FSLIC recap plan."[55]

James O'Shea of the *Chicago Tribune* called it "an incredible display of the U.S. League's legislative clout." He went on, "Virtually every congressman who received money from the high-flying and traditional thrifts voted the way the industry wanted."[56] *New York Times* reporter Nathaniel Nash said the vote was "a dramatic display of the influence of local thrift institutions on their elected officials."[57] The League applauded its triumph, writing its members, "Thank you for your part in achieving one of the greatest grass roots [sic] legislative victories in our history. Your calls, letters and visits to your members of Congress made the difference." [58]

Senator Cranston of California, Senator David Pryor of Arkansas, and House Speaker Wright were key actors in postponing recapitalization. Among other things, they used the recap bill as a bargaining chip against Gray and his team of regulators. Cranston reportedly put a hold on the recap bill at the behest of Charles Keating. [59] Pryor put a hold on the bill on behalf of Arkansas savings and loans (which had one of the highest failure rates in the country) and wrote to Gray: "I have put a 'hold' on the Senate recapitalization bill and am anxious to receive assurances from you that you will correct the abuses which have been taking place in Arkansas and other states" (meaning regulatory activity, not savings and loan abuses). [60]

Wright was particularly adept at using the recap bill as a way to extract concessions from regulators for his thrift benefactors. He put a hold on the recap bill twice, the first time on behalf of Craig Hall, a Dallas real estate syndicator who was one of the largest holders of real estate in Texas and chair of Resource Savings Association of Dallas. In 1986 Hall was unable to service the many loans he had from California and Texas thrifts and initiated a global restructuring of those loans under more favorable terms. However, Westwood Savings and Loan in Los Angeles refused to restructure its loans to Hall, because FHLB representative Scott Schultz had advised the thrift it was not in its best interest. Instead, Westwood told Hall it would foreclose on his properties.

Speaker Wright called Gray and asked him to intervene on Hall's behalf. [61] Gray soon learned that Wright had put a hold on the FSLIC recapitalization bill until something was done to accommodate Hall. As described in the special counsel's report on Wright's ethical violations, "Gray and Fairbanks [FHLBB chief of staff] thus determined that if they were to obtain a recapitalization bill, they would have to facilitate a restructuring of Hall's loans." [62] Gray removed

Schultz from the Westwood case and replaced him with a representative who agreed to the restructuring. Three days later Wright released the recap bill.

Wright's second hold on the bill was on behalf of Tom Gaubert, owner of Independent American Savings Association in Texas. Gaubert had been a Texas real estate developer before he bought controlling interest in the S&L in January 1983. Explaining the opportunities provided by deregulation, he reportedly told a friend, "I'm tired of playing Monopoly with my money. This way [through owning a deregulated S&L], we can use the depositors' money." [63]

Gaubert was a member of Coelho's "Speakers' Club," which for $5,000 assured members they could "obtain personal assistance in Washington." [64] As chair of the Democratic Congressional Campaign Committee, Coelho regularly went to the savings and loan industry for soft money. Brooks Jackson, an investigative reporter for the *Wall Street Journal* who gained access to the DCCC in the months preceding the 1986 elections, described Coelho's code of ethics in soliciting this critical soft money: "Doing official favors for donors was permitted. The unforgiveable sin was to make the connection explicit." Coelho once explained to Jackson, "I don't mind donors bringing up that they have a problem with the government. But don't ever try to create the impression with me, or ever say it, if you say it it's over, that your money has bought you something. That's a real delicate line there." [65]

Gaubert wrote checks for more than $15,000 in his first six months as a member of Coelho's Speakers' Club and was invited on the annual backpacking trip for the elite of the Democratic party. When Wright was up for reelection, Gaubert established a PAC called East Texas First, with offices located in a branch of Sunbelt Savings and Loan. The PAC brought in contributions from sixty-six Texas thrift owners and borrowers, principally Dallas developers who had received hundreds of millions of dollars in thrift loans. [66] Although such "independent expenditure committees" are required by law to be independent of any particular individual's campaign, this PAC inadvertently sent the Federal Election Commission a report of its activities under the heading "Wright Appreciation Fund."[67] The directors of Sunbelt were reportedly given "subsidies" by its owner to make $1,000 contributions to the PAC.[68] In 1986 Gaubert became treasurer of the DCCC, raising $9 million in that capacity.[69] The following year he chaired a fundraiser that brought in $1 million for Speaker Wright.[70]

At the same time that Gaubert was coordinating the thrift industry contribution to Democrats he was under investigation by the FHLBB. In December 1984 regulators had forced Gaubert to resign from Independent American, which by then had criminal referrals against it for serious regulatory violations.[71] Two years later he was prohibited from ever operating a federally insured thrift. It was then that Wright threatened FHLBB chair Edwin Gray that if he did not call off the investigation of Gaubert and Independent American, he (Wright) would hold up the recap bill. Gray refused and the recap bill was tabled, to be revived later in a watered-down version and only under increasing public pressure.[72] Commenting on the concessions made by the FHLBB and the special treatment that Texas thrifts received at Wright's request in the 1980s, one senior regulator remembered telling Gray, "'He [Wright] just increases the demands, and the extortion just gets worse and worse. . . . The guy won't stay bought.'"[73]

In fact, Wright attempted to insulate Texas savings and loans from regulatory intervention by Gray and his FHLB examiners on many other occasions. In October 1986 Wright responded to complaints from J. Scott Mann, operator of CreditBanc Savings in Austin, that regulators were harassing him. Forwarding the letter to Gray and enclosing his own cover letter, Wright told the FHLBB chair, "This kind of high-handed and arbitrary attitude [on the part of regulators] can only create fear, mistrust and a climate of great instability." Taking at face value Mann's accusations, Wright told Gray in no

uncertain terms that the regional FHLB was acting "clearly outside
the realm of acceptable regulatory behavior" and ended by issuing
a warning: "I look forward to hearing that conditions have im-
proved as a result of your direct personal involvement."[74]

Infamous Vernon S&L, owned by Don Dixon, was also the recipient of Wright's concern. By October 1983 examiners reported that
Vernon had tallied up "significant regulatory violations, unsafe and
unsound practices, lending deficiencies, inadequate books and records, and control problems." Subsequent examinations continued
to show sham transactions and recordkeeping inadequacies. In
1986 it was discovered that Vernon kept two sets of board minutes,
and in September 1986, when it was deeply insolvent, it was placed
under the supervision of the Texas Savings and Loan Department.
Roy Green, head of the Dallas FHLB, called Vernon "the worst-run,
worst-managed debacle that he knew of in the savings and loan
industry."[75]

At Coelho's request Wright agreed to intervene with regulators on
behalf of Dixon. Again, he called Gray and asked him to "look
into" Dixon's case. Subsequently, Wright said he was under the
impression that he had secured Gray's assurance that Vernon would
not be "closed down." Wright was reportedly irate when regulators
adopted a "consent to merger" resolution for Vernon (although
technically Gray had kept his word—a consent to merger is quite
different from "closing down"). Ultimately, Vernon was put into
receivership and Dixon was indicted and convicted of criminal misconduct. While Wright was unsuccessful in the end in staving off
the regulators in the Dixon case, what is remarkable is the attempt.
As the Phelan Report concludes, "It is clear that Wright was willing to
intervene on Dixon's behalf without performing even a rudimen-
tary investigation of Dixon's dispute with the Bank Board." And, "In
Vernon's case, Wright could not have picked a more unseemly
beneficiary of his influence."[76]

In addition to these intercessions on behalf of individual thrift owners, Wright went to bat for the whole Texas industry. While there is nothing intrinsically wrong with this, what is problematic is the persistence and intensity of this intervention on behalf of an industry that was so permeated with insider abuse at the time and his indifference to investigating pervasive allegations of abuse.[77] At least as important were the hardball tactics he employed, which on occasion bordered on blackmail. In one episode Wright had called Gray to register yet again his "deep concern about the way institutions are being treated in Texas."[78] Wright went on to say that he had heard that the director of regulatory affairs of the Dallas FHLB, Joe Selby (who was known as one of the most rigorous regulators in the country), was "a homosexual" and that he "had established a ring of homosexual lawyers in Texas" who handled thrift problems. He then asked Gray, "Isn't there anything you can do to get rid of Selby?" Selby stayed on at the FHLB, but as the *Phelan Report* notes, "Wright's request that Gray 'get rid of' Selby greatly exceeded the bounds of proper congressional conduct."[79]

The Coelho–Wright–Texas thrift network offers a dramatic example of the personal, political, and financial ties between key members of Congress and the thrift industry. Such ties were replicated throughout the country, most notably in California, Texas, Arkansas, and Florida, where thrift failures proliferated and losses soared. One senior official in Florida reported that to his knowledge *all* the Florida thrifts that managed to stay open after insolvency in the 1980s did so with the help of their owners' political connections.[80] The Keating case is by far the most widely publicized instance of influence peddling to stave off regulatory scrutiny of thrift fraud.

Charles Keating contributed heavily to political candidates at the state and federal levels and to both political parties. It is reported that he even contributed $50,000 to the campaign of an Arizona state attorney general who was running unopposed.[81] At the national level Keating and his associates contributed almost $2 million to political candidates, with the bulk of it, $1.4 million, going to the five senators who are now known as the Keating 5.[82]

Although in 1979 he had been charged by the Securities and Exchange Commission (SEC) with siphoning funds from an Ohio bank—charges that he settled—Keating was granted a charter in 1984 to operate Lincoln Savings and Loan, purchased through junk bonds sold by Drexel. When Gray issued his direct investment rule limiting speculative investments such as ADC loans and junk bonds, Keating sought an exemption for Lincoln and hired a stable of academics and lawyers to sing the praises of direct investments.[83] Alan Greenspan, former chair of the Council of Economic Advisers under President Gerald Ford and soon-to-be chairman of the Federal Reserve Board, wrote a letter to the FHLB of San Francisco in support of an exemption for Lincoln. In this letter Greenspan assured the regulators that under Keating's stewardship Lincoln had "transformed itself into a financially strong institution that presents no foreseeable risk to the Federal Savings and Loan Corporation" and hence "should be allowed to pursue new and promising direct investments."[84] For this service, Keating paid Greenspan $40,000.[85]

Keating even briefly managed to get one of his team a position on the Bank Board. During the congressional recess in November 1986, Don Regan announced that one of the two vacant seats on the Bank Board would go to Lee Henkel.[86] It was widely known that Keating was a major client of Henkel's law firm, and subsequent investigation revealed that Keating's American Continental Corp. had loaned Henkel and his business associates more than $100 million, some of which was in default.[87] They had close personal connections as well, socializing together at Keating's various resorts and serving together on John Connally's presidential campaign in 1980.[88] The first new rule Henkel proposed as a Bank Board member was a modification of the limit on direct investment that would have had the effect of exempting from the restriction only two thrifts in the country, one being Lincoln.[89]

When Congress reconvened after the winter recess, Senator Proxmire launched an investigation into Henkel's ties with Keating, and after five months Henkel was forced to resign, never actually having been confirmed by the Senate. Ultimately, the connections between Keating and Henkel and Henkel's favoritism toward Keating while on the FHLBB were too explicit to survive the confirmation process. Even the League is said to have been too "embarrassed" to support Henkel's appointment.[90] But his five-month tenure on the Bank Board is itself testament to Keating's remarkable political influence.

The costliest episode in the saga of Keating's political influence began in early 1987, as Lincoln was being investigated by the FHLB in San Francisco for poor underwriting of loans and investment irregularities. In April 1987 Senator Dennis DeConcini called Edwin Gray to a now infamous meeting in his office. In attendance at the meeting were Senators John McCain, John Glenn, and Alan Cranston, all of whom had received hefty campaign contributions from Keating. DeConcini, referring to Keating as "our friend at Lincoln," proposed that perhaps Lincoln could offer more home mortgages, in exchange for which Gray would void the direct investment rule and back off of Lincoln.[91]

The San Francisco regulators were soon summoned to another meeting with the senators, this time joined by Donald Riegle, who was to become chair of the Senate Banking Committee and who also had received generous donations from Keating. At this meeting, the five senators (the Keating 5) tried to persuade the regulators of the financial health of Lincoln and the absence of any "smoking gun" to prove misconduct.[92] Later that summer, M. Danny Wall replaced Edwin Gray as chair of the FHLBB. One of Keating's lawyers assured him in a May 1988 letter, "You have the Board right where you want them. . . . I have put pressure on [new Bank Board chair] Wall to work toward meeting your demands and he has so instructed his staff." [93] Wall moved the investigation of Lincoln to Washington, D.C., out of the hands of the "hostile" San Francisco regulators. The institution was not closed until two years later, a delay that cost taxpayers an estimated $2 billion.

In an unusual housecleaning, several of the most powerful members of the House and Senate were ousted for their part in the savings and loan crisis and their indiscreet involvement in not-so-folded lies. In one six-month period, Speaker of the House Jim Wright, Majority Whip Tony Coelho, and House Banking Committee Chair Fernand St. Germain lost their seats as a result of the scandal and other related improprieties. St. Germain had been investigated by the Department of Justice and the House Ethics Committee in the early 1980s for "serious and sustained misconduct" in his interactions with the thrift industry. While no further censure was forthcoming from his colleagues on the Hill, he was voted out of office in 1988. He subsequently became a Washington lobbyist for the S&L industry.

Wright's ouster was protracted and accompanied by detailed revelations of his links to highflying S&Ls in his home state of Texas. The outside counsel in Wright's ethics hearing devoted the vast bulk of his 279-page report to breaches of ethics related to interventions on behalf of Texas thrifts. [94] Perhaps not so curiously, his colleagues on the House Ethics Committee spent barely one page on this topic and, parting ways with the outside counsel, concluded that Wright had been "intemperate" but had not violated any official codes of ethics in his thrift activity. [95] As Waldman put it, perhaps "those living in a glass House chose not to throw stones." [96] The ethics committee focused instead on more idiosyncratic charges—such as the allegation that Wright had self-published a book that he "sold" for several thousand dollars in the 1980s in lieu of the traditional honoraria for speeches. A group of Republicans threatened to reopen the S&L issue on the House floor, but Wright had had enough and resigned on May 31, 1989.

Two weeks later Coelho resigned to preempt a similarly embarrassing routing. In the end what did Coelho in was the discovery that he had bought a $100,000 junk bond from Drexel Burnham Lambert, with half the financing coming from "a friend from Southern California"—namely, Thomas Spiegel, owner of Columbia S&L who was later indicted on numerous criminal charges. Not only was such a loan improper for the House majority whip, but he had failed to disclose it. Having witnessed Wright's demise, Coelho resigned rather than face a thorough investigation of what Brooks Jackson called his "honest graft."

POLITICAL COVER-UP: THE SOUTHWEST PLAN

By 1987 one-third of the savings and loan industry was officially insolvent, and many more S&Ls were insolvent on a tangible net worth basis.[97] In the presidential election of 1988, both sides were curiously silent about the savings and loan crisis and the pending taxpayer bailout. In September Michael Dukakis referred to the debacle once, and by that afternoon key Democrats in Congress warned him to stay away from the issue, which was as potentially damaging to Democrats as it was to Republicans.[98] As Lowy put it, "Too many officials from both parties had their fingerprints all over it."[99]

No doubt presidential nominee George Bush had his own personal reasons for avoiding discussion of the S&L scandal, as his youngest son, Neil, was caught in the middle of a potentially embarrassing investigation of wrongdoing at Silverado S&L.[100] More generally, however, the Republican administration did not want the specter of a vast taxpayer bailout hovering over the election. To this end, official estimates of the size of the crisis were consistently understated. So optimistic was Bank Board chair Wall that he became known among the staff at the Bank Board and the FDIC as "M. Danny Isuzu."[101] Lowy explains, "Danny Wall, the good

Republican soldier, was playing on the administration's team, keeping the 1987 punt of the problem into 1989 from coming to rest in the middle of the 1988 presidential campaign." [102] Wall himself describes it this way, referring to his numerous trips to Congress to estimate the amount of money required to resolve the crisis: "I was asked [about the size of the crisis] in a code that everyone understood. The code was: Will $10.8 billion be enough to get you to 1989? My answer was, yes, this is enough for the near future. . . . Everybody knew what we were talking about." [103]

When the White House interviewed the economist Dan Brumbaugh as a possible replacement for Gray as chair of the Bank Board (before appointing Danny Wall), he was asked if he would be willing "to keep a lid on reports of the S&L crisis." [104] At Wall's Senate confirmation hearing, he promised to "accentuate the positive." [105] And according to FHLB regulators in San Francisco, when they requested the latest computer run showing the depth of the crisis and the need for a taxpayer bailout, they were told it could not be supplied until after the election. [106]

But the facts were leaking out. A report commissioned by Governor William P. Clements, Jr., of Texas in early 1988 showed that 40 percent of all Texas thrifts were insolvent even on the basis of creative accounting practices but remained open, piling up losses of $5 billion a year. One week after the release of this report, Chairman Wall announced the "solution" known as the Southwest Plan, the political purpose of which was to show that the debacle could be cleaned up with the resources at hand.

The plan seems to have originated with the Dallas FHLB, whose officials believed that the Texas thrift crisis might be resolved by consolidating insolvent thrifts and selling them as packages to healthy institutions, thereby achieving economy of scale, infusing new capital into the industry, and, most important, avoiding the closing of these zombie thrifts whose depositors would have to be reimbursed. The chair of the FSLIC, Stuart Root, a former Wall Street lawyer and former president of the Bowery Savings Bank in New York, liked the idea. Remembering that the chairman at the Bowery, Bud Gravette, had had a similar idea for several failing New York banks in 1984, Root hired Gravette to study the feasibility of such a plan for Texas.[107] After evaluating the possibilities, Gravette's recommendation was to merge insolvent thrifts, according to a computer program he had developed, and sell them to some of the good thrift managers whose Texas institutions were still solvent.

Both the U.S. League of Savings Institutions and the Texas League strongly favored such a plan, which they saw as the only alternative to massive closures, and one that provided lucrative possibilities for mergers.[108] The problem with Gravette's plan was that there were very few solvent Texas thrifts with the kind of capital needed to enter into such acquisitions. Perhaps more important, it was unclear why any solvent thrift would want to take on institutions whose extensive bad assets had dragged them deep into insolvency. As Henry Gonzalez, chair of the House Banking Committee, put it when he heard of the plan, "They've taken a lot of dead horses and stitched them together into one big horse that's just as dead and stinks even more."[109]

In the absence of immediate takers and in the rush to get the Southwest Plan under way, Danny Wall put together a plan that contained a series of incentives for prospective buyers and that ultimately had little in common with Gravette's original idea. These incentives were of three general types, all carefully calculated to minimize any capital outflow from the FSLIC (since the costs were far beyond its capacity) and to put off for the future the government's obligations. These incentives included the FSLIC assumption of the thrift's bad assets, FSLIC IOUs of various sorts, and tax deductions. After an investigation by his committee, Gonzalez claimed that these incentives resulted in "virtual giveaways," with buyers receiving $78 in assets and tax benefits for every $1 they provided in capital.[110]

Here's how it worked. As the FSLIC assumed a thrift's bad assets, the purchaser only bought the institution's performing loans and good assets, with the government taking on its losers, thus enhancing the appeal of these otherwise debt-ridden institutions. In a further effort to entice potential buyers, the FSLIC issued several kinds of IOUs, in what turned out to be one of the most controversial ingredients in the plan. "Yield maintenance agreements" in some contracts gave the purchaser of zombie thrifts a government IOU or guarantee against future bad assets. For example, if in the future the thrift's loans did not generate a certain guaranteed yield, the FSLIC IOUs would make up the losses. Some of these agreements promised the purchaser a loan yield 2.75 percent above what it cost Texas thrifts on average to obtain deposits; thus if the deposit interest rate was 9 percent, the FSLIC guaranteed a loan yield of at least 11.75 percent, or the government would make up the difference. Other FSLIC IOUs promised to cover any losses incurred through the future sale of bad assets.

Tax deductions sweetened the deals even more. First, tax deductions on purchase, as "goodwill," could be used to offset any taxes due on the purchaser's other enterprises. According to the congressional testimony of the director of an independent consulting firm that studied these deals, "Almost all of the supposed capital provided by the investors in these transactions was recovered immediately from tax benefits." [111] More incredible were the tax deductions allowed under a 1981 tax law due to expire at the end of 1988. According to the interpretation of this law, payments made against FSLIC IOUs were not taxable, but *the losses that these FSLIC payments covered could still be used as deductible losses.* In other words, if a thrift sold a bad asset at a loss, FSLIC IOUs made up for the loss, yet at the same time the thrift could claim the loss as a tax writeoff.[112] Prefacing his comments "You may not believe this, but it's true," Martin Mayer writes, "The government made up the loss and then paid a second time in the form of reduced tax receipts." [113] The losses to the

government from this double-dipping were exacerbated by the fact
that purchasers had a pronounced incentive to sell their assets at the
worst possible loss, since they were both compensated for the loss
and took a tax deduction that increased with the size of the
"loss." [114]

Finally, in some cases the FHLBB offered pocket charters to insure
against the possibility that the FSLIC could not make good on its
IOUs. There was some question as to whether Congress would
stand behind the debt that the FSLIC had incurred through the
issuing of these notes. Bank Board member Larry White was reportedly concerned that the FSLIC IOUs violated the constitutional principle that "no money shall be drawn from the Treasury, but in
consequence of appropriations made by law." [115] Mayer describes
the IOUs "as a form of counterfeiting by a government agency." [116]
Given the uncertainty of the FSLIC's ability to stand by its IOUs
(which came to be called "Wall paper" after Bank Board chairman
Wall), [117] secret pocket charters were sometimes issued at the time
of purchase, to be activated should the FSLIC renege on its obligations. These charters would enable buyers to start up a new "bad
bank" into which it could dump its bad assets, for which the government would then be responsible. The existence of these pocket
charters was not revealed until 1990. [118] Mincing no words, Paul
Zane Pilzer calls the "generous incentives" contained in these deals
"a wholesale raid on the Treasury of the United States." [119] Recognizing that such lucrative deals might later be challenged, the FSLIC
even promised to cover any and all legal fees associated with problems connected to the deals. [120]

The chaotic process through which the deals took place compounded the cost to taxpayers. First was Wall's choice of director
for the plan. Instead of hiring someone experienced and capable
of fending off the hard-hitters in the thrift industry to supervise
the packaging of thrifts and taking bids, Wall appointed Thomas
Lykos, a thirty-one-year-old junior Republican staff member on the

securities subcommittees of the Senate Banking Committee and the House Energy and Commerce Committee. Lykos was considered a political insider, but he had never negotiated a complex financial deal, prompting William Black to say, "The appointment . . . sent a clear message of what mattered under the Plan." [121]

Second was the frenzied pace at which the deals were concluded. Because the 1981 tax law allowing for the deduction of fictitious losses was to expire on the last day of 1988, the FSLIC rushed to finalize the deals. According to Black, this was "the most expensive aspect of emphasizing the tax benefits . . . [since] [t]he last thing any negotiator wants is to create a situation where the other party knows you must reach a deal by a particular deadline." [122] As Lowy explains it, "Negotiating against the clock when you have to do a deal and the other side doesn't, isn't recommended to achieve the best results . . . especially when the players on the other side include some of the sharpest negotiators in the country." [123] In addition to weakening their bargaining leverage, the deadline substantially decreased the amount of time the FSLIC could spend on any given deal. The FSLIC handled 109 failed thrifts in its Southwest Plan, finalizing most of the transactions in the last days of December in what one reporter calls a "pressure-cooker atmosphere." [124] Five deals were announced on New Year's Eve. Thomas Vartanian, who had been a member of the FHLB and was now a lawyer representing many successful bidders in these deals, told *Wall Street Journal* reporters, "It was like they [the regulators] were playing tennis blindfolded and with one arm behind their back." [125]

Unlike what the Gravette plan had envisioned, most of the purchasers were not well-managed, solvent thrifts. In some cases failing thrifts were allowed to purchase these packages. More frequently the buyers were high financiers like Ronald Perelman of the Revlon Group, the Caroline Hunt Trust Estate, and the Robert M. Bass Group. Noting that only those with huge amounts of taxable income could benefit from the lucrative tax benefits of these giveaway transactions, one independent expert testified to Congress, "It was almost as if the government were playing Robin Hood in reverse."[126]

There is considerable evidence that instead of soliciting bids from the widest possible swath of potential buyers, certain favored—or "preferred"—buyers were targeted.[127] The system operated like this. S&L packages were put together roughly along the lines used in the Gravette plan, but which defunct thrifts these packages contained was technically kept secret and the bidding was to be done "blind."[128] Ordinary bidders said that their requests for general information on the packages and on the bidding process itself went unanswered; one prospective bidder interviewed by the *Economist* reported that he had telephoned Lykos's office 102 times and never received a response.[129] In contrast, favored bidders were told which packages to bid on and were privy to inside information about their contents.[130] A Dallas lawyer who had successfully completed many of these deals told the *Economist* that the process was "byzantine and backroom."[131] It is even reported that "exclusives" were granted to some important bidders, like Robert Bass.[132] The vast majority of these favored bidders were either heavy contributors to the Republican party (most were members of President Bush's Team 100, meaning they had contributed at least $100,000 to the Bush campaign) or friends of senior Bank Board officials.[133]

According to Black, the "preferred acquirer" system was protected through the maintenance of control over the bidding process. Most important, independent financial analysis of the relative merit of various bids was eschewed, relying instead on the input of the Dallas FHLB whose direct ties to the Texas thrift industry should have made its evaluations suspect. Although the FSLIC had the resources to hire outside consultants to study the deals, it hired law firms with no particular financial expertise. When San Francisco FHLB regulators expressed misgivings about the advisability of particular preferred deals, they were forbidden to pursue their critique.

In one incident the regulators met with a supervisor from Washington, D.C., and presented their objections to the sale of a thrift in their jurisdiction. The supervisor conceded that she agreed with the regulators' objections but would recommend the purchase anyway. She explained that her office—the Office of Regulatory Activities (ORA)—had come under fire from the FSLIC, which, "in a play on the scientific name for killer whales, 'Orca,' " referred to their office as "ORA the deal killers." She said that she had instructions from Washington not to kill any more deals.[134]

The first Southwest Plan deal in many ways set the stage for the rest, and it is exemplary of the inefficiencies and political intrigue that permeated this effort to cover up the scope of the crisis. The deal involved Southwest Savings Association in Dallas. Southwest had almost $1.5 billion in assets in 1988 and under the chairmanship of C. Todd Miller, who was also the vice-chair of the Dallas FHLB, had been one of the most profitable and well-run thrifts in Texas. But by the spring of 1987 Southwest was verging on insolvency, probably in part because of the high deposit interests—or the "Texas premium"—it had to pay to compete with Texas highfliers.[135]

What made Southwest unusual was that it was 90 percent owned by the Caroline Hunt Trust Estate, established on behalf of Caroline Hunt and with a net worth in 1987 of approximately $900 million.[136] What was troubling for Hunt was that she had signed a "net worth maintenance" agreement with the FHLBB stipulating that if the net worth of Southwest ever fell below the regulatory requirement, her estate would make it up. Having already poured $22.9 million into Southwest under this agreement and with the sinking thrift losing $3 million of its capital base every month, Caroline Hunt stood to lose substantial amounts.

The deal offered her under the Southwest Plan promised salvation. It called for Southwest Savings to purchase for $25 million in new capital four other insolvent Texas thrifts. In return Southwest

Savings would get $483 million in IOUs from the FSLIC to cover all the thrift's bad assets. In addition, it guaranteed a yield from new assets of at least 2.75 points above the cost of deposits; so that if deposits in Texas on average cost 10 percent interest, yields were guaranteed by the FSLIC at 12.75. In the first year after the deal was concluded, the FSLIC had to provide Southwest with another promissory note worth $200 million to cover these guarantees.

Not only were all legal fees covered in the deal, but they were calculated in such a way as to ensure costly lawsuits. Pilzer provides a good example. Let us say that there was a particular $10 million bad loan, and Southwest Savings paid legal fees of $1 million in an effort to collect from the borrower. These legal fees could be rolled onto the bad asset, so that the FSLIC IOU would be $11 million. Incredibly, the FSLIC's yield maintenance agreement then provided a 2.75 percent premium over the cost of new funds on this $11 million, not the original $10 million bad asset. As Pilzer explains, "In short, this feature of the agreement made it profitable for the thrift to sue people regardless of whether the suits had any merit." [137]

Probably the most controversial aspect of this deal was that it allowed Caroline Hunt to renege on her commitment to Southwest to make up for its capital shortages, thus potentially saving her hundreds of millions of dollars, a tab that taxpayers ultimately picked up. The director of the FSLIC, Stuart Root, called the Hunt deal "a loss leader"; by 1990 the new thrift had a negative net worth of $350 million. [138] In this first stage of the thrift "bailout," all that was accomplished was that one of the richest people in America was bailed out by the FSLIC. [139] It was indeed Robin Hood in reverse.

When asked why Tom Lykos and the FSLIC gave in to the hard-hitting negotiating of Hunt's team, Danny Wall said Southwest Savings was the "only qualified bidder." But the package and criteria for bidding were established by Lykos after reviewing prospective bidders; that review was conducted by the Dallas Federal Home

Loan Bank, whose vice-chair was C. Todd Miller, Southwest's CEO. One of the thrifts sold to Southwest in the deal, Lamar Savings Association, had tried to bid on the package itself, and was prepared to contribute $1.6 billion in new capital. The FSLIC reportedly did not even consider its bid.[140]

Another of the Southwest Plan deals—the Bluebonnet deal—was called by Senator Howard Metzenbaum "an abomination, the worst case" in the 1988 cover-up.[141] James Fail had been indicted in 1976 for securities fraud connected to one of his insurance companies in Alabama, and was prohibited from ever again entering the insurance industry in that state.[142] Despite the fact that this background might have "presumptively disqualified" him as a bidder, Fail was allowed to purchase fifteen insolvent thrifts in one Southwest Plan transaction.[143] Fail put up $1,000 of his own money and borrowed the remaining $70 million from his own insurance companies and a variety of other sponsors. In return he got $3 billion in tax breaks that he could apply to his moneymaking ventures; in his first year as owner of Bluebonnet, Fail received another $371 million in subsidies.[144] An outraged Senator Metzenbaum declared, "It is no longer appropriate to call Mr. Fail the 'buyer' in this transaction. The Bluebonnet deal was a gift."[145]

Senate hearings into the Bluebonnet transaction focused on the bidding process for this "gift." Fail's lobbyist in the deal making was Robert J. Thompson, a former aide and close friend of George Bush and a close personal friend of a senior Bank Board official. Thompson was so well connected that he was able to address FHLBB chair Wall as "Dear Danny" in a letter requesting that the board assign a special liaison to Fail's case.[146] Thompson even was supplied a draft of the Bank Board's report on Fail's legal problems and participated in preparing the government's response.[147] Fail was late in submitting his bid, and a rival bid being considered at the time would have saved the government an estimated $100 million.[148] In fact, the Dallas Bank Board had originally opposed Fail's eligibility based on his earlier indictment, but the Dallas board chairman, George Barclay, overruled his staff. Barclay admitted that it was "entirely possible" he had done so after receiving telephone calls from Washington officials urging him to recommend the Fail deal.[149]

The sweetest of the Southwest deals went to Ronald Perelman of the Revlon Group, whose private wealth is estimated at over $5 billion, making him one of the richest people in the United States.[150] This transaction, which produced the largest thrift in Texas, merged First Texas, Gibraltar S&L, and Vernon. Perelman put in $65 million of his own capital and borrowed another $250 million to inject $315 million into the new First Gibraltar. In return he got $7.1 billion in good assets, a $5.1 billion IOU to cover his new thrift's bad assets, and an estimated $461 million tax credit in the first year alone.[151] Perelman later sold First Gibraltar for a $1 billion profit, but he will continue to use $3 billion in "net operating losses" to offset taxes on his other enterprises over fifteen years.[152] When Perelman's deal, which was signed late at night on December 27 in the offices of the Dallas Federal Home Loan Bank, was described to the House Banking Committee in 1989, District of Columbia congressman Walter Fauntroy asked incredulously, "Why is it only white folks who get that kind of deal?"[153] In a 1995 cover story on Perelman and his empire, *Business Week* characterized the First Gibraltar transaction as "a hugely generous and controversial deal."[154]

The Southwest Plan ultimately consisted of fifteen transactions involving eighty-seven insolvent Texas thrifts with combined assets of $12 billion.[155] Bank Board chair Wall had estimated that the plan could resolve Texas thrifts for $6 to $7 billion; it ended up costing more than $80 billion. The director of an independent consulting firm that studied the Southwest Plan testified before Congress that these transactions cost the government up to 40 percent more than would have outright liquidation.[156] One journalist called the Southwest Plan "the most colossal deception yet." [157] A *Fortune* magazine reporter called it the "screwiest S&L bailout ever." [158] Congressman Gonzalez of Texas, who had replaced St. Germain as chair of the House Banking Committee, said of the plan, "When this is over, it's going to make the Watergate people look like a Boy Scout troop of honor." [159]

Political intrigue thus permeated the Southwest Plan twice. The plan was born of the political necessity to cover up the thrift crisis and keep the real taxpayer bailout quiet until after the 1988 election. It was to this end that Wall insisted that thrifts could be resolved with the funds at hand. And it was to this end that tax credits and IOUs were used, putting off to the future the cost of the resolutions and ratcheting up the final tab. But political fraud—as well as outright incompetence and inefficiency—permeated the plan itself, with favored buyers being targeted for special treatment and rival bidders who might have saved the government money being shunned.

IMPLICATIONS

William Greider, in an award-winning PBS documentary and in his book *Who Will Tell the People?* claims that American democracy has been subverted by the power of affluent special interests to woo policy makers and dictate the parameters of public discourse. In one arena after another, Greider marshals dramatic evidence for this instrumentalist model of the sabotage of representative democracy by "organized money." According to Greider, the unrivaled influence of this organized money and the pervasive deal making associated with it constitute no less than "the slow death of constitutional democracy in our time," a "grotesque distortion" of our representative system of government. [160]

Dan Clawson, Alan Neustadtl, and Denise Scott come to the same conclusion in their recent study of corporate PACs. Starting from the notion that power is not so much the ability to force people to act against their will as the more generalized capacity to "shape the field of action," they argue that in the American political arena "business is different" from any other interest group. By this they mean that the power of corporate PACs is enhanced not only by their disproportionate resources and carefully calculated campaign contributions but also by the unrivaled social legitimacy of business in America. This legitimacy translates into political capital unlike that enjoyed by any other group. Underscoring the benefit of the doubt conferred by this social legitimacy, Clawson, Neustadtl, and Scott draw an admittedly extreme comparison:

When a member of Congress accepts a $1000 donation from a corporate PAC, goes to a committee hearing, and proposes "minor" changes in a bill's wording, those changes are often accepted without discussion or examination. The changes "clarify" the language of the bill, perhaps legalizing higher levels of pollution for a specific pollutant or exempting the company from some tax. The media do not report on this change, and no one speaks against it. On the other hand, if a PAC were formed by Drug Lords for Cocaine Legalization, no member of Congress would take its money. If a member introduced a "minor" amendment to make it easier to sell crack without bothersome police interference, the proposed change would attract massive attention, the campaign contribution would be labeled a scandal, the member's political career would be ruined, and the wording change would not be incorporated into the bill.[161]

The evidence is widespread that our democratic process has been badly distorted by monied interests and the private deal making that has all but replaced public policy making and precludes democratic accountability. Enhancing the edge already enjoyed by business interests with substantial resources at their disposal is the invaluable political capital their unique social legitimacy grants them. Politics as usual in this scenario is special access for monied and culturally privileged interests and a pervasive system of—in Reisman's term— "folded lies."

In some ways, then, the political favors granted the savings and loan industry in the 1980s were rather ordinary, as were the cover-ups and side steps. The political frauds and deal making documented here cost hundreds of billions of dollars in a taxpayer bail-out and brought the U.S. financial system to the brink of disaster, but the *process* through which these frauds were perpetrated was politics as usual, as many have described it.[162] This is perhaps the most sobering insight we can derive from this extraordinary scandal—its ordinariness.

But the scandal is not so ordinary in that it has exposed what normally remains concealed. For a brief moment it made explicit the implicit bribery at the heart of our political system. Robert Clarke, former comptroller of the currency, noted that in many ways the behavior of S&L executives in the 1980s was no different from that of financial managers at other times and in other sectors. What was different was that the economic collapse in Texas and elsewhere exposed wrongdoing that otherwise would have gone unde-tected.[163] "When the economic tide goes out, you find out who's swimming naked," he said.[164] Clarke was referring to the Ponzi schemes and other swindles perpetrated by thrift operatives, but the same can be said of the political frauds that facilitated these transactions and protected the perpetrators. What was unusual was not that political deals were cut and favors traded but that the tide went out, all too briefly revealing the naked underside of a political system in which money buys access and some interests are more "special" than others.

One more quality sets the S&L fiasco apart from politics as usual. Clawson, Neustadtl, and Scott refer to the substantial social legiti-macy from which business interests benefit in the political arena. They argue that corporate power goes beyond even the cynical "one dollar, one vote" aphorism, since business interests enjoy a taken-for-granted status unlike that of any other interest group. This taken-for-granted legitimacy derives in part from the stereotype of responsible businesspersons and the social status conferred on them and in part from the connection between business interests and the rest of the economy. Not only do business executives exude social respectability, but the realization of business interests is perceived to be integrally linked to a healthy economy and employment opportunities.[165]

For most of this century savings and loans were small-town institutions run by local bankers in a highly regulated environment, but by the mid-1980s deregulation had attracted a new breed of thrift owner with a dramatically different relationship to the local economy. In place of the traditional bankers of the past, thrifts were increasingly owned and operated by those from outside the industry—real estate developers in particular, but also dentists, carpet salesmen, and others without experience in banking and without the benefit of that status. Some—James Fail is a good example—even had prior indictments on their records. One senior investigator noted the transformation in thrift personnel, using conventional stereotypes as his explanation for thrift fraud: "They [former thrift executives] dressed in blue suits, they had polished shoes, they were very honest people. They may have come from a family of banking of tradition [sic]. The people who came in and bought the S&Ls in the early 1980s have none of these [qualities]." [166] Given the widely held view of the role of respectability and social status in privileging business interests, it is telling that the influence of the thrift industry increased—peaking with the 1987 FSLIC recap vote—just as the social respectability and "blue suit" status of thrift operators declined.

More important, this political clout came at the expense of the larger economy. While it may be true that business interests typically accrue legitimacy through their perceived connection to broader economic benefits such as job preservation or economic growth, key policy makers in the S&L scandal can scarcely use that justification for the deal making that brought the financial system to the brink of collapse and multiplied the federal deficit many times over. When this tide went out, it revealed the raw power of personal, career, and financial interests unadorned by the rhetoric of a larger national interest.

At the same time it is important to note that this official complicity in the thrift debacle varied across the agencies and institutions of government. Remember that by the mid-1980s Edwin Gray and the FHLBB launched a determined crusade to contain the crisis while key members of Congress regularly sought to thwart them. This interagency struggle is an important subplot in this story of political intrigue and suggests that a uniformly instrumentalist view of the relationship between the state and monied interests may be overly simplistic. We will return to these issues in the conclusion, but first we look at the government response to the crisis that it had for so long chosen to ignore.

The looting of the nation's savings and loans was finally brought to a quiet end in 1989. After years of looking the other way, and before an unknowing public could express its outrage, a thrift bailout plan was introduced and enacted shortly after President Bush took office. Hardly anyone noticed the legislation, which represented the largest taxpayer bailout in history. As one commentator observed, "The biggest bailout in history was enacted with a small fraction of the public debate accorded to prohibiting flag burning or the funding of allegedly obscene art." [1] It is no wonder that the legislation passed so quietly; as we have seen, politicians had left their fingerprints all over the S&L fiasco.

The ravaged state of the savings and loan industry and the insolvency of the FSLIC finally forced the government to take legislative steps to reregulate thrifts and to end their financial hemorrhaging. The Financial Institutions Reform, Recovery and Enforcement Act of 1989 (FIRREA) was the Bush administration's bailout plan. It was approved by Congress within six months and went into effect in August 1989. The bill raised $50 billion over three years through the sale of bonds to be paid back over forty years. This money was to be used largely to finance the federal seizure of hundreds of insolvent savings and loans and to provide funds to cover insured deposits. Since it was financed by bonds, more than half of the final bailout cost will consist of interest payments. In July 1996 the General Accounting Office predicted the total tab would be close to $500 billion.[2]

Many of the deregulatory measures instituted in the 1980s were repealed by FIRREA. For example, the law required that thrifts hold at least 70 percent of assets in home mortgages or mortgage-backed securities to obtain below-market-rate advances from the Federal Home Loan Bank and to take tax deductions for loan loss reserves. It also prohibited thrifts from investing in junk bonds with insured deposits and required that any existing junk bonds be sold by 1994; it limited loans to one borrower to 15 percent of the thrift's capital; it prevented states from providing more lenient regulations for state-chartered thrifts than federal standards allow; and, for the first time, it tied capital requirements to the investment risk of a thrift's portfolio.

Recognizing the organizational impediments to effective regulation that existed in the past, Congress also revamped the regulatory agencies that oversee thrifts, abolishing the FHLBB and the FSLIC. The latter's responsibilities were transferred to a division of the Federal Deposit Insurance Corporation, which had previously insured only commercial banks. The examination and enforcement functions once performed by the FHLBB are located in the new Office of Thrift Supervision. The Resolution Trust Corporation was formed to manage and dispose of seized thrift assets. (The RTC ceased operations in early 1996 when all assets had been sold.)

Finally, and most important for our analysis, FIRREA provided new tools for law enforcement in pursuing financial fraud in the thrift industry. One of the most significant was a civil forfeiture provision for thrift-related offenses, making it possible to seize defendants' assets before they could be transferred offshore, consumed, or otherwise "disappear." It also provided for increased penalties for financial institution crimes committed after August 9,

1989 (from five years to twenty years in prison per offense), and extended the statute of limitations for such crimes from five to ten years. While it did not affect the many offenses committed prior to 1984, the new statute of limitations constituted official recognition of the large workloads of investigators and the unprecedented backlog of financial fraud cases. At the same time FIRREA authorized substantial increases in FBI agents and prosecutors to work these cases, as well as $75 million annually for three years to enhance the Justice Department's efforts to prosecute financial fraud.

A related law, enacted on November 9, 1990, strengthened some of the provisions of FIRREA and added new ones. Title 25 of the Crime Control Act of 1990, also known as the Comprehensive Thrift and Bank Fraud Prosecution and Taxpayer Recovery Act of 1990, focused almost entirely on law enforcement efforts and enhanced sanctions against financial institution fraud. It increased penalties for concealing assets from government agencies and obstructing their functions and placing assets beyond their reach, as well as obstructing examination of a financial institution.[3] The law also increased maximum statutory penalties from twenty to thirty years imprisonment for a range of violations, including false entries on reports, bribery, embezzlement, mail and wire fraud, and intentional misapplication of thrift funds, reserving the severest sanctions for "financial crime kingpins." The Financial Institutions Fraud Unit was established in the Office of the Deputy Attorney General, to be headed by a special counsel for a period of five years. A presidential appointee, the special counsel was to supervise and coordinate investigations and prosecutions of financial institution crimes and manage civil enforcement and resource issues. Finally, the act increased the $75 million allocated to enforcement by FIRREA to $162.5 million per year for fiscal years 1991 through 1993.[4]

The purposes of FIRREA and the Crime Control Act of 1990 were to restructure the regulatory apparatus of the thrift industry, provide resources for cleaning up the industry, and generally increase the capacity of the state to deal with financial institution fraud. But the scope of the debacle and accompanying fraud still left regulators and enforcement officials with a herculean task. The RTC reported that since its inception in 1989 through July 1992, it had merged, sold, or managed 652 failed thrifts. During this period, the government had spent close to $196 billion to resolve these institutions.[5]

Law enforcement caseloads were enormous. Assistant Attorney General W. Lee Rawls gave Congress the following statistics on investigative workloads.

During FY 1991, the FBI received 28,150 criminal referrals from financial institutions, bank supervisory agencies, and other complainants. These referrals produced 5,490 new FBI investigations. . . . As of September 30, 1991, the FBI had 8,678 FIF [financial institution fraud] matters under investigation. Of those, a total of 4,336 represented major cases where the loss or exposure to the financial institution was $100,000 or more. . . . Through the first quarter of FY 1992 (as of 12-31-91), the FBI received 7,491 criminal referrals resulting in the initiation of 1,762 new cases. It also had 8,715 FIF matters under investigation. Of those, a total of 4,495 represented major cases.[6]

Congressional hearings repeatedly pointed to the backlog of complex criminal cases and the limited ability of federal enforcement agencies to respond effectively. In April 1990 there were 1,298 "inactive cases," each involving over $100,000, which under official definitions were designated "significant," but there were not enough FBI agents or U.S. Attorneys to investigate or prosecute them.[7] The Secret Service even picked up some of the spillover from the massive FBI workload and undertook investigations of S&L crime.

Two central aspects of the government bailout concern us here. First, the unprecedented response to financial institution fraud (in terms of the resources committed to the effort and the criminal sanctions pursued) was based primarily on the need to curtail financial losses in a failing industry whose capital was government insured. More specifically, the law enforcement effort was directed less at penalizing S&L offenders for their crimes than at rescuing the industry, shoring up investor confidence, and containing the loss of government-insured capital. Second, even given this unprecedented response to white-collar crime, the effort was constrained by systemic limitations on enforcement and the overwhelming scale of the disaster.

CRIME CONTROL OR DAMAGE CONTROL?

Attorney General Richard Thornburgh prefaced a Justice Department report on savings and loan fraud with this promise: "The American public can be assured . . . that prosecution of white collar crime—'crime in the suites'—and particularly savings and loan crimes, will remain a top priority of the Department of Justice." [8] In a speech to U.S. Attorneys in June 1990 President Bush stated, "We will not rest until the cheats and the chiselers and the charlatans [responsible for the S&L disaster] spend a large chunk of their lives behind the bars of a federal prison." [9] The president was unequivocal about his plans for attacking financial institution fraud: "We aim for a simple, uncompromising position. Throw the crooks in jail." [10]

This get-tough-on-crime approach to the thrift offenders is strikingly at odds with the earlier collective denial and avoidance tactics. Undoubtedly President Bush hoped to gain political mileage from an emphatic response to the worst financial fraud epidemic in U.S. history, even if (or maybe, particularly because) that response was several years late. But this was not just empty political rhetoric. By 1989 both the legislative and executive branches were giving considerable attention to savings and loan fraud. FIRREA had allocated substantial resources to financial fraud efforts, and almost immediately the number of FBI personnel assigned to financial fraud investigations climbed from 822 to 1,525. The total Department of Justice budget for financial fraud went from $80,845,000 to $212,236,000.[11]

Special task forces and working groups were established. The Bank Fraud Working Group in Washington, D.C., brought together top officials from the Office of the Comptroller of the Currency, the Department of Justice, and the Treasury Department to improve communication, provide an arena for policy discussions, and generally coordinate the enforcement effort. In late 1983 a special task force (Texcon) was established in Dallas to deal with the overload of criminal referrals involving S&L fraud related to land purchases and condominium development along I-30 east of Dallas. While Texcon processed the I-30 cases, the Dallas Bank Fraud Task Force (Thriftcon) dealt with the numerous other S&L cases still being referred to the Dallas FBI. The Department of Justice increased the Dallas FBI staff by 19 special agents and added support personnel and equipment. When Thriftcon began operations in 1987, it included 27 FBI agents, 21 Department of Justice and Northern District of Texas attorneys, 4 Office of Thrift Supervision (formerly FHLBB) officials, and 17 Internal Revenue Service agents. By 1990 Thriftcon was staffed by 94 full-time agents. By the spring of 1992 it included 150 law enforcement personnel from four different Justice Department sections or agencies and two Treasury Department divisions.[12] With this infusion of resources, the number of prosecuted S&L offenders grew quickly. From October 1988 to April 1992, more than 1,100 defendants were formally charged in "major" savings and loan cases and 839 were convicted.[13] Major financial fraud investigations increased by 54 percent from 1987 to 1991. The FBI opened more than 260 major case investigations every month, and by early 1992 more than 4,300 financial fraud investigations were under way, approximately 1,000 involving savings and loans.[14] At no time in its history has the U.S. government allocated so many resources and devoted so much of its law enforcement effort to white-collar crime.[15]

The question is, Why? Two major explanations stand out. The first is simply that the unprecedented epidemic of thrift fraud quite naturally required a corresponding, unprecedented response. The second possibility, postulated by some researchers, is that this assault on financial fraud was an indication of the erosion of official tolerance for white-collar crime. There is a common flaw in both of these explanations: If there was indeed a crackdown on white-collar crime, it was highly *selective*. While Congress, the Justice Department, and the thrift regulatory agencies took an aggressive approach to financial institution fraud, corporate and business crime in other sectors was ignored by comparison. Since the Reagan administration in the early 1980s, sanctions against employers who violate health and safety standards have plummeted.[16] Despite the fact that hundreds of thousands of U.S. workers are killed and disabled annually from work-related accidents and illnesses, employer convictions almost never result in criminal prosecution, much less imprisonment. (The production of asbestos will result in 170,000 deaths from lung cancer and other related diseases; yet none of the corporate executives who deliberately concealed the dangers have been criminally charged.) The U.S. Food and Drug Administration continues to be reluctant to recommend criminal prosecution of corporate executives who conceal the hazards of their products or deliberately fabricate data attesting to their safety.[17] Indeed, if we focus on traditional forms of corporate crime, there is no evidence of any crackdown.

So the explanation must lie elsewhere. Let us look at the details of this government response to thrift fraud. It is noteworthy that priority was placed on financial institutions that were on the verge of failure or already insolvent and in which fraud played a significant

role in the collapse. The official definition of a "major case"—cases
to which top priority is assigned—refers to dollar losses, the role of
insiders, and the like, as discussed earlier. Yet government officials
consistently told us that among the most important factors determining priority is *whether the alleged fraud contributed to the insolvency.* Ira
Raphaelson, at the time special counsel for financial fraud in the
Deputy Attorney General's Office, told a Senate subcommittee that
whether cases are treated as major ones depends on dollar losses
and the role fraud played in an institution's failure.

Senator Dixon: "How do you define a major case?"

Mr. Raphaelson: "If it involves an alleged loss of more than $100,000 or
involves a failed institution."

Senator Dixon: "There are at least 4300 cases over $100,000?"

Mr. Raphaelson: "Or involving a failed institution, it might be less than
$100,000. But *because it is linked to a failure, we still consider
it a major case.*" [18]

At the same hearing the General Accounting Office summarized
for the Senate subcommittee the number of major cases being investigated, defining such cases as "those involving failed institutions
or alleged losses of $100,000 or more." [19] Referring to their priori-
tization of cases, as well as likely sentence severity, one FBI agent in
Florida gave an example: "If you steal over $5 million and you make
the bank fail, you've popped the bubble on the thermometer there!"
The same Florida agent tied the influx of federal resources for financial fraud investigations to the economic importance of these
cases. A few years ago, he explained, "we as financial crimes or
financial fraud investigators were vying for manpower in this office
along with [drugs and public corruption] squads. We had to share
the white-collar crime staffing . . . with these people. Now that
we've had such dramatic increases in the number of failed institutions in the last year and a half, they're being investigated here and

Congress has appropriated huge amounts of funds to target that."[20]

In addition to the "major case" specification, in June 1990 the Office of Thrift Supervision, the Resolution Trust Corporation, and the Federal Deposit Insurance Corporation developed a matrix with which to establish the priority of thrift fraud investigations and used it to draw up a list of the "Top 100" thrifts for investigative purposes. Among the most important ingredients in this matrix were the financial health of the institution, whether fraud had contributed to insolvency, and the economic effect on the larger community.[21]

Enforcement statistics confirm that these priorities were central determinants of the response to thrift crime. A GAO report reveals that of the approximately one thousand major thrift cases under investigation in fiscal year 1991, one-third involved failed institutions and the other two-thirds were for investigations of fraud that contributed to major losses.[22] Thriftcon in Dallas handled only insolvent institution cases. Indeed, the task force was established in 1987 when it was brought to the attention of officials in Dallas that eighteen thrifts in the area were on the verge of collapse. The following incident suggests that as a matter of policy, when alleged fraud did not result in demonstrable losses, no further investigation was pursued. In response to a query from Congress about criminal referrals made in connection with Silverado Savings and Loan, the Department of Justice explained that one of the referrals in question was dropped: "This matter involved no demonstrable loss; prosecution was declined in the United States Attorney's Office, District of Colorado."[23]

In other words, the crackdown on financial fraud seems to have been driven less by crime control concerns than by the need to control the financial damage. Substantial evidence attests to the importance attributed to this damage control. Congressman Henry Gonzalez, chair of the House Committee on Banking, warned FBI director William Sessions of the urgency of dealing with thrift crime: "The issue is very, very serious. We can not allow . . . a loss of faith in the deposit insurance system. . . . Confidence is at the root of everything because if we lose the confidence of the people, no system will stand up to that." [24] GAO director Harold Valentine told a Senate subcommittee that bank and thrift fraud and the financial collapse to which they contributed were "perhaps the most significant financial crisis in this nation's history." [25] The Department of Justice referred to it as "the unconscionable plundering of America's financial institutions." [26] A senior staff member of the Senate Banking Committee explained the attention being given to thrift fraud: "This industry is very close to the heart of the American economy. We teetered on the edge of a major, major problem here. Well . . . we got a major problem, but we teetered on the edge of a major collapse. . . . You know, all these [financial] industries could bring down the whole economy!" [27]

Bank fraud and thrift fraud are of course not new. Investigators and regulators report that abuse by thrift insiders was frequent in the 1960s and 1970s but that it attracted little attention because the institutions were generally thriving. One regulator who said that fraud has always existed in thrifts claimed that "[hot prices in real estate are] the only thing that pulled everybody's asses out for years." [28] The government response to thrift fraud thus has little to do with punishing crime per se; instead, it is crisis prevention, aimed at stopping further damage to financial institutions that lie "close to the heart of the American economy."

A number of other studies have noted the role of regulatory agencies in shoring up investor faith by minimizing uncertainty and risk and generally stabilizing the financial system. Susan Shapiro's study of the Securities and Exchange Commission, for example, shows that SEC officials see themselves as protectors of the securities and exchange system rather than as its adversaries. [29] Nancy Reichman underlines the stabilizing effect of regulating risks in the stock market. As she puts it, "Regulations . . . harness . . . uncertainty." [30]

Mitchell Abolafia observes a similar dynamic in the commodities futures market, where regulations "structure anarchy."[31] And Peter Yeager points out that there is substantial business support for the enforcement of regulations that "protect the integrity of the marketplace."[32] As Laureen Snider explains, "Controlling this type of corporate crime [violations of economic regulations] turns out to be in the interests of the corporate sector overall, as well as being compatible with state objectives. Such laws protect the sanctity of the investment market, which is central to the ability of corporations to raise money by issuing shares."[33]

Consistent with this regulatory literature, the government crackdown on the savings and loan industry and its bailout were driven by the need to limit financial losses and stabilize the economy. And the mission was all the more urgent since this industry and the capital it was losing were government insured. The government's response to the savings and loan debacle can be seen, then, as an effort directed less at penalizing thrift wrongdoers for their misdeeds than at limiting damage to the industry, preventing comparable damage in other financial sectors, and containing the hemorrhage of government-insured capital. An upper-echelon official in Washington, D.C., when asked to comment on this interpretation, said simply, "You hit the nail right on the head."[34]

THE RESOURCE PROBLEM: THE S&L FIASCO AS "ALASKAN OIL SPILL"

Despite the unprecedented influx of resources, the thrift cleanup was chronically behind schedule. The concepts "system capacity," "resource saturation," and "system overload," employed to analyze the impact of increased workload demands on criminal justice agencies, may be useful here.[35] Two dimensions of system capacity are particularly relevant to the government's response to the savings and loan disaster. The first has to do with the difficulty of detecting, investigating, and sanctioning such complex financial fraud and the related demand for enormous infusions of resources and expertise. Second is the unprecedented scale of this epidemic of fraud and the related resource and logistical constraints.

The hidden and complex nature of many white-collar and corporate crimes, especially financial frauds, makes them particularly difficult to detect and sanction. As Jack Katz notes in this regard, white-collar crimes are woven into ordinary business routines and are often well hidden by intricate and misleading paper trails.[36] Numerous studies point to the limited capacity of criminal justice agencies to respond to such illegalities.[37] And financial crimes of the sort involved in the S&L scandal are perhaps the most complex white-collar offenses ever dealt with by authorities. One FBI agent described these cases.

When it comes to these insider, conspiratorial things, they are extremely complex, they are disguised. . . . The problem is figuring out what the crime is—what did they do, how did they do it. And then can I explain to a court of law, to people who are high school graduates or less. I spent, I think, about five and a half months where all day, every day, I sat in a room with boxes and boxes of records. You look through these things to see where the money went. . . . It's difficult. To figure out what's happened to these things is really tough.[38]

The high degree of complexity present in these financial frauds and the fact that much of the essential information was controlled by thrift insiders produced a new breed of case for even experienced enforcement agents. As one high-ranking FBI official noted, a change in expectations regarding "efficiency" in investigating these crimes was needed.

I think it's worth mentioning the efficiency ratio of bank fraud embezzlement cases. When the attorney general gets up and talks about statistical data, we show the bars and pie graphs and everything else, and look at what we used to do and what we're doing now, and it's two different animals. I know now the average agent working in financial institution fraud in the FBI used to get 4.7 convictions per year, and that was a base used for the barometer for efficiency in the field division. That was when we were working cases that had a vast preponderance of outsiders submitting false loan applications, or tellers embezzling funds, and when we had complete cooperation from the management, and the records were there on the premises, and generally things were current. The witnesses were the insiders. They were the victims. Now we run into this stuff where we are targeting the individuals who are the custodians of the records, and many times you have to put together a case without their assistance. They're totally different animals, and our efficiency ratio shoots down. It looks like we're being less efficient but it's just different cases.

Complexity was sometimes deliberately constructed by perpetrators of fraud to disguise their offenses as normal business transactions and put off wary regulators. One investigator described his experience: "I have got a little financial background. I have been here for a while. It took the regulators a while to explain to me what they were doing, and the regulators said it took them a while to figure it out too. You have a Keating. Keating said, 'You don't understand my land deals and my junk bond deals.' [David] Paul said, 'You don't understand my junk bonds. You're too stupid.' "

These cases have sometimes taken several years and millions of dollars to investigate and prosecute. One FBI agent estimated the time spent on investigations: "From the time we open the investigation until we get it to the indictment stage . . . I don't know any case that has taken less than six months, and some have taken three years. The really big cases—two or three years." Another investigator explained, "You have to subpoena massive amounts of documents, attempt to locate witnesses, attempt to put together things that were disguised. . . . That takes a lot of time. . . . Typical things—land flips, straw borrowers, money being diverted, in this case, laundered along the way—took quite a bit of paperwork and review just to find out where it all went. This was a heck of a lot of work right here, just in this one case."

Moreover, the complexity of these cases made it difficult for prosecutors to present them persuasively to a jury. As one investigator described it, "These things get so convoluted and complicated that you really have a hard time discerning the end of an investigation. You have a hard time convincing the prosecutor that they ought to prosecute this case, and then you have a virtually impossible time with the jury."

In response to the time and budget constraints posed by these cases, and to simplify them for presentation to juries, investigators and prosecutors developed a streamlined "rifle-shot" approach. The gist of this strategy was to focus on one or two clear and serious violations of the law that would be relatively easy to document and explain to a jury, rather than attempt to piece together the whole fabric of complex illegal transactions—an endeavor that could take many years with no certain payoff. As one investigator explained the approach, "The theory is not meant to prove a global picture in which these people caused the downfall of the institution. The theory is to pick out the best and most egregious case that has jury appeal, that has hard facts, that can be proven and understood by a jury. . . . So you may have ten or fifteen things, and you focus your investigation on those prime areas that you think are going to take you into the courtroom and get the guilty pleas."

An FBI agent also related the rifle-shot approach to the complexity of these cases and the enormous resources they require.

The Bureau [FBI], I think, is very much up-front on this, that you could stay in there with a bevy of agents . . . and investigate every criminal allegation because many of these places were such rats' nests. You could investigate them for a decade and still not be sure that you got everything that they were involved in. So, with the resources you have, you have to say, all right, this guy's a bad actor, we want to be able . . . to see that he gets a substantial criminal sentence without having spent an inordinately long amount of time because we've got these other cases that are backing up over here.

This rifle-shot technique was the government's response to the obstacles of investigating and prosecuting thousands of complex cases in which it was difficult to distinguish convoluted, but legitimate, business transactions from fraud. While saving time and resources, it of course left much criminal activity undetected and unprosecuted and inevitably resulted in less prison time for those offenders who were convicted. As one official explained, "We started out originally with the strategy that was much more global and we found it consumed way too many resources. . . . Now what we've tried to do is the much more focused strategy. . . . The problem with not putting together the entire story is if he only pleads guilty to one or two counts, he may not get significant jail time."

An RTC official expressed dismay over the crimes that go unprocessed due to time limitations and the rifle-shot strategy.

What I'm hoping to be able to do . . . is to go back to these hot smoldering ashes—because they are by no means cold, they are still very active—sift through them deeper, get into . . . the very sophisticated convoluted fraud schemes that I believe are there, and pull together the network of fraudulent schemes between these incestuous relationships of these various institutions that I believe are there but unfortunately resources and time constraints have let us . . . look at only pieces of it. But I still think that there is more there to be found.

It is unlikely that this already overextended official will have time to return to cases that have already been processed and recover from the "smoldering ashes" a picture of the broader network of criminal

activity.[39] The point here is that this ad hoc approach, while mandated by the system's limited capacity to process these cases in their
entirety, inevitably leaves much criminal activity uncovered.

Compounding these difficulties is the sheer scale of the thrift
fraud. Frustrated officials repeatedly addressed this issue in interviews, as they spoke of the impossibility of investigating and processing the thousands of offenders involved. A top federal law enforcement official expressed it succinctly: "There was a time
[when] . . . we were having trouble keeping people from giving us
too much to deter, the groundswell. . . . Did we clean it up? Are we
cleaning it up? No. We are addressing. Are we addressing it quickly
enough? Probably not."

Another official with a dramatic flair contrasted the size of the job
with the available resources: "I feel like it's the Alaskan oil spill. I
feel like I'm out there with a roll of paper towels. That's as close as
I can come to it. The task is so huge, and what I'm worrying about
is: where can I get some more paper towels? . . . I stand out there
with my roll and I look at this sea of oil coming at me, and it's so
colossal and at the same time people are yelling at me, 'The birds
and fish are dying! Do something! Do it faster!' I'm going as fast as
I can."

An enforcement official in Washington, D.C., explained that while
financial institution fraud efforts had received funding increases,
the volume of cases had created huge bottlenecks. Not only were
the funding increases still inadequate, but more general limitations
existed in the system as a whole. He explained, "The greatest stum-
bling block is the lack of resources. . . . It's not just the lack of agents
investigating. It's lack of prosecutors, lack of judges, lack of places
to book." An FBI agent expressed his frustration: "There's so much
going on. . . . And a lot of these people are very bright, exceedingly
bright people. You easily catch the dumb ones and some of the
bright ones, but the exceedingly bright ones . . . I have to believe it

continues. They outfund us. They have more money to do it, to outstrategize us, and it continues. I know they're there."

Another FBI agent, when asked to estimate the proportion of fraud that was being detected and processed, was straightforward in his response: "I guess it's the old iceberg theory. . . . We probably see more of the stupid people, and by definition we're gonna catch a whole lot less of the smarter people. I don't have any way of knowing how much of the actual crime we are uncovering and prosecuting, but . . . it's probably a very minuscule amount."

So, despite the unprecedented federal response to savings and loan fraud, there are limits to system capacity. While systemic limits are critical in understanding the constraints of crime control more generally, they are particularly important in the savings and loan context. For while the imperatives of shoring up the financial system enhanced the urgency of the endeavor, the complexity of these cases and their sheer numbers virtually ensured system overload and a severely limited response. Overwhelmed by the complexity of the cases and the unprecedented volume of S&L frauds, state officials were limited to "cleaning up the oil spill with paper towels."

There is little doubt that the complexity and scale of S&L fraud limited the government response and left large portions of "the iceberg" undetected. However, the system capacity argument is itself limited in its ability to account for some components of the S&L enforcement effort—most notably sentencing patterns. We now turn to a more detailed discussion of the prosecution and sentencing of S&L offenders and the limitations of the system capacity argument.

PURSUING WHITE-COLLAR CRIMINALS

 One of the controversies that emerged in the wake of the savings and loan crisis was the perceived failure of federal authorities to respond quickly and decisively to fraud. Journalists as well as members of Congress charged that law enforcement officials allowed their agencies to be overwhelmed by an avalanche of thrift fraud cases and tended to focus on high-profile offenders while letting large numbers of more ordinary, but extremely costly, cases languish in bureaucratic limbo.[1]

Early evidence supported the critics. In a report to a congressional subcommittee in 1987, the FBI admitted that because of personnel and resource shortages, "banks in the Los Angeles Division are faced with having only about ten percent of referrals actually investigated."[2] In hearings held in the spring of 1990, Congressman Douglas Barnard reported that as of February 1990 the FBI had 21,147 "unaddressed" referrals and complaints related to financial institution fraud, with 1,012 of those involving losses of over $100,000.[3] Congressman Frank Annunzio—seated under a banner that asked "When Are the Savings and Loan Crooks Going to Jail?"—opened hearings held a few months later with this statement: "Frankly, I don't think the administration has the interest in pursuing Gucci-clad white-collar criminals. These are hard and

complicated cases, and the defendants often were rich, successful
and prominent members of their upper-class communities. It is far
easier putting away a sneaker-clad high school drop-out who tries
to rob a bank of a thousand dollars with a stick-up note, than a
smooth-talking S&L executive who steals a million dollars with a
fraudulent note."[4] Similar criticisms were voiced by journalists,
who frequently suggested political motivations behind the failure
of law enforcement officials to pursue high-level S&L crooks.[5]

Consistent with our informants' observations, the official law enforcement response to these criticisms often focused on system capacity. In a speech to the National Press Club in 1990, then Attorney
General Thornburgh used a sports metaphor to criticize prac-
titioners of what he called "inside baseball" (presumably like
Monday morning quarterbacks) who complained about the "do-
nothing Justice Department." He justified the department's relatively poor "season" in 1989 in combating S&L fraud by stating,
"We were playing all-out, everywhere we could—we'd been doing
that for two years—but sometimes with barely nine men on the
field."[6]

Law enforcement officials also insisted that comparing referrals
and indictments was not a valid way to measure performance, since
a single referral might implicate a number of individuals; conversely, one crime might elicit a number of referrals from different
parties. In testimony before the Senate Banking Committee, the
special counsel for financial institution fraud stated, "A referral does
not necessarily result in an investigation let alone an indictment.
Conversely, a single referral may result in multiple cases. A number
of regulatory agencies may generate multiple referrals on the same
incident or even dozens of referrals on the same person. Such multiple referrals based on a single event may result in only single prosecution [sic]."[7]

From this point of view, no single unit of analysis would allow one to evaluate the Justice Department's efforts. A frustrated Senator Richard Bryan of Nevada expressed it this way:

This kind of language . . . drives the public crazy. . . . It seems like we're going through a Hamlet-like soliloquy to be a case or not to be a case. When the decision is made to investigate, that is when a case, in the law enforcement parlance, is begun. All right. . . . However, until an investigative case is indicted or a complaint is filed in court, the Justice Department does not count it as a case. Thus . . . any effort to compare regulatory referral numbers to investigate cases initiated by the law enforcement agencies with prosecutions by the Justice Department, will be forever comparing apples and something from a different food group.[8]

Later Senator Bryan told the special counsel who was attempting to defend the administration's performance in prosecuting thrift fraud, "Not every case referred to a prosecutor by an investigative agency reaches the standards that you as an experienced prosecutor would recognize is worthy of going to trial. I concede that. . . . But, somehow there ought to be a system set up . . . as to the number of cases referred, the disposition of those cases, the number of cases prosecuted, of those prosecuted which cases deal with financial institutions that failed. And what the disposition [was]."[9]

Although the Justice Department never created such a system, we have put together the disparate data provided to us by various agencies and compiled the track record Senator Bryan was looking for. Despite the remonstrations of law enforcement officials, there is one common unit of analysis in both referrals and indictments: the individual. For the following analysis, we isolated and counted the number of individuals cited in Category I referrals and those indicted in S&L-related cases. We counted each individual only once to remove the possibility of multiple referrals of the same individual, the major complaint that Justice officials had lodged against those who used referrals to estimate the incidence of crime.

Our analysis of prosecution efforts is admittedly complicated by the fact that there is often a long lag time between referral and indictment, making within-year comparisons problematic. Even if all referrals led to indictments, given the time between referral and indictment, one would not expect the number of indictments to equal the number of referrals in a given year. Over time, however, one would expect the numbers to more closely approximate each other as referrals submitted in any given year would result in indictments in future years.

We were fortunate to discover that the Office of Thrift Supervision in Texas and California had computerized systems for monitoring criminal referrals and indictments within their districts, although at the time we did our study no national system had yet been developed. Thus in these two states we were able to calculate the odds of indictment for individuals named as suspects in criminal referrals.

To begin, we obtained a computerized list of individuals named in Category I referrals in Texas between January 1, 1985, and March 16, 1993. We then created a file consisting of 1,568 individuals, with variables including the numbers of referrals in which they were named, the total dollar losses reported in those referrals, and other information gathered from referrals. These names were then matched to a separate file maintained by the Dallas OTS on indictments, convictions, and sentences (ICS). The ICS file contained information collected from a variety of sources, including the Executive Office of the U.S. Attorneys "Major S&L Case" survey. By matching information from the two files, we were able to calculate the total number of individuals cited in Category I referrals over the eight-year period and the proportion of those individuals who had been indicted by the end of that period.

We followed the same procedure in assembling the California

data. First we obtained a separate referral file consisting of all "Priority" (Category I) referrals filed in the state between January 1, 1987, and December 31, 1993, and produced a list of individual suspects cited in these referrals. These names were then matched against the ICS file to determine which ones had been indicted.

Table 6 shows the proportion of individuals indicted by the year of their first referral. These data reveal that of the 1,515 individuals cited in referrals in Texas between 1985 and March 1993, approximately 13 percent (194) had been indicted by May 1993. In California 6.1 percent (82) of the 1,339 individuals cited in referrals between 1987 and the end of 1993 had been indicted by December 1993. The lag period between referral and indictment is reflected in the fact that individuals first referred in the earlier years were much more likely to have been indicted. For example, among individuals first referred in Texas in 1986, nearly 30 percent had been indicted by May 1993. Of those first referred in 1992, only 7 percent had been indicted.

We can assume, however, that the vast majority of individuals first cited in 1988 who would ever be indicted, had been indicted by 1993. Of the 132 individuals first referred in Texas in 1986, only 3 were indicted after 1990; of the 285 suspects referred in 1987, only 1 was indicted after 1991. Thus we estimate that in Texas roughly 14 percent of all persons suspected of major thrift crimes will ever face prosecution. Likewise, using 1988 as our baseline year, the number of suspected California thrift fraud offenders who will ever be indicted is approximately 25 percent.

Of course, these data do not indicate with any precision the number of S&L crooks who got away. Criminal referrals represent reports of *suspected* fraud. These allegations are not subject to the evidentiary standards required for an indictment, much less a conviction, and therefore should not be regarded as definitive indicators of criminal events. In the case of S&Ls, as in white-collar crime in general, the line between criminality and simple abuse is often a fine one, and

Table 6
Individuals Criminally Referred and
Indicted in Texas and California

Year	Individuals Named in Texas Referrals		Individuals Named in California Referrals	
	N	Percentage Indicted	N	Percentage Indicted
1985	32	21.9	NA	NA
1986	132	29.5	NA	NA
1987	285	15.4	86	24.4
1988	421	13.8	52	25.0
1989	224	10.7	56	30.4
1990	186	6.5	102	9.6
1991	188	3.7	268	4.1
1992	43	7.0	315	2.2
1993	4	0.0	460	0.7
Total	1,515	12.8	1,339	6.1

Source: Data from Office of Thrift Supervision, Dallas and San Francisco.

what regulators see as fraud may be interpreted under the more rigorous gaze of prosecutors as irresponsible and reckless but not necessarily criminal.

We hypothesize, however, that nonevidentiary factors also played a part in this large gap between referrals and indictments. Here we touch on a larger theoretical issue that has dominated academic discussions of white-collar crime since the field was first defined by Edwin Sutherland in the 1940s: the apparent reluctance of criminal justice agents to pursue white-collar offenders with the same vigor they apply to more common street criminals.

REVISITING THE WHITE-COLLAR CRIME ADVANTAGE

As Sutherland explained it in his *White Collar Crime,* the differential treatment of corporate offenders and street criminals is derived from three kinds of factors. First, judges and other criminal justice personnel identify with white-collar offenders whose social standing is similar to their own, and are reluctant to view them as criminals. Second, white-collar offenders often have more resources at their disposal and are able to mount formidable legal defenses to counter allegations of criminal misconduct. Third, laws are formulated in such a way as to exclude much white-collar misbehavior from the category of crime. Recent research has addressed Sutherland's groundbreaking theory of white-collar crime—some refuting his basic contention of favoritism toward white-collar criminals and others attempting to modify his analysis and extend it to intragroup comparisons of white-collar offenders.

One school—espousing what we might call the "alternative sanctions" argument—claims that while powerful white-collar offenders might be treated differently, this is less indicative of class favoritism than of practical matters, such as the availability of alternative sanctions for these offenders. Susan Shapiro, for example, based on her analysis of securities violations in the United States, argues that "any apparent discrimination against lower status offenders in prosecutorial discretion is more readily explained by greater access to legal options than by social standing." She therefore calls for a reconceptualization of Sutherland's thesis, asserting that "arguments that attribute the leniency accorded white-collar offenders to class bias misunderstand the structural sources of leniency." [10]

Similar arguments have been offered by Chicago school economists, notably Richard Posner. Drawing on the work of Gary Becker, Posner points out that efficient legal institutions will seek to minimize costs and maximize gains by penalizing white-collar offenders with monetary sanctions obtained through less costly civil or administrative procedures rather than seeking imprisonment through the cumbersome criminal justice system.[11] (It should be noted that these arguments do not refute the notion of de facto favoritism toward white-collar offenders. Instead they merely shift the cause of that favoritism from deliberate class bias of individual prosecutors to systemic, structural factors. Nonetheless, since its proponents intend this as a refutation of Sutherland's theory, we will take it here at face value.)

Similarly, the "system capacity" argument discussed in the last chapter directs attention away from Sutherland's focus on class advantage to address the inherent limitations of the criminal justice system in dealing with these complex crimes. This perspective focuses on the practical difficulties that white-collar offenses pose to investigators and prosecutors as a limiting factor on the use of criminal sanctions. As we have seen, white-collar crimes are often very complex, require special expertise on the part of investigators, and can be very difficult to explain to juries. For these reasons, investigators and prosecutors may be reluctant to initiate criminal cases against suspected white-collar offenders unless the chances of conviction are high.[12] While the result may be leniency toward white-collar offenders, the reason has less to do with direct class influence than with more "neutral" systemic features of the crimes themselves and the criminal justice process.

Others who work in the white-collar crime area have modified Sutherland's basic "class advantage" theory, using it to explain differential treatment *within* white-collar populations. They suggest, for example, that powerful white-collar offenders are protected from criminal sanctions less by virtue of their social class or status and more by their position within, or in relation to, the organization in which the crimes are committed (admittedly, social class and organizational position are likely to be related).[13] White-collar individuals in high organizational positions, such as CEOs of large corporations, may be able to evade prosecution because of their ability to distance themselves from the crimes, leaving lower-level white-collar employees—those organizationally closer to the crimes—to "hold the bag." Organizational structure can thus serve as a buffer between the higher-level white-collar offender and social control mechanisms, at the expense of lower-level employees.

Indictment Rates   We can now examine the data more closely to determine if any of the above explanations help to account for the decision of prosecutors not to proceed with indictments, or to file charges against some suspected savings and loan offenders but not others. Table 7 shows the proportion of individuals with various characteristics who had been indicted by March 1993 (in Texas) or December 1993 (in California). There is no support in these data for the alternative sanctions theory. From that perspective, the relatively low rates of criminal prosecution of savings and loan offenders might be explained by the availability of civil remedies. Civil actions might be preferable to criminal actions because of the generally lower standard of evidence required. As public pressure mounted to recoup losses from the S&L debacle, federal authorities might have seen civil measures as more effective mechanisms for producing cash settlements.

This pressure to pursue civil rather than criminal sanctions may have been increased further by the nature of the available civil remedies in these cases. The predominant form these took was professional liability claims filed by regulators against individuals holding professional liability insurance policies. These policies—the equivalent of malpractice insurance for physicians—indemnified thrift directors and officers as well as their accountants and attorneys against civil claims (see chapter 2). But the policies often contain clauses declaring them void if criminal wrongdoing is involved.

The RTC and the FDIC filed professional liability claims against more than eight hundred individuals in California and Texas in the period covered by our data. However, there is little support for

Table 7

Selected Characteristics of Suspects and Offenses
in Texas and California

Characteristic	Individuals Named in Texas Referrals		Individuals Named in California Referrals	
	N	Percentage Indicted	N	Percentage Indicted
Dollar Loss				
Less than 100,000	490	7.1	124	6.5
100,000–999,999	442	10.6	1,006	4.8
1,000,000–9,999,999	358	16.5	188	10.6
More than 10,000,000	225	23.6	21	28.6
Number of Referrals				
1	1,114	8.6	1,247	5.7
2–5	350	19.0	87	14.4
6–10	35	51.4	4	0
More than 11	16	43.8	1	0
Suspect's Position				
Director	146	13.0	35	22.9
Officer	393	16.8	67	14.9
Employee	60	18.3	75	26.7
Stockholder	19	21.1	6	50.0
Borrower	530	11.3	954	2.3
Agent	30	16.8	13	0
Appraiser	32	6.3	6	0
Account holder	12	0	31	3.2
Other	284	9.5	150	12.0
Unknown	9	0	2	0
Civil Suit Filed				
Yes	87	30.0	24	37.5
No	1,428	11.8	1,315	5.6

Source: Data from Office of Thrift Supervision, Dallas and San Francisco.

the claim that civil sanctions are used as substitutes for criminal prosecution. Certainly, the use of civil suits cannot explain the large gap between criminal referrals and indictments we note in our data, since the overwhelming number of those named in criminal referrals were never cited in civil claims. As we can see in table 7, of the 2,854 individuals cited as criminal suspects in either of the two states, only 111 (3.9%) were also the subject of professional liability claims.

Further, the data in table 7 reveal that civil suits were often used in conjunction with criminal prosecution against those suspected of defrauding thrift institutions. In Texas 30 percent of those who were named in civil suits were also criminally indicted (mostly, independent of a referral). Similarly, in California almost 38 percent of those subject to civil actions were also charged in criminal cases. This finding is consistent with the statements of prosecutors who told us that, particularly in egregious cases, they would pursue thrift fraud offenders from every possible angle, while it contradicts the notion of alternative sanctions proponents that civil remedies are a substitute for criminal sanctions.

There is only weak support in our data for recent modifications of Sutherland's class advantage thesis and its application to comparisons within groups of white-collar offenders. Remember, this argument would suggest that among institutional insiders, lower-level employees would more likely be the targets of prosecution than officers (presidents, vice presidents, CEOs, etc.), because they lack the "organizational shield" to insulate them from prosecution. By the same logic, members of boards of directors are in a better position than officers to disclaim direct knowledge of criminal events. Board directors are generally required to approve the transactions undertaken by an institution's officers, particularly large loans. However, in corrupt thrift institutions that were dominated by powerful and charismatic officers, the board of directors often simply rubber-stamped their decisions.[14]

In both states we find that employees were indeed more likely than officers to be indicted. In Texas 18.3 percent of the employees who had been cited were indicted, compared to only 16.8 percent of the officers. In California the differences were more substantial: 26.7 percent of the employees cited, versus 14.9 percent of the officers, were actually indicted for crimes. Comparing directors and officers in both states produced mixed results. While in Texas directors were less likely than officers to be criminally indicted, in California directors were more likely to face criminal charges.

Although there is thus some ambiguous support for this alteration of Sutherland's theory, the data on borrowers are inconsistent with this approach. The single largest group of thrift fraud suspects in both states was borrowers (often in collaboration with insiders), yet they were considerably less likely than either officers or employees to be indicted, particularly in California, where only 2.3 percent of suspected borrowers were ever charged. Despite the presumed greater ability of highly placed insiders to shield themselves behind the organization, it was borrowers—who enjoyed no such organizational shield—who were more likely to avoid indictment.

Neither are our data entirely consistent with a system capacity model. According to this approach, the reason white-collar crimes are less rigorously prosecuted than street crimes is that their complexity and the limited resources of the criminal justice system discourage aggressive prosecution. The important variables are caseload pressures and resources and the general capacity of the criminal justice system to process these cases. At first glance, our data seem to confirm the validity of this perspective. Faced with a deluge of complex, time-consuming thrift fraud cases, federal prosecutors were forced to set priorities. More specifically, this meant setting a threshold of dollar losses below which prosecution would not be pursued.[15]

From a system capacity perspective, then, we would expect to see some triage effect, with a higher rate of indictment for those whose crimes resulted in larger dollar losses, a finding that would also be consistent with our more general "damage control" thesis discussed in the last chapter. Table 7 confirms this expectation, particularly for Texas. As we can see, as the total losses from an individual's suspected criminal activity increase, so does the likelihood that he or she will eventually be indicted. For the 490 individuals in Texas whose suspected crimes produced losses of less than $100,000, only 7.1 percent had been indicted by March 1993. In contrast, where total losses topped $10 million, the chances of indictment in Texas were more than three times greater (23.6%). In California the pattern is slightly less clear. Even there, however, individuals associated with crimes involving higher losses were generally more likely to be criminally indicted.

It also seems clear that, in Texas anyway, a triage mentality operated to target those who were named in multiple referrals. Table 7 shows that for the nearly three-fourths of the sample who were cited in only one referral, the chances of being indicted were slim—fewer than one out of ten (8.6%) had been indicted by March 1993. The chances of indictment increased dramatically for those named in six to ten referrals; over half (51.4%) of these had been charged with crimes by the end of the period. (From a more pessimistic view, this also means that nearly half of those individuals named in numerous Category I referrals had not been indicted.) It appears, then, that Texas prosecutors focused their attention and limited resources on individuals responsible for multiple and costly thrift crimes and gave less consideration to onetime offenders whose suspected crimes had less monetary impact. Because relatively few (7%) of the California suspects were named in more than one referral, the data reveal little about the relationship between number of referrals and indictments there.

Logistic regression results, shown in table A in the appendix, tend to confirm these findings from our bivariate analysis.[16] The best predictors of indictment were the dollar losses from the individual's suspected crimes and the number of times he or she was cited as a suspect in criminal referrals (REFERNO); a subject's position in the institution and the existence of civil remedies had no effect on the likelihood of indictment.[17]

Before jumping to conclusions about the centrality of dollar losses in explaining the likelihood of indictment (and thereby lending support to the system capacity perspective), it will be useful to examine the data on sentencing patterns.

Sentencing   What happened to the relatively few individuals who were brought up on criminal charges in thrift-related crimes? How many were convicted, sentenced to prison, and fined? Stephen Pizzo and Paul Muolo stated their view with characteristic drama in a *New York Times Magazine* article: "Does crime pay? For the white-collar criminals who played leading roles in the savings and loan debacle, the answer appears to be a resounding yes. . . . Many have gone unpunished, and most of those who have faced prosecution were handed short sentences or probation. Even their court-imposed criminal fines and financial restitution remain largely uncol-lected."[18] Pizzo and Muolo cite the outcomes of cases involving a number of well-known S&L crooks to support their contention. But more precise, statistically sound data must be examined before such conclusions can be reached with confidence.

Since October 1988, the EOUSA has been collecting data on "major S&L prosecutions" from U.S. Attorneys Offices and the Dallas Bank Fraud Task Force. The data we analyze here include major S&L prosecutions charged via indictment or "information" (essentially a plea bargain) from October 1, 1988, through March 18, 1992.

Table 8 shows that as of March 18, 1992, more than 1,000 defendants had been charged by U.S. Attorneys in major S&L cases. Of those, 580 had been sentenced, 451 (78%) to prison. Of those sentenced to prison, the median prison term was less than two years (22 months). Despite several highly publicized cases in which long

Table 8
Major S&L Cases (October 1, 1988, to March 18, 1992)

Cases	646
Defendants charged	1,098
Defendants convicted and sentenced	580
Defendants sentenced to prison	451
Median prison term (mos.)	22
Median loss per case (indictment/information)	$500,000
Total losses	$8,222,398,550
Total restitutions	$335,620,349
Total fines	$11,917,061

Source: Data from Executive Office of the U.S. Attorneys.

prison terms were imposed, for example, the thirty-year sentence imposed on Woody Lemons (the former chairman of the board at the notorious Vernon S&L in Texas), few convicted offenders received lengthy prison terms. The more detailed breakdown in table 9 shows that only 26 defendants, representing 4 percent of all those sentenced, received prison sentences of ten years or more, and just 78 (13%) received sentences of five years or more.

Most of these convicted offenders will be eligible for parole after serving as little as one-third of their full sentences. In some cases sentences have simply been reduced. For example, Don Dixon and Fast Eddie McBirney—two of the most notorious of the Texas high-fliers—won early release from prison after serving a small fraction of their terms. Dixon, who had been sentenced to two consecutive five-year terms, was allowed by U.S. District judge Joe Fish to serve only one of those sentences, which was then reduced from five to four years.[19] McBirney, sentenced to fifteen years in 1993, was released on parole after serving less than two years in prison. U.S.

Table 9
Prison Sentences in Major S&L Cases
(October 1, 1988, to March 18, 1992)

	N	Percentage of Sentenced Defendants
Total sentenced defendants	580	100
Defendants sentenced to prison	451	78
Length of prison term		
0–4.9 years	357	65
5+ years[a]	78	13
10+ years	26	4

Source: Data from Executive Office of the U.S. Attorneys.
[a] Some of these defendants also appear in the 10+ category.

District judge Robert Maloney, who reduced McBirney's sentence by two-thirds, cited his "extraordinary cooperation."[20]

While these EOUSA cases represent losses of over $8 billion, only $335 million in restitutions and only $11.9 million in fines had been ordered. This represents the amount of restitution that had been ordered in these cases, not the amount actually collected. In 1990 at a conference in Indianapolis, the OTS, RTC, and FDIC identified one hundred thrift referrals that they felt should receive top priority in investigations, given their particularly egregious nature and the estimated losses involved. A GAO report to Congress analyzing the indictment record for these "Top 100" referrals revealed that while a total of $83.6 million had been ordered in fines and restitutions in those cases, only $365,000, or less than one-half of one percent, was actually collected.[21] An investigation by the Associated Press (AP) on the collection of fines and restitutions imposed on S&L offenders produced similar results. The AP analysis focused on 109

S&L defendants who, as part of plea agreements, had agreed to pay a total of $133.8 million in fines and restitutions. A review of court records revealed that by the time the results were published in February 1993, only $577,540—again less than one-half of one percent—had been collected.[22] A recent GAO report reveals that a total of $26 million has been collected in restitutions in all savings and loan cases.[23]

Table 10 takes a closer look at the status of the 1,098 individuals charged since October 1988. The data reveal that of defendants whose cases had been adjudicated, the great majority were convicted: 761 (91%) were convicted, and only 74 (9%) were acquitted or had their cases dismissed. These high rates of conviction are typical for white-collar cases prosecuted at the federal level. In contrast to cases of street crime, where prosecutors are often forced to file charges first and then rely on evidence hastily assembled by the police, in white-collar cases prosecutors often take considerable time to assemble airtight evidence and screen out weaker cases

Table 10
Status of Defendants in Major S&L Cases (March 18, 1992)

	N	Percentage
Total defendants	1,098	
Awaiting trial	260	
Charged (not awaiting trial)	838	100
Convicted	761	91
Convicted and sentenced	580	
Convicted, awaiting sentencing	181	
Acquitted	53	6
Dismissed	21	2
Other	3	

Source: Data from Executive Office of the U.S. Attorneys.

before deciding to seek an indictment. In other words, these conviction rates probably result from the highly selective screening of cases prior to the indictment stage.

When we look at the individual characteristics of those who have been sentenced, we find a pattern similar to that discussed with regard to indictments. First, there is no evidence for the notion that institutional position shields one from a prison sentence, nor does it have any effect on the length of prison terms. Table 11 shows that the proportion of convicted defendants receiving prison sentences varied little across position categories. If we exclude the "unknown" category and appraisers (there was only one), the percentage of those convicted who received a prison sentence ranged only from 71 to 88 percent. More variance was observed in the length of prison sentences: the median was 48 months for thrift stockholders, 36 months for directors, and only 12 months for employees. Contrary to the notion that highly placed individuals can shield themselves, those higher up in the institution received the severest punishments.

Neither does the alternative sanctions perspective receive any support from these sentencing data. We might anticipate, according to this approach, that when individuals are subject to both civil and criminal sanctions, prosecutors and judges might temper the severity of the criminal sanctions. The data presented in table 11 report exactly the opposite results. Convicted defendants subject to civil suits were more likely to be sentenced to prison (91% vs. 77%) and on average received longer prison terms (48 months vs. 21 months).

The system capacity argument again appears to receive some tentative support. Although dollar losses do not influence the likelihood of a prison sentence for convicted offenders (remember, the variance here is minimal), as dollar losses increase, so does the length of the prison sentence. Similarly, many of these offenders victimized more than one institution, and the greater the number of institutional victims, the longer the prison term imposed.

Table 11

Sentences in Relation to Defendant's Position and Offense in Major S&L Cases (October 1, 1988, to March 18, 1992)

Characteristic	N	Percentage Sentenced to Prison	Median Prison Sentence (mos.)
Dollar Loss			
Less than 100,000	125	70	12
100,000–999,999	225	80	16
1,000,000–9,999,999	164	76	36
10,000,000–99,999,999	57	90	36
More than 100,000,000	9	89	30
Number of Victim Institutions			
1	466	79	18
2–5	98	72	36
6+	15	73	72
Unknown	1	100	10
Defendant's Position			
Officer	118	83	22.5
Director	25	88	36
Employee	61	80	12
Stockholder	9	78	48
Borrower	151	77	24
Agent	12	75	21
Appraiser	1	0	—
Account holder	38	79	18
Attorney for institution	22	82	18
Other	133	71	18
Unknown	10	100	24

Continued on next page

Table 11—Continued

Characteristic	N	Percentage Sentenced to Prison	Median Prison Sentence (mos.)
California	90	78	20
Texas	119	81	36
Civil case filed			
Yes	32	91	48
No	548	77	21

Source: Data from Executive Office of the U.S. Attorneys.

Focusing on our two target states, we see that median sentence length in Texas (36 months) was considerably longer than the national average (22 months), while California (20 months) was closer to the national median. We suspect that this may have to do with the higher losses involved in thrift fraud in Texas.

Here again, a more sophisticated multivariate analysis is helpful. In table B in the appendix, we present the results of a multivariate analysis of the influence of the variables presented in table 11 on severity of sentence, measured in terms of months sentenced to prison. For defendants who did not receive prison sentences, this variable was coded as 0. In the second column of table B we present the results of an ordinary least squares (OLS) analysis. However, it could be argued that since the dependent variables used here are limited, truncated at zero, the appropriate statistical technique would be a Tobit model. Using an OLS model in which the distribution of the observations in the dependent variable is non-normal, one runs the risk of producing biased and inconsistent parameter estimates.[24] For this reason we also estimated a Tobit model using the same independent and dependent variables. Tobit models calculate maximum-likelihood estimates of the model parameters. As can be seen, the results from the two models are not substantially different. We present both models here to satisfy the curiosity of the statistically minded.

The results of the multivariate analysis are consistent with the bivariate results presented in table 11. The two variables dollar loss (LOSS) and number of victimized institutions (VICNO) were statistically significant ($p < .01$ and $p < .001$, respectively), while none of the position variables were significant predictors of sentence length. As we suspected, the tendency of Texas judges to impose harsher sentences on S&L offenders observed in table 11 is related to the greater average cost of thrift crimes in that state. When other variables are held constant, sentences for Texas were not significantly longer than they were in other parts of the country. The coefficient for CIVIL was positive and significant ($p < .001$), indicating that individuals convicted of thrift fraud and subject to professional liability suits received *severer* sentences than those not subject to civil actions, once again putting to rest the notion that civil suits are used as an alternative sanction.

What this quantitative analysis of sentences indicates is that on the whole sentence lengths for these convicted savings and loan offenders varied with the estimated cost of their offenses, not their occupational position or their exposure to civil sanctions. It seems, then, that a triage mentality emerged in the context of this epidemic of white-collar crime and that within this group of white-collar offenders, the likelihood of indictment and the length of the prison term varied directly with the cost of the crime. But what does this say about the ability of the system capacity theory to explain the relative treatment of white-collar offenders and their street crime counterparts?

Strikingly, when this triage explanation is used to examine the

Table 12

Prison Sentences for S&L Offenders
and Selected Federal Offenders

	Mean Prison Sentence (mos.)
S&L offenders	36.4
All federal offenders, convicted of	
Burglary	55.6
Larceny	27.5
Motor vehicle theft	38.0
Counterfeiting	29.1
Federal offenders, with no prior convictions, convicted of	
Property offenses (nonfraudulent)	25.5
Public order offenses (regulatory)	32.3
Drug offenses	64.9

Sources: Data from *Federal Criminal Case Processing, 1980–90* (Washington, D.C.: U.S. Department of Justice, Bureau of Justice Statistics, 1992), 17; *Compendium of Federal Justice Statistics, 1988* (Washington, D.C.: U.S. Department of Justice, Bureau of Justice Statistics, 1991), 43.

differential treatment of white-collar and street criminals, it is stood on its head. As we see in table 12, when we compare our data on S&L sentences with data on sentences imposed on federal defendants convicted of burglary, larceny, car theft, and counterfeiting, we find that these latter offenders often received longer sentences—and in the case of burglars, far longer sentences—despite the fact that the cost of these crimes almost never approached $500,000, the average per S&L offense. Compared to the mean prison sentence of 36.4 months for S&L offenders, burglars were sentenced on average to 55.6 months and car thieves received a 38-month sentence.

In this case, then, there is a strong *inverse* relationship between the average cost of the crime and the severity of the sentence.[25] Tom Smith, director of Public Citizen in Texas, was probably right when he complained of Dixon and McBirney's early prison releases, "If someone had walked in and stuck a gun in front of a cashier in a 7-Eleven store and stolen money of this magnitude, they'd be in jail for a very long time." [26]

It might be argued that thrift offenders received relatively light sentences because they were first-time offenders with no prior record. While this assumption that S&L criminals had no prior record is generally valid (but not universally so), many thrift offenders were cited in multiple referrals over a period of several years. We can nonetheless compare our sample of S&L offenders to first-time federal offenders. The bottom half of table 12 shows the mean prison sentence for federal defendants convicted of two broad categories of offenses, who had no prior criminal convictions. We see here that average prison sentences imposed on first-time property offenders was only somewhat shorter than sentences imposed on these highfliers whose crimes cost on average $500,000. And the average sentence imposed on first-time drug offenders was almost double that of these highfliers.[27]

What this analysis suggests is that while a system capacity model might help explain the prioritizing of cases *within* the savings and loan context, it cannot account for the differential treatment of white-collar offenders and street criminals of which Sutherland spoke more than forty years ago. Granted, white-collar cases *are* complex and do require substantial resources to prosecute, but given the high price tag attached to these crimes, no system capacity model can make sense of less than rigorous prosecution efforts. It certainly cannot make sense of the lenient sentencing of these offenders *after* they have been successfully prosecuted.

Given these findings—that neither organizational position nor exposure to civil penalties differentiates among offenders within this white-collar population and that prioritizing cases according to crime seriousness can only explain differences within this group but not between this group and other federal offenders—it would seem important to return to Sutherland's original formulation. That is, what is the nature of the differential treatment of white-collar offenders and ordinary street criminals, and how can we explain these differences? Our analysis has highlighted the relative leniency accorded these offenders. Future research needs to tease out the exact nature of this class advantage and its sources.

SUMMING IT UP

We have examined quantitative data from a variety of sources to address fundamental questions about the government response to fraud in the savings and loan industry. Our most important findings can be summarized as follows:

· In Texas only one out of every seven individuals suspected of committing major crimes at thrift institutions will be prosecuted for those crimes. In California roughly one out of four suspected thrift offenders will ever be indicted.

· Of those charged in major S&L cases, a relatively high proportion (91%) were convicted and of those, most (78%) were sentenced to prison.

· The likelihood of indictment for suspected offenders in Texas and California was influenced by the dollar losses associated with those crimes and, in Texas, with the number of crimes the individual was suspected of committing. Similarly, the length of prison sentences for those convicted varied directly with dollar losses and the number of institutions victimized.

· Little support was found for the organizational position modification of Sutherland's class advantage theory. Indeed, insiders' positions in the thrift had only a slight influence on the likelihood that they would be indicted, while borrowers (who did not enjoy an inside position and the shield it might accord) were less likely than insiders to be indicted. The length of prison sentence imposed was unrelated to the organizational position of thrift offenders.

· Similarly, no evidence was found to support an alternative sanctions model. In fact, being the subject of a civil action increased both the likelihood of indictment for these thrift fraud suspects and the length of their prison sentences.

· Compared with the sentences imposed on other federal offenders and considering the high financial costs resulting from their crimes, S&L offenders received relatively short prison sentences. The median length of prison sentences for these offenders nationally was less than two years (22 months), with a mean of just over three years (36.4 months).

These findings are generally consistent with the qualitative data generated from our interviews. They suggest once again that losses due to thrift fraud are much higher than the 3 to 5 percent of bailout costs that some experts have estimated (see chapter 1). According to data from the Executive Office of the U.S. Attorneys, losses in the relatively small proportion of cases that led to indictments and convictions totaled more than $8 billion by 1992. Given the large amount of reported fraud that did not result in indictments (six out of seven in Texas), total losses due to fraud must be several times higher.

Like the interview data presented in the last chapter, these data also reveal a criminal justice system that is swamped by the largest set of white-collar crimes in American history, involving vast networks of sophisticated offenders. Efforts to establish priorities to deal with the overload have been only partially successful, as large numbers of individuals suspected of committing serious financial crimes will go unpunished.

The data also confirm the differential treatment accorded white-collar offenders, even when their crimes bring the financial system to the brink of disaster. While two generations of white-collar criminologists since Sutherland have pointed to this differential treatment, recent work has attempted to refute the notion of class (and, more to the point, corporate) advantage in the criminal justice system. The relative leniency these white-collar offenders enjoyed despite the seriousness of their crimes suggests the continued relevance of Sutherland's groundbreaking work and the importance of continuing to explore the bases for that leniency.

Finally, the findings reported here regarding indictment and sentencing patterns are consistent with our proposition that the S&L cleanup was driven primarily by damage control concerns rather than criminal justice or crime control concerns. While it was imperative to close down these fraud-ridden and insolvent institutions and contain the financial losses, it was apparently less urgent to punish the white-collar perpetrators of these financial frauds as if they were common criminals.

CONCLUSION

As we write this, in mid-1996, the Whitewater hearings in Congress drag on. The Republican leadership has, at least thus far, not produced a smoking gun to implicate the Clintons in criminal wrongdoing related to the real estate venture they invested in or their associations with Madison Guaranty Savings and Loan. As with many cases in the S&L imbroglio, there will probably never be definitive answers to all the questions concerning the potentially fraudulent transactions at Madison or the specific role played by various actors.[1] Whatever the outcome of these hearings, it is indicative of the powerful mix of economics and politics in the S&L fiasco that the families of both President Clinton and former President Bush (see chapter 3) have been implicated.

In tracing the course of the S&L industry in the 1980s, we have shown how these previously conservative, small-town institutions came to occupy such a central place in the high-finance world of economic intrigue and political influence peddling. Deregulation, combined with generous deposit insurance, set the stage for the explosive growth of these institutions as well as the epidemic of financial fraud that accompanied that growth.[2] Refuting economists and industry consultants who contend that impersonal economic forces and bad business judgment brought down the industry, we have pointed to crime and fraud as central ingredients in the collapse. Drawing from primary data as well as extensive published reports, we have documented the role of thrift insiders and the vast networks of outside participants that made these crimes possible, delayed their prosecution, and multiplied their costs.

A number of important implications for the study of white-collar crime follow from this analysis. The first has to do with the practical issue of how we locate and measure white-collar crime when it is so frequently disguised behind ordinary business transactions. As we discussed in chapter 1, the definition of crime has been a long-standing problem for white-collar criminologists, and one that is not easily resolved. Since Paul Tappan opened fire half a century ago with the argument that only those activities that have been successfully prosecuted are the proper realm of criminologists, those who study white-collar crime have addressed the scientific and practical limitations of such a narrow approach.[3] Not only does the official definition of crime dramatically limit the population of legitimate study, but more important, it directly contradicts a guiding principle of the white-collar crime tradition—that a large amount of such crime goes undetected and/or unprosecuted precisely because it is "white-collar." And as Gilbert Geis has so aptly noted, what is important in distinguishing who is criminal is not how he or she has been treated by the criminal justice system but what he or she has actually done.[4]

Tappan's point, however, cannot be ignored. If so much white-collar crime remains hidden, how can we as scholars get our arms around it? We have presented one possibility here. Taking one industry as our case study, we used criminal referrals, official reports, case histories of specific institutions and actors, and deductive analysis to expose extensive insider fraud. The deductive analysis was critical to this effort. By laying out the logical components of alternative explanations for the thrift crisis (gambling for resurrection, incompetence, and fraud) and their respective predictions regarding how managers would behave and which institutions would fail, we were able to test these hypotheses against the empirical reality. Assuming rational (or at least not consistently irrational) behavior on the part of thrift managers, only the insider fraud explanation is consistent with that empirical reality. Perhaps most important, the costliest failures studied by the GAO included *all* of those characteristics that a fraud hypothesis would predict, such as massive growth, inadequate underwriting, and manipulation of books and records, and are inconsistent with alternative accounts.

A second, more theoretical contribution stems from our analysis of specific forms of thrift fraud. While the complex schemes at the heart of the thrift crisis were often intricately woven and involved multiple layers of deception, nonetheless three basic forms of fraud—hot deals, looting, and covering up—predominated. What is noteworthy about this insider abuse is that it is qualitatively different from the corporate crime studied first by Sutherland and subsequently by several generations of white-collar crime scholars. Most important, hot deals and looting comprise a kind of hybrid—crime by the corporation against the corporation, or collective embezzlement. Sharing qualities of both corporate crime and traditional embezzlement, but distinct from both, these crimes were collective endeavors in which top management ran their own institutions into the ground for personal gain. It would seem, then, that the old dichotomies of the white-collar crime literature—organization as "weapon" or organization as "victim"; "organizational crime" or "occupational crime"—need to be amended to account for what may be an increasingly common form of fraud.

Third, we have argued that the new financial era—what has been called the casino economy—may be particularly vulnerable to such collective embezzlement. Much as violations of worker safety standards or environmental protection laws are to the industrial production process, collective embezzlement may be the signature crime of finance capitalism. Institutions such as thrifts, investment firms, banks, insurance companies, and pension funds, whose primary function is to manage other people's money, may be especially susceptible. As a congressional subcommittee investigating insurance company fraud put it, "Pirates and dolts . . . will plague an attractive industry such as insurance, where customers hand over large sums of cash in return for the promise of future benefits." [5] Unrestrained by investments in infrastructure and with little of their own capital at stake, those who handle other people's money in the casino society truly operate in a "criminogenic environment." [6] Add to this the steady stream of cash that federal deposit insurance assured, and the thrift industry was ripe for a "bust-out."

We do not want to oversimplify this distinction between industrial and finance capitalism, or to overdraw the correlation between the two contexts and the types of crime that can be predicted in those contexts. Clearly, the industrial and financial sectors are empirically interdependent, if analytically distinct. Furthermore, traditional corporate crime can be found in the financial sector (as, for example, when the primary goal of insider trading is to boost corporate profits), just as collective embezzlement might periodically victimize a manufacturing enterprise. Neither is this analysis meant to imply that collective embezzlement in the financial sector is somehow more destructive or morally repugnant than traditional corporate crime in the "good old days" of productive industrial capitalism. Workers who have lost life or limb in industrial accidents, or communities subjected to high levels of exposure to toxic industrial waste, would no doubt contest such a foolish notion. Instead, the point here is to highlight the different logics underlying the industrial and financial "production" processes and to link different types of crime to those processes so that we can understand and predict the patterns that emerge over time.

One final question arises about this pattern. If finance capitalism is so vulnerable to collective embezzlement, does this mean that massive fraud is chronic and inevitable? We address this issue in more detail in our discussion of policy recommendations. For now, it should be pointed out that the S&L industry was particularly susceptible to collective embezzlement due to federal deposit insurance and the continuous flow of cash that this government underwriting assured. In most other contexts, the ability to construct what are in effect Ponzi schemes is limited by the need to persuade potential "customers" of the legitimacy of the enterprise and the security of their investments. So while the casino economy may open up vast new opportunities for fraud, realizing those opportunities entails the not insignificant challenge of defrauding investors while continuing to attract their business.

A fourth theme that emerges from this study is the striking similarity between these networks of fraud and organized crime. As we have seen, in important ways these "corporate" crimes were different from the crimes by the corporation for the corporation on which so much of the literature has focused. But the more specific point here is that the ways in which they differ, and the direct connection between these financial frauds and the political fraud that facilitated them, suggest that these crimes more closely resemble organized crime than traditional corporate crime. While there have been a number of other attempts to rethink the boundaries between corporate and organized crime, some of these efforts continue to make ad hominem distinctions between the two while others neglect the important role of political participation that distinguishes organized crime.[7] If we take as our definition of organized crime that it is premeditated, motivated by personal gain, organized by networks, continuous, and facilitated by the participation of public officials, then the corporate actors we have focused on here did engage in organized crime.

The classification of thrift fraud as organized crime challenges the prevalent view of crime by corporate offenders as by definition distinct from other types of crime. White-collar criminologists have spent much of the last twenty-five years attempting to debunk myths about what the "real" criminal looks like. But we have not been very successful. As Michael Levi puts it, white-collar offenders are still perceived as "essentially decent people" while organized criminals are "essentially nasty people."[8] These stereotypes no doubt help to explain the relatively lenient sentencing of thrift offenders that we found here. Recognizing certain types of fraud by corporate executives as organized crime allows us to advance beyond the ad hominem definitions that have constrained our theoretical vision, have contributed to the very stereotypes that white-collar criminologists intended to debunk, and have resulted in differential—some would say irrational—sentencing patterns.

Last but not least, in terms of the importance of its theoretical implications, is the role of government complicity in the S&L crisis. As we have seen, political fraud accompanied and made possible the financial fraud that is the more obvious protagonist in this story. While it is impossible to document intent in every case discussed here, nonetheless the role of implicit bribery, or folded lies, was critical not only in the deregulation that set the stage for this disaster but also in shielding thrift offenders from regulatory scrutiny and in constructing the ill-fated Southwest Plan through which generous benefactors could further benefit.[9]

There is an interesting parallel between the conceptual and methodological difficulties of identifying white-collar crime and the similar difficulties of determining the boundaries of political bribery. In both cases the distinction between fraud and legitimate business and political practices is blurred and often depends on subjective issues such as intent. Just as in the case of white-collar crime, however, it would be naive and analytically shortsighted to confine our analysis of political corruption to those few cases that have been so egregious or incompetently managed to elicit an official reproach. Instead, we have pieced together from official records and government documents, as well as personal interviews and extensive secondary sources, as complete a picture of government collusion as possible. While this picture is no doubt incomplete, and there may be some cases in which we have implied fraudulent intent when in fact there was none, nonetheless the broad picture of political participation in the crisis is striking.

What are the theoretical implications of these findings of government collusion? Specifically, what does the pattern of that collusion reveal about the nature of the state and its relationship to various forms of white-collar crime, in particular collective embezzlement?

COLLECTIVE EMBEZZLEMENT AND THE STATE

One way to view the government role in the S&L crisis is as a massive regulatory failure. It might be useful, then, to consider more carefully what kind of regulations failed. Sociologists have long made a distinction between "social" regulations (such as occupational safety and health standards), which are aimed at controlling production processes, and "economic" regulations (such as insider trading restrictions), which regulate the market and stabilize the economy.[10] While the former protect workers and consumers against the excesses of capital—and tend to cut into profits—the latter regulate and stabilize the capital accumulation process, and historically have been supported by affected industries.

This distinction is consistent with a structural approach to the state, which emphasizes the "objective relation" between the state and capital.[11] This objective relation guarantees that the state will operate in the long-term interests of capitalists independent of their direct participation in the policy-making process or mobilization of resources. Central to this objective relation under capitalism, the state must promote capital accumulation since its own survival depends on tax revenues derived from successful profit-making activity, as well as the political stability that is contingent on economic growth. In this structuralist rendition, the state enjoys relative autonomy. In direct contrast to the instrumentalist model espoused by William Domhoff and others, structuralists argue that state managers are not captive to individual capitalist interests and indeed are capable of violating those interests to pursue the broader and more long-term interests of capital accumulation and political legitimacy.[12]

Regulation scholars who borrow from this perspective have generally focused on social—rather than economic—regulation. This literature addresses the lax enforcement of social regulations and ties that laxity to the capital accumulation function of the state and the perceived costs of interfering with profitable industry.[13] These scholars also note that the legitimation mandate of the state periodically requires that it respond to political demands to protect worker safety, reduce environmental hazards, or enforce labor standards. The point, however, is that active enforcement of social regulation occurs primarily in response to public pressure and legitimation concerns and recedes once political attention has shifted elsewhere and state legitimacy is no longer threatened.[14]

In contrast, when the goal is economic regulation, according to this structural model, the state tends to assume a more rigorous posture. Despite occasional protests from the individual capitalists at whom sanctions are directed, the state rather vigorously enforces regulations that stabilize the market and enhance economic viability. Unlike social regulations, which are implemented primarily in response to on-again/off-again legitimation needs, economic regulations are integral to the capital accumulation process and are thus more consistently and urgently pursued.[15] For example, research on the Securities and Exchange Commission, discussed in chapter 4, has shown that while the SEC is by no means omnipotent in the face of its powerful Wall Street charges, nonetheless it rather routinely seeks criminal sanctions and relatively stiff monetary fines for elite offenders.[16]

But what of collective embezzlement? If the structural logic is valid, then the state should have an altogether different relationship to collective embezzlement in the thrift industry than to traditional corporate crimes in the manufacturing sector. For one thing, the structural model would predict—and the empirical literature supports this prediction—that the state would take violations of economic regulations quite seriously. And we would expect that enforcing *banking* regulations, which lie at the very heart of the economic system, would be among the state's highest priorities and would thus be a showcase for enforcement.

In addition, remember that collective embezzlement is aimed not at enhancing corporate profits but at personal gain at the expense of the institution. In the S&L context, it not only decimated individual institutions but also threatened the demise of the whole industry, and with it the financial stability of the U.S. economy. As the senior staff member of the Senate Banking Committee put it, "All these financial industries could bring down the whole economy." [17] For the state, whose functions include capital accumulation and long-term economic stability, containing this collective embezzlement should have been a top priority.

Instead, the state not only failed to avert the crisis, it was complicitous in establishing the conditions in which it developed and in shielding thrift offenders from detection. This complicity of government officials sharply contradicts the structuralist notions of relative autonomy and the priority placed on economic regulation and long-term financial stability and seems to add substantial credibility to the instrumentalist model of the impact of raw economic power and influence peddling.

But there is more to it than this. While it is true that the U.S. League of Savings and Loans and its individual members exerted considerable influence in Congress, at the same time a vitriolic struggle between members of Congress and the FHLBB raged behind the scenes.[18] By all accounts, Edwin Gray and his staff at the FHLBB were stunned by the escalating thrift crisis in Texas and elsewhere and approached their assignment with urgency. After watching a homemade videotape of miles of abandoned condominiums east of Dallas financed by the insured deposits of Empire Savings and Loan, Gray spent the rest of his tenure at FHLBB attempting to reregulate thrifts and encountering resistance from the industry, the White House, and Congress.

This clash between regulators who were alarmed at the pending disaster and key members of Congress who protected their thrift benefactors refutes not only the structural notions of uniform state purpose and relative autonomy but also instrumentalists' depiction of state actors as simply lackeys of monied interests. It suggests instead that relative autonomy may vary across the institutions that together comprise the state. Members of Congress, whose political careers depend on a steady influx of campaign funds, may be particularly susceptible to the demands of those with the resources to make large campaign contributions. Civil servants in regulatory agencies, while certainly not immune to political pressures and financial temptation, may for structural reasons be less susceptible to such pressures and periodically may take a more rigorous enforcement approach in the interests of economic stability.

This account of the evolution of the thrift crisis suggests the need for a synthetic model of state action. As we have seen from the literature, the state is capable of concerted action and rigorous regulation in the interest of financial stability, consistent with structural theory. But the real-life political actors who make up the state have their own political and career interests and are susceptible to a variety of external influences. Thus while the state has a structural interest in economic stability and, therefore, in containing collective embezzlement, instrumental influences on state actors can—and periodically do—derail that agenda.

This revisiting of state theory within the S&L context is of more than theoretical interest, for it has a number of important policy implications.

POLICY RECOMMENDATIONS

On July 27, 1995, Texas Republican Jack Fields, chair of the House Subcommittee on Telecommunications and Finance, introduced legislation to dilute the powers of the SEC and loosen restrictions on securities brokers. Among other things, the law would have cut the number of commissioners on the SEC from five to three; require the agency to weigh the benefits of each securities regulation against the cost it exacts on business; limit brokers' liability to investors; relax requirements about the amount of information investors must be provided about the securities they purchase; and do away with disclosure rules for firms contemplating a corporate takeover. Congressman Fields said of his proposed legislation, "This initiative represents the most significant revision of federal regulation of financial markets since the Great Depression." [19] *Business Week* questioned the move, citing the role of the SEC in "keep[ing] U.S. markets the safest in the world" and reasoning, "You would think the SEC would be the last place targeted by reg-slashers on Capitol Hill." [20]

According to the finance counsel to the House subcommittee that drafted this bill, the reform was a way for congressional Republicans to say, "Here, Wall Street, look what we want to do for you." [21] In their zeal to court heavy campaign contributors on Wall Street, however, the bill's sponsors apparently went too far. Wall Street executives quickly protested that the SEC is critical to shoring up investor confidence and stabilizing the financial system. The general counsel for PaineWebber said of the bill, "[It] is really fixing something that isn't broken." [22] As of this writing, Fields was apparently reconsidering some of the bill's more radical provisions.

The attack on the SEC may be a vendetta against its chairman, as *Business Week* believes, or a botched effort to woo Wall Street investment firms, but it is by no means an isolated instance of efforts at financial deregulation in recent years. [23] Nor are Republicans the only ones on board. In 1994 Congress approved and President Clinton enthusiastically endorsed the lifting of barriers prohibiting banks from operating branches across state lines beginning in 1997 (formerly, banks were required to establish independent subsidiaries for their regional operations). While the measure will save banks operating costs, critics point out that it will also increase the rate of acquisitions and mergers already under way, leaving the banking industry in the hands of a few financial giants.[24]

As a result, small-town institutions and their deposits, some of which are funneled back into their local communities, are at risk of being taken over by national conglomerates. More important here, the flip side of the economy of scale achieved by the industry's consolidation may be an "economy of fraud": Not only do incentives and opportunities increase with the cash flow, but the repercussions of fraud rise geometrically as a handful of banking giants controls the nation's insured deposits. As one *New York Times* financial writer put it, referring to the increase in interbank transactions but equally relevant to the repercussions of bank mergers, "If the interbank market can swiftly transmit funds from one part of the system to the other, it can just as rapidly transmit—and spread through the system—the problems of any one bank."[25] Just as ominous as the potential for fraud and its ripple effects, this potential was all but ignored in congressional debate on the legislation, which passed the Senate by an overwhelming 94 to 4. Less than a decade after the height of the worst epidemic of financial crime in American history, the financial services industry is being revamped with no concern for the issue of fraud. The point here is not to argue that fraud is inevitable in such an environment, although there are good reasons to predict that the opportunities for fraud will increase. The more fundamental point is that these reforms are under way *without regard* for that possibility.

In the mid-1980s a *Business Week* cover story sounded a note of caution against what it saw then as "a political environment generally favoring deregulation."[26] Despite their stunning miscalculation that the thrift industry would survive without a bailout, *Business Week* commentators accurately foresaw the continued dangers of deregulating the casino economy. "Only when fear overcomes greed," they said, "will the casino society rein itself in."[27] As it turned out, they were overly optimistic on two counts. Not only did the S&L industry require a massive bailout, but that crisis and the fear it temporarily instilled have been quickly forgotten if the recent round of deregulation and the cavalier attitude with which it is undertaken are any indication. "Greed" apparently trumps "fear."

Future research might be directed at this paradox of increasing financial deregulation coming on the heels of the most catastrophic experiment with deregulation in history. This conspicuous neglect of recent history confirms the limitations of a pure structuralist model of the state and highlights the need for a more nuanced and empirically grounded understanding of political action. This research might draw from our study to further integrate white-collar criminology and state theory, two traditions that have remained largely distinct despite their clear overlaps in subject matter and theoretical domains.

The recent spate of deregulatory action also suggests the urgency of delineating a minimum set of policy guidelines or lessons to be learned from the S&L debacle. We offer here recommendations at three levels. First, policy changes—whether in the form of statutes or administrative regulations—must be carefully scrutinized with an eye for their criminogenic features. In light of what we now know about the potential for financial fraud given the right conditions, it is irresponsible to launch reforms of the financial system without an extended discussion of how these changes will affect the possibility for fraud.

Among the most obvious red flags are policies that would limit disclosure requirements, reduce capital requirements for financial institutions, encourage accounting gimmicks, offer government insurance for risky speculation, facilitate juggling of insured and noninsured accounts, reduce or emasculate internal controls, or otherwise increase the opportunities or reduce the risks associated with insider fraud. As a way to at least focus attention on these issues, perhaps major revisions of economic or financial policy should be accompanied by a "fraud impact statement," to borrow the vernacular of environmental policy makers.

The second set of recommendations relates to the nature of regulatory oversight and examination. Foolhardy policies in the early 1980s set the stage for S&L fraud, but inadequate regulatory supervision allowed it to flourish. When confronted with his misdeeds, one of the most prolific of thrift embezzlers, Charles Bazarian, asked, "So where were the regulators?"[28] Of course it suited Bazarian to place the blame on regulators for not effectively controlling his fraudulent impulses, but the broader point is still valid. If an industry is structured so as to offer ample opportunities for fraud—and the financial services industry may be prototypical—it is critical to set in place a rigorous system of oversight that stymies those who are tempted.

The question then is, What kind of regulatory control is most likely to be effective in this context? Some regulation scholars now argue that under certain circumstances cooperative approaches focusing on persuasion might work better in eliciting compliance than confrontational approaches.[29] Given the central role of deliberate insider abuse in the S&L scandal, however, the cooperative approach would probably have been ineffective in this environment.[30] Indeed, it seems unlikely that collective embezzlement will be discouraged by any but the most vigorous law enforcement approach. As a start, serious public debate of these issues is critical. The alternative is to court disaster in a casino society that refuses to rein itself in.

In this regard, it should be noted that in contrast to the regulatory catch-22 surrounding the enforcement of social regulations or the imposition of sanctions for crimes that advance corporate profits, the state has an unequivocal interest (both long-term and short-term) in containing collective embezzlement. The recognition of this new form of fraud for what it is, and the understanding of its objective relationship to the state and economic stability, might open up new regulatory space for deterrence and rigorous sanctions. After all, the looting described here—and its relationship to the state—is different in effect from traditional bank robbery only in its magnitude and destabilizing effect on the rest of the economy.

More broadly, our analysis suggests the need to revisit the role of monied interests in the political process. William Greider speaks of "the slow death of constitutional democracy in our time," as organized money dominates not just the electoral process but the governing process as well. Greider argues that ordinary people have effectively been cut out of the democratic dialogue, as "democratic expression" has become "too expensive for most Americans to afford."[31] As "mock democracy" replaces the genuine article, more and more Americans are alienated from politics, disdainful of politicians, and cynical about the process through which they are chosen. One symptom of this collapse of democracy, and the correlative distrust of government, is the meager rate at which Americans vote—between one-third and one-half of eligible voters, depending on whether it is a presidential election. Minimizing the role that organized money plays in that process, through whatever measures can pass constitutional muster, would be a critical first step toward restoring the democratic process.

Profound political reform is thus urgent if we are to preserve more than the pretense of democracy. Beyond that, and more relevant to this study, it is critical to shoring up financial stability in this age of global economic transformation. While structural relations between the state and capital may allow—even dictate—a strict response to collective embezzlement, we have seen that this response is subject to sabotage by those with the resources and motive to woo policy makers. And as one S&L regulator told us, "It was always the worst S&Ls in America that were able to get dramatically more political intervention."[32] Unless the ability to acquire such intervention is limited—for example, through strict campaign finance

reform—our capacity to check lucrative financial fraud will continue to be compromised.

Financial fraud of the sort described here is of course not new. In
the early twentieth century, congressional hearings revealed that the
officers of National City Bank made interest-free loans to themselves
for $2.4 million just days before the bank was declared insolvent.[33]
In 1905 the New York State legislature learned that insurance executives were spending policy makers' money on extravagant parties
and prostitutes.[34] The more recent case of Equity Funding Life
Insurance Company strikes even closer to home. The president and
chairman of Equity led a far-ranging conspiracy of twenty-two men
to bilk the insurance company and its customers out of hundreds of
millions of dollars between 1970 and 1974 through fabricating
transactions and siphoning off funds. So neither the collective embezzlement described in this book nor regulatory negligence is
unprecedented. What is new is the epic proportions of these financial crimes and the increasing dominance of the finance capitalism
on which they are based. Add to this the latest deregulatory zeal,
and the casino society seems destined to unleash ever greater opportunities for fraud with ever higher price tags.

The culmination of industrial capitalism in the United States by
the mid-twentieth century brought a proliferation of studies on
white-collar crime and the role of prevailing economic and market
structures in fueling it. Future research must build on this rich
tradition to explore the implications of the shift away from an
economy centered on manufacturing to one increasingly dominated by financial transactions and speculation. If, as previous research has shown, the structure of the economy influences the
nature of corporate crime and the government response to it, then
criminologists and state theorists face new challenges as the casino
economy evolves. It is urgent that we take up that challenge, not
only because it is worthwhile theoretically to understand, for example, the S&L crisis but also because only in this way can we build the
groundwork for averting such crises in the future.

APPENDIX

Table A
Results of Logistic Regression of Indictment/No Indictment
on Selected Independent Variables, Texas and California

Variable	Texas (N = 1,489)		California (N = 1,318)	
	Coefficient	Odds Ratio	Coefficient	Odds Ratio
LOSS	.0612***	1.0631	.1154*	1.1330
	(.0176)		(.0445)	
REFERNO (number	.1600***	1.1735	−.1443	.8824
of referrals)	(.0380)		(.2233)	
POSITION				
DIRECTOR	−.2907	.7478	−.3449	.7083
	(.3039)		(.6079)	
EMPLOYEE	.7202	2.0549	.7548	2.1272
	(.3860)		(.4946)	
STOCKHOLDER	.6047	1.8307	1.6614	5.2666
	(.6670)		(1.0459)	
BORROWER	−.2792	.7564	−1.1130*	.3286
	(.2158)		(.4628)	
AGENT	.3115	1.3654	—	—
	(.5397)			
APPRAISER	−1.2015	.3007	—	—
	(.7667)			
ACCOUNT HOLDER	—	—	−.5747	.5629
	(1.1200)			
OTHER	−.3947	.6739	−.5277	.5900
	(.2657)	(.4721)		

Continued on next page

Table A—Continued

Variable	Texas (N = 1,489)		California (N = 1,318)	
	Coefficient	Odds Ratio	Coefficient	Odds Ratio
TEXAS DISTRICTS				
B	−.7840***	.4570	—	—
	(.2103)			
C	−.5205	.5942	—	—
	(.4941)			
D	.0759	1.0738	—	—
	(.2179)			
CALIFORNIA DISTRICTS				
A	—	—	−.3761	.6865
			(.3721)	
B	—	—	−.6357	.5295
			(.7730)	
C	—	—	.2367	1.2671
			(.4334)	
CIVIL	.4383	1.5500	.7732	2.1667
	(.3005)		(.5512)	
CONSTANT	−2.4296***		−2.0197**	—
	(.3051)		(.7738)	
Log likelihood	−503.561		−220.4304	
Model chi-square	−145.17***		173.38	

Source: Data from Office of Thrift Supervision.
Notes: Standard errors are in parentheses. In the Texas model 16 observations were dropped because of a lack of variance in the response variable for ACCOUNT HOLDER and 1993. In the California model 19 cases were dropped because of a lack of variance in the response variable for AGENT and APPRAISER. Omitted categories for indicator variables are for Position, OFFICER; for Districts, District A in Texas and for District D in California. To save space, coefficients and odds ratios are not reported for year variables.
*p < .05   **p < .01   ***p < .001

DISCUSSION OF TABLE A

When researchers are forced to rely on data assembled by government agencies for administrative purposes, a certain amount of control over the quality of those data is lost. In the data used above one has to be concerned about the possibility of sampling bias. In both states many more individuals were cited as suspects in referrals than were indicted. But, of those indicted, a substantial proportion had not been cited in referrals. This means that criminal referrals do not represent the population of all suspected S&L crimes. Rather, both the incidents described in the referrals and the events that form the basis for the indictments can be assumed to be overlapping subsets of the population of all alleged incidents of thrift-related fraud. We have no a priori reason to believe that the two subsets of suspected crimes differ in any substantive ways, that the suspected crimes that form the basis for indictments against individuals not cited in referrals differ significantly from the crimes described in the referrals. Yet the nature of the data pointed to a potential problem of sample selection bias.

To test for the influence of sample selection bias on our analysis we followed the procedures outlined by Richard Berk.[1] First, a subset of indicted individuals from the indictment files for whom complete information was available ($N = 370$) was selected. A dichotomous variable was created in each file indicating whether the individual had been cited in a criminal referral. This variable was then regressed on the major independent variables used in the main analysis producing a correction, or "hazard," term, a quantity indicating the likelihood that the individual would have been cited in a referral and thus the likelihood that he or she would have appeared in the sample. The hazard term was created by first using an equation that took the form:

$$Z = \beta_o + \beta_i Z_i$$

Where β_o is a constant, β_i is a vector of logistic regression coefficients, and X_i is a vector of variable levels. Next, Z was entered into the equation:

$$\text{Prob(referral/no referral)} = \frac{1}{1+e^{-z}}$$

The result was a hazard term indicating the likelihood of inclusion in the sample. This variable was then entered as a regressor into the equations that formed the main analysis.

These "corrected" models revealed no substantive differences with the "uncorrected" models. With one exception, none of the coefficients gained or lost significance. In the California corrected model BORROWER became insignificant, the result of collinearity between that variable and the hazard term. The problem of multicollinearity is a common problem in these models.[2] Thus we decided that sample selection processes had not seriously biased our sample. For this reason in table A we report the results from the uncorrected models.

Table B
Results of Tobit and OLS Analyses of Influence of Selected Variables on Length of Prison Sentence for Defendants Sentenced in Major S&L Cases (October 1, 1988, to March 16, 1992)

Variable	Tobit Model Coefficients	OLS Model Coefficients
LOSS	.0002** (.00007)	.0002** (.00006)
VICNO (number of victimized institutions)	.4801*** (.1289)	.4655*** (.1044)
DEFNO (number of defendants in case)	−.0552 (.0444)	−.0393 (.0347)

Table B—Continued

Variable	Tobit Model Coefficients	OLS Model Coefficients
POSITION		
DIRECTOR	−.3446	−.2830
	(.9221)	(.7480)
EMPLOYEE	−.5288	−.4670
	(.6439)	(.5194)
AGENT	−1.6406	−1.3408
	(1.2487)	(.9908)
BORROWER	.2380	.2944
	(.5065)	(.4089)
STOCKHOLDER	1.5920	1.6078
	(1.3880)	(1.1233)
CUSTOMER	−.8240	−.4592
	(.5424)	(.6040)
ATTORNEY	1.4922	1.0947
(for S&L)	(1.5226)	(1.2530)
OTHER	−.8240	−.5129
	(.5426)	(.4352)
UNKNOWN	−.3691	−.1296
	(.8946)	(.7142)
CIVIL	3.3177***	3.1289***
	(.8030)	(.6554)
TEXAS	.7561	.7386
	(.4425)	(.3573)
CALIFORNIA	.4832	.3011
	(.4920)	(.3962)
CONSTANT	2.5021	2.9436
	(.4362)	(.3519)
Chi-square	75.52***	—
R^2	—	.1497

Source: Data from Executive Office of the U.S. Attorneys.
Notes: Position category APPRAISER dropped because of lack of variance in the response variable. Omitted position category is OFFICER. N = 580.
*$p<.05$ **$p<.01$ ***$p<.001$

DISCUSSION OF TABLE B

One approach to the quantitative analysis of sentencing severity breaks down the process into two stages: the decision to incarcerate (the so-called in/out decision) and, for those defendants sentenced to prison, decisions about the length of the term imposed. Statistical models are then estimated for each of these decisions. In some settings these models may accurately reflect the sentencing process, where, for example, plea negotiations focus first on the decision to incarcerate and later on sentence length. However, this approach may misrepresent the actual sentencing process and may provide faulty statistical models, particularly in the second model of sentence length where by definition the sample has been modified to exclude cases receiving nonincarcerative sentences. For this reason here we estimate models of the sentencing process that include all the cases, in which the dependent variable is months in prison and where those cases receiving nonincarcerative sentences are assigned a value of zero.

Problems arise when ordinary least squares regression techniques are used to analyze data sets where the dependent variable is "limited," that is, cannot fall below or exceed certain values and in which a significant proportion of the cases have values at the upper or lower limits. To overcome these difficulties, researchers often use Tobit models that produce maximum-likelihood estimates of the parameters. However, the interpretation of coefficients produced by Tobit models is not as straightforward as it is in OLS models. Therefore, in the above analysis we report the results of both the OLS and the Tobit models.

NOTES

1.   National Commission on Financial Institution Reform, Recovery and Enforcement (NCFIRRE), *Origins and Causes of the S&L Debacle: A Blueprint for Reform*, Report to the President and Congress of the United States (Washington, D.C.: Government Printing Office, July 1993), 4; Robert A. Rosenblatt, "GAO Estimates Final Cost of S&L Bailout at $480.9 Billion," *Los Angeles Times*, 13 July 1996, D1, D2; U.S. General Accounting Office (GAO), "Financial Audit: Resolution Trust Corporation's 1995 and 1994 Financial Statements," letter report (GAO/AIMD-96-123), 2 July 1996.

2.   We use the terms *thrift* and *savings and loan* interchangeably throughout the book.

3.   Quoted in James Bates, "Columbia S&L Puts Its Loss at $226.3 Million," *Los Angeles Times*, 26 October 1989, D1–D2.

4.   Calvin Trillin, "Zsa Zsa's Crowd Knows Why the Rich and Famous Deserve a Capital-Gains Cut," *Los Angeles Times*, 4 October 1989, B7.

5.   Edwin H. Sutherland, "White-Collar Criminality," *American Sociological Review* 5 (1940): 1–12; and *White Collar Crime* (New York: Dryden, 1949).

6.   These interviews are referred to throughout as "personal interview," in the interest of confidentiality.

7.   Jack Katz ("Legality and Equality: Plea Bargaining in the Prosecution of White-Collar and Common Crimes," *Law and Society Review* 13 [1979]: 431–459) has noted in this regard that the investigative and prosecutorial functions are often one and the same in white-collar crime work; see

also Jack Katz, "The Social Movement Against White-Collar Crime," in *Criminology Review Yearbook*, ed. Egon Bittner and Sheldon Messinger (Beverly Hills, Cal.: Sage Publications, 1980), 161–184.

8. Personal interview.

9. Personal interview.

10. See chapter 5 for further discussion of these issues.

11. 12 USC 1421 *et. seq.*; 12 USC 1724 *et. seq.*

12. William K. Black, "Substantive Positions of S&L Trade Associations, 1979–1989," unpublished staff report no. 1 (1993), NCFIRRE.

13. P.L. 96–221.

14. P.L. 97–320.

15. Michael M. Thomas, "The Greatest American Shambles," *New York Review of Books*, 31 January 1991, 32.

16. U.S. GAO, "Thrift Industry Restructuring and the Net Worth Certificate Program," Report to the Congress (GAO/GGD-85-79), 24 September 1985, 7.

17. Federal Home Loan Bank System, *A Guide to the Federal Home Loan Bank System* (Washington, D.C.: Federal Home Loan Bank System Publishing, 1987), 11.

18. House Committee on Government Operations, Subcommittee on Commerce, Consumer, and Monetary Affairs, *Fraud and Abuse by Insiders, Borrowers, and Appraisers in the California Thrift Industry*, Hearings before the Subcommittee, 100th Cong., 1st sess., 13 June 1987, 12–13.

19. House Committee on Government Operations, *Combatting Fraud, Abuse and Misconduct in the Nation's Financial Institutions: Current Federal Efforts Are Inadequate*, Report by the Committee, 100th Cong., 2d sess., 13 October 1988, H. Rept. 100-1088, 62.

20. Cal. Stats. 1983 c. 1091.

21. House Committee on Government Operations, Subcommittee on Commerce, Consumer, and Monetary Affairs, *Fraud and Abuse by Insiders, Borrowers, Appraisers*, 21, 18.

22. GAO, "CPA Audit Quality: Failures of CPA Audits to Identify and Report Significant Savings and Loan Problems," Report to the Chairman, House Committee on Banking, Finance, and Urban Affairs (GAO/AFMD-89-62), 2 February 1989, 2.

23. *Business Week*, "The Casino Society," 16 September 1985, 78–90.

24. Thomas, "American Shambles," 31.

25. L. William Seidman, "Seidman Lectures," in *Focus on the 90s: Economics at Home, Turmoil Abroad*, ed. Mel G. Grinspan (Memphis, Tenn.: Rhodes College, 1992), 36; emphasis added.

26. *Business Week*, "Casino Society," 78.

27. House Committee on Banking, Finance, and Urban Affairs, Subcommittee on Financial Institutions Supervision, Regulation and Insurance, *Financial Institutions Reform, Recovery, and Enforcement Act of 1989* (H.R. 1278), Hearings before the Subcommittee, 100th Cong., 1st sess., 8, 9, 14 March 1989, 286.

CHAPTER ONE: "BAD GUYS" OR RISKY BUSINESS?

1. James S. Granelli, "Keating Indicted for Fraud, Jailed," *Los Angeles Times*, 20 September 1990, A1.

2. Sheryl Stolberg, "Keating Trades His Business Suit for Prison Blues," *Los Angeles Times*, 21 September 1990, D1.

3. Lawrence J. White, *The S&L Debacle: Public Policy Lessons for Bank and Thrift Regulation* (New York: Oxford University Press), 117.

4. Bert Ely, "FSLIC's Losses—When and How They Accumulated" (Alexandria, Va.: Ely & Co., 1990), 2. Unpublished papers.

5. Robert E. Litan, "Deposit Insurance, Gas on S&L Fire," *Wall Street Journal*, 29 July 1993, A10.

6. Martin Lowy, *High Rollers: Inside the Savings and Loan Debacle* (New York: Praeger, 1991), 161, 4.

7. Robert J. Samuelson, "S&L's: Much More than Sleaze," *Washington Post*, 7 July 1993, A21.

8. Lowy, *High Rollers*, 4.

9. Bert Ely, "Crime Accounts for Only 3% of the Cost of the S&L Mess" (Alexandria, Va.: Ely & Co., 1990), 2. Unpublished papers.

10. U.S. Department of Justice, "Attacking Financial Institution Fraud," *Second Quarterly Report to Congress, Fiscal Year 1992*.

11. The NCFIRRE (*Origins and Causes of the S&L Debacle*, 71) concurs with

our appraisal of Ely's approach: "Strong methodological reasons favor discounting [Ely's] conservative estimate."

12. Samuelson, "S&L's," A21; Lowy, High Rollers, 4; Gary Hector, "S&L's: Where Did All Those Billions Go?" Fortune Magazine, 10 September 1990, 88; Ely, "FSLIC's Losses," 9; Litan, "S&L Fire," A10.

13. Ely, "FSLIC's Losses," 11.

14. Edwin H. Sutherland, "Is 'White Collar Crime' Crime?" American Sociological Review 10 (1945): 132–139; Paul W. Tappan, "Who Is the Criminal?" American Sociological Review 12 (1947): 96–102; Ernest W. Burgess, "Comment," American Journal of Sociology 56 (1950): 32–33; Leonard Orland, "Reflections on Corporate Crime: Law in Search of Theory and Scholarship," American Criminal Law Review 17 (1979–1980): 501–520; Gilbert Geis, "White Collar Crime: What Is It?" in White Collar Crime Reconsidered, ed. Kip Schlegel and David Weisburd (Boston: Northeastern University Press, 1992), 31–52.

15. Tappan, "Who Is the Criminal?" 100, 97, 100.

16. Sutherland, "Is 'White Collar Crime' Crime?" 132–139; Sutherland, White Collar Crime.

17. Geis, White Collar Crime: What Is It? 36.

18. William K. Black, "The Incidence and Cost of Fraud and Insider Abuse," unpublished staff report no. 13 (1993), NCFIRRE. It should not be lost on the reader that this relatively infrequent, and incompetent, form of bank robbery is the only type of crime included in Ely's calculations.

19. Ibid., 6.

20. Laurie Holtz, speech at Florida International University, 20 March 1991, 7.

21. Tappan, "Who Is the Criminal?" 100.

22. Stephen Pizzo, Mary Fricker, and Paul Muolo, Inside Job: The Looting of America's Savings and Loans, 2d ed. (New York: HarperCollins, 1991), 41–54; U.S. GAO, "Thrift Failures: Costly Failures Resulted from Regulatory Violations and Unsafe Practices" (GAO/AFMD-89-62), Report to Congress, 16 June 1989, 22.

23. Pizzo, Fricker, and Muolo, Inside Job, 66.

24. Ibid., 50.

25. House Committee on Government Operations, *Combatting Fraud*, 38.

26. James O'Shea, *Daisy Chain: How Borrowed Billions Sank a Texas S&L* (New York: Pocket Books, 1991), 59–70.

27. Ibid.

28. Black, "The Incidence and Cost of Fraud and Insider Abuse."

29. Susan Hightower, "S&L Swindlers Get Early Withdrawal from Prison," *San Diego Union-Tribune*, 31 July 1994, I1.

30. A Phoenix accountant reported that Michael Milken advised Keating to buy a California thrift as a way to secure funds for ACC. Whatever the truth to that story, Milken put up the $51 million to purchase Lincoln through the sale of junk bonds (Pizzo, Fricker, and Muolo, *Inside Job*, 389).

31. Ibid., 350, 390.

32. Black, "The Incidence and Cost of Fraud and Insider Abuse."

33. Pizzo, Fricker, and Muolo, *Inside Job*, 400.

34. Ibid., 432–433.

35. GAO, "Thrift Failures: Costly Failures Resulted from Regulatory Violations," 17. These 26 thrifts were responsible for more than 57 percent of the FSLIC's losses between 1985 and 1987.

36. Quoted in Lowy, *High Rollers*, 160.

37. Charles A. Deardorff, "The Relationships between the Incidence and Cost of Abuse and Fraud by Insiders and the Concentration of Thrift Ownership" (Office of Thrift Supervision, San Francisco, 1991). Unpublished manuscript.

38. NCFIRRE, *Origins and Causes of the S&L Debacle*, 4.

39. U.S. GAO, "Failed Thrifts: Internal Control Weaknesses Create an Environment Conducive to Fraud, Insider Abuse, and Related Unsafe Practices," statement of Frederick D. Wolf, Assistant Comptroller General, before the Subcommittee on Criminal Justice, House Committee on the Judiciary, 22 March 1989 (GAO/T-AFMD-89-4), 11.

40. "Major" cases are defined as those in which "a) the amount of fraud or loss was $100,000 or more, or b) the defendant was an officer, director or owner . . . or, c) the schemes involved multiple borrowers in the same institution, or d) involves [sic] other major factors" (U.S. Department of Justice, Office of the Attorney General, *Attacking Financial Institution Fraud, Fiscal Year 1992* [First Quarterly Report to Congress], 9).

41.   Marvin Collins, Interview in *Corporate Crime Reporter* 6, no. 4 (27 January 1992): 16.

42.   GAO, "Failed Thrifts: Internal Control Weaknesses"; FHLBB, cited in House Committee on Government Operations, *Combatting Fraud*, 51.

43.   Resolution Trust Corporation, *RTC Review* (Washington, D.C.: Government Printing Office, 1992), 11.

44.   Office of Thrift Supervision, Dallas District Office, "Correlation between Insider Fraud and Reported Insolvency." Unpublished report, April 1990.

45.   George A. Akerlof and Paul M. Romer, "Looting: The Economic Underworld of Bankruptcy for Profit," *Brookings Papers on Economic Activity* 2, edited by William C. Brainard and George L. Perry (Washington, D.C.: Brookings Institution, 1993), 30, 28.

46.   NCFIRRE, *Origins and Causes of the S&L Debacle*, 71. Crippen is quoted on p. 82; Levitas, on p. 86.

47.   Ibid., 70. These estimates of the role of fraud in bringing thrifts to insolvency are consistent with similar estimates for insolvent commercial banks. An Office of the Comptroller of the Currency study of 171 banks that failed between 1979 and 1987 found that "material fraud" was a factor in the failure of 11 percent of those institutions and "insider abuse" played a significant role at 35 percent of them (Fred Graham and James Horner, "Bank Failures: An Evaluation of Factors Contributing to the Failure of National Banks," in *The Financial Services Industry in the Year 2000: Risks and Efficiency* [Chicago: Federal Reserve Bank of Chicago, 1989], 405–435). More recently, the GAO analyzed data on all of the 286 banks that failed in 1990 and 1991 and estimated that insider fraud had contributed significantly to 36 percent of those failures (49% of these institutions had had criminal referrals filed against them) (U.S. GAO, "Bank Insider Activities: Insider Problems and Violations Indicate Broader Management Deficiencies," Report to Congress [GAO/GGD-94-88], March 1994).

48.   Ely, "Crime Accounts for Only 3%."

49.   We are indebted to William Black, former deputy chief counsel at the Office of Thrift Supervision in San Francisco, for many of the concepts in the following deductive analysis.

50. GAO, "Thrift Failures: Costly Failures Resulted from Regulatory Violations," 15.

51. Lawrence J. White, The S&L Debacle, 41, 75; House Committee on Banking, Finance, and Urban Affairs, Effectiveness of Law Enforcement against Financial Crime, Hearing before the Committee, Dallas, Texas, 101st Cong., 2d sess. pt. 1, 11 April 1990, 610; ibid., 23–30, 175–192; Lowy, High Rollers, 74–76, 175–192.

52. House Committee on Banking, Commerce and Urban Affairs, Effectiveness of Law Enforcement against Financial Crime, pt. 1, 610.

53. GAO, "Thrift Failures: Costly Failures Resulted from Regulatory Violations," 31–39.

54. Lowy, High Rollers; Jonathan R. Macey and Geoffrey P. Miller, "Why Bank Regulation Failed: Designing a Bank Regulatory Strategy for 1990's," Stanford Law Review 45 (1992): 289–309.

55. Black, "The Incidence and Cost of Fraud and Insider Abuse."

56. William K. Black, "ADC Lending," unpublished staff report no. 2 (1993), NCFIRRE.

57. Ely, "FSLIC's Losses," 6.

58. Business Week, "Casino Society," 82.

59. Personal interview.

60. GAO, "Thrift Failures: Costly Failures Resulted from Regulatory Violations," 15.

61. Norman Strunk and Fred Case, Where Deregulation Went Wrong: A Look at the Causes behind Savings and Loan Failures in the 1980s (Chicago: U.S. League of Savings Institutions, 1988), 89.

62. Quoted in House Committee on Banking, Finance, and Urban Affairs, Effectiveness of Law Enforcement against Financial Crime, 449.

63. GAO, "Thrift Failures: Costly Failures Resulted from Regulatory Violations"; NCFIRRE, Origins and Causes of the S&L Debacle; Black, "ADC Lending" and "The Incidence and Cost of Fraud and Insider Abuse."

64. Pizzo, Fricker, and Muolo, Inside Job; personal interviews.

65. GAO, "Thrift Failures: Costly Failures Resulted from Regulatory Violations," 42.

66.   Cited in House Committee on Banking, Finance, and Urban Affairs, *Effectiveness of Law Enforcement against Financial Crime*, 185.

67.   GAO, "Thrift Failures: Costly Failures Resulted from Regulatory Violations," 92, 93.

68.   Resolution Trust Corporation, *Annual Report* (Washington, D.C.: Resolution Trust Corporation, 1989), 12.

69.   Lowy, *High Rollers*, 131.

70.   Black, "ADC Lending," 2.

71.   Strunk and Case, *Where Deregulation Went Wrong*, 132–134.

72.   House Committee on Banking, Finance, and Urban Affairs, *Investigation of Lincoln Savings and Loan Association*, Hearings before the Committee, 101st Cong., 1st sess., pt. 2, 1989, 576–595.

73.   James R. Barth, *The Great Savings and Loan Debacle* (Washington, D.C.: AEI Press, 1991), 66.

74.   Thomas, "American Shambles," 32.

75.   Quoted in Pizzo, Fricker, and Muolo, *Inside Job*, 254.

76.   Maggie Mahar, "The Great Collapse: Commercial Real Estate Is on the Skids across the Nation," *Barron's*, 22 July 1991, 11.

77.   Holtz, speech at Florida International, University, 30.

78.   Lowy, *High Rollers*, 88.

79.   It should be noted that inflation was under control by the mid-1980s and conservative thrifts were able to ride out the original interest rate crisis and ultimately report substantial real profits.

80.   House Committee on Banking, Finance, and Urban Affairs, *Effectiveness of Law Enforcement against Financial Crime*, 30.

CHAPTER TWO: THRIFT CRIME DEMYSTIFIED

1.   In this so-called scandal, it was revealed that members of Congress systematically overdrew on their House "bank" accounts—which were really part of the House post office. While the public was encouraged to draw parallels to their own household banking, such overdrafts were technically allowed and cost taxpayers nothing.

2.   P. J. O'Rourke, "Piggy Banks," *Rolling Stone*, 24 August 1989, 43.

3.   David Weisburd et al., *Crimes of the Middle Classes: White-Collar Offenders in the Federal Courts* (New Haven: Yale University Press), 60.

4.   18 USC 215; 18 USC 656, 961c; 18 USC 1344; 18 USC 1001; 18 USC 1005; 18 USC 2, 371.

5.   Konrad Alt and Kristen Siglin, Memorandum on bank and thrift fraud to Senate Banking Committee members and staff, 25 July 1990, 3–5, 4.

6.   House Committee on Government Operations, *Combatting Fraud*, 180–181; Pizzo, Fricker, and Muolo, *Inside Job*, 236–237.

7.   O'Shea, *Daisy Chain*, 75.

8.   Personal interview.

9.   O'Shea, *Daisy Chain*, 32; personal interviews.

10.   O'Shea, *Daisy Chain*, 34–35.

11.   Pizzo, Fricker, and Muolo, *Inside Job*, 14.

12.   A study by the economist M. Ray Perryman documents this effect, blaming the Texas real estate recession at least in part on the overbuilding in which Texas S&Ls engaged (House Committee on Banking, Finance, and Urban Affairs, *Investigation of Lincoln Savings and Loan Association*, 473–476).

13.   Ibid., 126–128.

14.   Martin Mayer, *The Greatest Ever Bank Robbery: The Collapse of the Savings and Loan Industry* (New York: Charles Scribner's Sons, 1990), 6.

15.   Ibid., 4–5, 7.

16.   Quoted in Mayer, *The Greatest Ever Bank Robbery*, 9.

17.   House Committee on Government Operations, Subcommittee on Commerce, Consumer, and Monetary Affairs, *Fraud and Abuse by Insiders, Borrowers, and Appraisers*, 306–307.

18.   Alt and Siglin, Memorandum on bank and thrift fraud, 5.

19.   House Committee on Government Operations, Subcommittee on Commerce, Consumer, and Monetary Affairs, *Adequacy of Federal Efforts to Combat Fraud, Abuse, and Misconduct in Federally Insured Financial Institutions*, Hearings before the Subcommittee, 100th Cong., 1st sess., 19 November 1987, 79–80, 129–130.

20.   House Committee on Banking, Finance, and Urban Affairs, *Effectiveness of Law Enforcement against Financial Crime*, pt. 1, 799–872.

21.   A study by James Barth, former chief economist for the Office of Thrift Supervision (the thrift regulatory agency that replaced the FHLBB

in 1989), reported that from 1980 to 1988, 489 savings and loans that stayed open after they were insolvent lost over $40 billion while operating in the red (cited in Joel Glenn Brenner, "S&L Bailout: How Delays Drove Up Cost," *Washington Post*, 11 March 1990, H1).

22.   Personal interviews; Pizzo, Fricker, and Muolo, *Inside Job*, 277–278.
23.   Alt and Siglin, Memorandum on bank and thrift fraud, 5.
24.   O'Shea, *Daisy Chain*, 110.
25.   Black, "The Incidence and Cost of Fraud and Insider Abuse"; William K. Black, " 'Cash Cow' Examples," unpublished staff report no. 6 (1993), NCFIRRE.
26.   "Special deals" was the code name Renda and his co-conspirators used to refer to their nominee loan and linked financing schemes.
27.   Quoted in Pizzo, Fricker, and Muolo, *Inside Job*, 127.
28.   Ibid., 114. Quote on p. 133.
29.   Ibid., 154.
30.   Personal interview.
31.   NCFIRRE, *Origins and Causes of the S&L Debacle*, 48.
32.   William K. Black, "Thrift Accounting Principles and Practices," unpublished staff report no. 20 (1993), NCFIRRE, 24.
33.   Ibid., 9; NCFIRRE, *Origins and Causes of the S&L Debacle*, 9.
34.   NCFIRRE, *Origins and Causes of the S&L Debacle*, 49.
35.   House Committee on Government Operations, *Combatting Fraud*, 34.
36.   Pizzo, Fricker, and Muolo, *Inside Job*, 39.
37.   Office of Thrift Supervision, "United States of America before the Office of Thrift Supervision: In the Matter of Thomas Spiegel, Former Director and Chief Executive Officer, Columbia Savings and Loan Association; Re: Order No. 90-1619," Notice of Charges against Thomas Spiegel, 4 September 1990.
38.   Black, " 'Cash Cow' Examples."
39.   Gregory Crouch, "McKinzie Guilty of Looting Savings and Loan," *Los Angeles Times*, 30 March 1990, D1.
40.   Michael Binstein, "A Confederacy of Greed," *Regardie's*, July 1989, 31.
41.   Pizzo, Fricker, and Muolo, *Inside Job*, 274.
42.   Binstein, "A Confederacy of Greed," 30.

43.   Pizzo, Fricker, and Muolo, *Inside Job*, 404–405; Lowy, *High Rollers*, 152–153.

44.   Lowy, *High Rollers*, 152.

45.   Mayer, *The Greatest Ever Bank Robbery*, 77; Pizzo, Fricker, and Muolo, *Inside Job*, 405; Lowy, *High Rollers*, 152–153.

46.   *Los Angeles Times*, "CenTrust Chairman Sentenced to 11 Years," 2 December 1994, D2.

47.   GAO, "Thrift Failures: Costly Failures Resulted from Regulatory Violations," 21.

48.   Ibid.

49.   Ibid.

50.   Office of Thrift Supervision, "In the Matter of Thomas Spiegel," 32.

51.   O'Shea, *Daisy Chain*, 217–218.

52.   Pizzo, Fricker, and Muolo, *Inside Job*, 406.

53.   Black, " 'Cash Cow' Examples," 1.

54.   Binstein, "A Confederacy of Greed," 27.

55.   Ibid., 28.

56.   GAO, "Thrift Failures: Costly Failures Resulted from Regulatory Violations," 21.

57.   Personal interviews.

58.   Edwin H. Sutherland, *White Collar Crime: The Uncut Version* (New Haven: Yale University Press, 1983), 231.

59.   Donald R. Cressey, *Other People's Money: A Study of the Social Psychology of Embezzlement* (Glencoe, Ill.: Free Press, 1953).

60.   Stanton Wheeler and Mitchell Lewis Rothman, "The Organization as Weapon in White Collar Crime," *Michigan Law Review* 80, no. 7 (1982): 1405.

61.   James W. Coleman, "Toward an Integrated Theory of White Collar Crime," *American Journal of Sociology* 93 (1987): 407.

62.   Wheeler and Rothman, "The Organization as Weapon," 1406.

63.   James Bates, "Columbia S&L Puts Its Loss at $226.3 Million," *Los Angeles Times*, 26 October 1989, D1; *Business Week*, "Casino Society," 16 September 1985, 78–90.

64.   Quoted in Bates, "Columbia S&L," D1.

65.   James Grant, "Michael Milken, Meet Sewell Avery," *Forbes 400*, 23 October 1989, 61.

66.   *Business Week*, "Casino Society," 90.

67.   GAO, "Thrift Failures: Costly Failures Resulted from Regulatory Violations," 51.

68.   Ibid., 40.

69.   House Committee on Government Operations, Subcommittee on Commerce, Consumer, and Monetary Affairs, *Adequacy of Federal Efforts*, 99–100.

70.   House Committee on Government Operations, Subcommittee on Commerce, Consumer, and Monetary Affairs, *Fraud and Abuse by Insiders, Borrowers, and Appraisers*, 321–322.

71.   GAO, "Thrift Failures: Costly Failures Resulted from Regulatory Violations," 41, 44–45.

72.   House Committee on Government Operations, Subcommittee on Commerce, Consumer, and Monetary Affairs, *Fraud and Abuse by Insiders, Borrowers, and Appraisers*, 308.

73.   O'Shea, *Daisy Chain*, 216.

74.   Pizzo, Fricker, and Muolo, *Inside Job*, 430.

75.   There was much less variation in the crimes committed by outsiders acting on their own without the assistance of institutional insiders. In fact, their crimes generally took two basic forms: *diversion of loan proceeds* from their intended purposes and filing *false documents* to obtain loans. Typical of the former was the owner of a development company who paid himself $583,000 for "consulting fees" out of a $4.7 million construction loan. Use of false documents commonly involved the filing of fake appraisals that greatly inflated the value of property pledged as security for loans. Finally, we used a *miscellaneous* category for the offenses that did not seem to fit these two basic forms of outsider fraud.

76.   GAO, "CPA Audit Quality," 5.

77.   Mayer, *The Greatest Ever Bank Robbery*, 294; Pizzo, Fricker, and Muolo, *Inside Job*, 489.

78.   Pizzo, Fricker, and Muolo, *Inside Job*, 407.

79.   Ibid., 406.

80. Quoted in Michael Waldman, *Who Robbed America? A Citizen's Guide to the Savings & Loan Scandal* (New York: Random House, 1990), 49.

81. David W. Myers, "Accounting Firm to Pay $186.5 Million to Settle Claims," *Los Angeles Times*, 10 August 1994, D1.

82. Jerry Knight, "Deloitte & Touche Agrees to Pay $312 Million in S&L Settlement," *Los Angeles Times*, 15 March 1994, D2.

83. Myers, "Accounting Firm," D1.

84. Quoted in Waldman, *Who Robbed America?* 50.

85. David G. Savage, "High Court to Rule on Lawyer Liability in S&L Failures," *Los Angeles Times*, 30 November 1993, D1.

86. *Los Angeles Times*, "Attorney to Testify against S&L Client," 8 November 1993, D6.

87. Government lawyers estimate that pending claims against lawyers and accountants are worth more than $1.5 billion. It is unlikely, however, that they will recover even a fraction of that amount, due to two U.S. Supreme Court decisions in June 1994 that will make it more difficult for the government to win these lawsuits. In one decision, the Court ruled in favor of a narrow definition of "malpractice"; in the other, it allowed for the voiding of cases filed after the filing deadline. (James S. Granelli, "Supreme Court Gives Protection to Third Parties in S&L Cases," *Los Angeles Times*, 14 June 1994, D1, D3; Civil Action no. 91-2226 CRR, *Resolution Trust v. Gardner*, In the United States District Court for the District of Columbia, 2–3).

88. *Resolution Trust v. Gardner*, 3.

89. Lowy, *High Rollers*, 73–74.

90. Ibid., 75.

91. Texas Governor's Task Force on the Savings and Loan Industry, reprinted in House Committee on Banking, Finance, and Urban Affairs, *Effectiveness of Law Enforcement against Financial Crime*, pt. 1, 220–277.

92. Personal interviews.

93. Quoted in House Committee on Government Operations, Subcommittee on Commerce, Consumer, and Monetary Affairs, *Fraud and Abuse by Insiders, Borrowers, and Appraisers*, 26.

94. GAO, "Financial Audit."

95. House Committee on Banking, Finance, and Urban Affairs, *Effectiveness of Law Enforcement against Financial Crime*, pt. 1, 802.

96. House Committee on Banking, Finance, and Urban Affairs, *Effectiveness of Law Enforcement against Financial Crime*, pt. 2, 20.

97. GAO, "Thrift Failures: Costly Failures Resulted from Regulatory Violations," 51–53.

98. Collins, Interview, 15.

99. Ibid., 16.

100. House Committee on Banking, Finance, and Urban Affairs, *Effectiveness of Law Enforcement against Financial Crime*, pt. 2, 20.

101. Personal interview.

102. House Committee on Banking, Finance, and Urban Affairs, *Effectiveness of Law Enforcement against Financial Crime*, pt. 1, 804–872.

103. William Weld, speech before the Fidelity and Surety Committee of the American Bar Association, 23 January 1987.

104. Geis, "White Collar Crime: What Is It?" 35.

105. Coleman, "Toward an Integrated Theory of White Collar Crime," 427.

106. Gilbert Geis, "White Collar Crime: The Heavy Electrical Equipment Antitrust Cases of 1961," in *Criminal Behavior Systems: A Typology*, ed. Marshall B. Clinard and Richard Quinney (New York: Holt, Rinehart and Winston, 1967), 140–151.

107. Harvey A. Farberman, "A Criminogenic Market Structure: The Automobile Industry," *Sociological Quarterly* 16 (1975): 438–457.

108. Francis T. Cullen, William J. Maakestad, and Gary Cavender, *Corporate Crime under Attack: The Ford Pinto Case and Beyond* (Cincinnati: Anderson Press, 1987); Mark Dowie, "Pinto Madness," in *Crisis in American Institutions*, ed. Jerome Skolnick and Elliot Currie (Boston: Little, Brown, 1979), 26–34.

109. Wheeler and Rothman, "The Organization as Weapon," 1425.

110. Peter Asch and J. J. Seneca, "Is Collusion Profitable?" *Review of Economics and Statistics* 58 (1969): 1–12; Marshall B. Clinard et. al., *Illegal Corporate Behavior* (Washington, D.C.: Government Printing Office, 1979); George Hay and Daniel Kelly, "An Empirical Survey of Price-Fixing Conspiracies," *Journal of Law and Economics* 17 (1974): 13–39; Richard A. Posner, "A Statistical Study of Antitrust Enforcement," *Journal of Law Enforcement and Economics* 13

(1970): 365–420; Marc Riedel, "Corporate Crime and Interfirm Organization: A Study of Penalized Sherman Act Violations," *Graduate Sociology Club Journal* 8 (1968): 74–97.

111. John Braithwaite, "White-Collar Crime," *Annual Review of Sociology* 11 (1985): 1–25; Michael Levi, "Crisis? What Crisis? Reactions to Commercial Fraud in the United Kingdom," *Contemporary Crises* 11 (1987): 207–221; Susan P. Shapiro, "Collaring the Crime, Not the Criminal: Reconsidering the Concept of White-Collar Crime," *American Sociological Review* 55 (June 1990): 346–365; Diane Vaughan, "The Macro-Micro Connection in White-Collar Crime Theory," in *White-Collar Crime Reconsidered,* ed. Kip Schegel and David Weisburd (Boston: Northeastern University Press, 1992), 124–145.

112. Marshall B. Clinard and Richard Quinney, eds., *Criminal Behavior Systems: A Typology,* 2d ed. (New York: St. Martin's Press, 1973), 188.

113. Wheeler and Rothman, "The Organization as Weapon."

114. Estes Kefauver, *Crime in America* (New York: Greenwood Press, 1968).

115. *President's Commission on Law Enforcement and Administration of Justice Task Force Report: Organized Crime* (Washington, D.C.: Government Printing Office, 1967), 1–6.

116. Ralph Salerno and John S. Tomkins, *The Crime Confederation: Cosa Nostra and Allied Operations in Organized Crime* (Garden City, N.Y.: Doubleday, 1969), 89.

117. Donald Cressey, *Theft of the Nation: The Structure and Operations of Organized Crime in America* (New York: Harper and Row, 1969), 109.

118. Howard Abadinsky, *Organized Crime* (Boston: Allyn and Bacon, 1981); Annelise Graebner Anderson, *The Business of Organized Crime: A Cosa Nostra Family* (Stanford, Cal.: Hoover Institution Press, 1979); Clinard and Quinney, *Criminal Behavior;* M. R. Haskell and Lewis Yablonsky, *Criminology: Crime and Causality* (Boston: Houghton Mifflin, 1983).

119. Gordon Hawkins, "Organized Crime and God," in *The Honest Politician's Guide to Crime Control,* ed. Norval Morris and Gordon Hawkins (Chicago: University of Chicago Press, 1969), 203–235; Jay S. Albanese, "What Lockheed and La Cosa Nostra Have in Common: The Effect of Ideology on Criminal Justice Policy," *Crime and Delinquency* 28 (1982): 211–232; Alan A. Block, "History and the Study of Organized Crime," *Urban Life*

6(1978): 455–474; Dwight C. Smith, Jr., "Paragons, Pariahs, and Pirates: A Spectrum-Based Theory of Enterprise," *Crime and Delinquency* 26 (July 1980): 358–386.

120. Alan A. Block, *East Side, West Side: Organized Crime in New York, 1930–1950* (Cardiff, Wales: University College Cardiff Press, 1980), 10.

121. Ibid.

122. Albanese, "What Lockheed and La Cosa Nostra Have in Common."

123. James W. Meeker and John Dombrink, "Criminal RICO and Organized Crime: An Analysis of Appellate Litigation," *Criminal Law Bulletin* 20 (July–August 1984): 309–320; James W. Meeker, John Dombrink, and Henry N. Pontell, "White-Collar and Organized Crime: Questions of Seriousness and Policy," *Justice Quarterly* 4 (March 1987): 73–98.

124. Smith, "Paragons, Pariahs, and Pirates."

125. Michael D. Maltz, "On Defining 'Organized Crime': The Development of a Definition and a Typology," *Crime and Delinquency* 22 (1976): 342.

126. Sutherland, "White-Collar Criminality"; James W. Coleman, *The Criminal Elite: The Sociology of White Collar Crime* (New York: St. Martin's Press, 1985); Coleman, "Toward an Integrated Theory"; Farberman, "A Criminogenic Market Structure"; Geis, "White Collar Crime: The Heavy Electrical Equipment Antitrust Cases."

127. Kitty Calavita, "The Demise of the Occupational Safety and Health Administration: A Case Study in Symbolic Action," *Social Problems* 30 (1983): 437–448; Theodore Lowi, *The End of Liberalism* (New York: W. W. Norton, 1969); Laureen Snider, "Cooperative Models and Corporate Crime: Panacea or Cop-out?" *Crime and Delinquency* 36 (1990): 373–390; Peter Yeager, *The Limits of Law: The Public Regulation of Private Pollution* (Cambridge: Cambridge University Press, 1991).

128. Personal interview.

CHAPTER THREE: THE POLITICAL CONNECTION

1.   Edwin J. Gray, "Warnings Ignored: The Politics of the Crisis," *Stanford Law and Policy Review* 2 (Spring 1990): 139.

2.   W. Michael Reisman, *Folded Lies: Bribery, Crusades, and Reforms* (New York: Free Press, 1979), 9.

3.   Amitai Etzioni, "Keating Six?" *The Response Community* 1 (1990–91): 1.

4.   Joseph A. Grundfest, "Son of S&L—The Sequel: The Conditions that Caused the Crisis Are Still with Us," *Washington Post*, 3 June 1990, D1.

5.   Waldman, *Who Robbed America?* 61.

6.   Ibid.

7.   Ibid., 63. In recognition of the temptations implicit in such honoraria, the House banned them in 1989; they are still permissible in the Senate, as long as they do not exceed 27 percent of the individual's Senate salary.

8.   Personal interview.

9.   Personal interview.

10.   House Committee on Banking, Currency, and Housing, Subcommittee on Financial Institutions Supervision, Regulation and Insurance, *Failure of Citizens State Bank of Carrizo Springs, Texas, and Related Financial Problems*, Hearings before the Subcommittee, 94th Cong., 2d sess., 30 November and 1 December 1976, pt. 1, 3.

11.   Ibid., 580.

12.   Congressman Gonzalez continued to be a strong advocate for regulation and oversight and voted against both deregulation bills in 1980 and 1982. In 1988 he replaced St. Germain as chair of the House Banking Committee.

13.   Depository Institutions Deregulation and Monetary Control Act (DIDMCA) of 1980; Garn–St. Germain Depository Institutions Act of 1982.

14.   Quoted in Brooks Jackson and Paulette Thomas, "Waning Power: As S&L Crisis Grows, U.S. Savings League Loses Lobbying Clout," *Wall Street Journal*, 7 March 1989, A1.

15.   House Committee on Banking, Finance, and Urban Affairs, Subcommittee on General Oversight and Investigation, *Findings of Booz Allen and Hamilton Study of FHLBB*, Hearings before the Subcommittee, 100th Cong., 1st sess., 14 May 1987, 30.

16.   Ibid. In one instance in 1981 the League was able to get the sponsorship of 99 members of the House and 40 senators for a bill that permitted thrifts to sell tax-exempt "All Savers Certificates" that cost government coffers more than $4 billion in lost revenue and in the end did not enhance

the financial health of the thrift industry. Representative Sam Gibbons of Florida, a sponsor of the bill, was overheard lamenting, "This is the worst turkey I've ever introduced" (quoted in Jackson and Thomas, "Waning Power," A1).

17. Quoted in Jackson and Thomas, "Waning Power," A1.

18. Two years later during House hearings on the S&L debacle, a curious incident occurred. An oblique reference to St. Germain's role in the S&L crisis was made when the former Banking Committee chair's portrait was temporarily removed from the hearing room to make way for a banner that read "PUT THE SAVINGS AND LOAN CROOKS IN JAIL." Congressman Parris of Virginia protested, with more than a smattering of defensiveness, "I love your sign, but I regret you had to remove the portrait of the former committee chairman in order to put up a sign. . . . We hope you will return him to his position of honor after this hearing is completed. . . . Who are the crooks? Who are we talking about? Are we talking about Members of the Senate? Are we talking about former Members of the House?" (House Committee on Banking, Finance, and Urban Affairs, Subcommittee on Financial Institutions Supervision, Regulation and Insurance, *When Are the Savings and Loan Crooks Going to Jail?* 33).

19. Mayer, *The Greatest Ever Bank Robbery,* 23.

20. Ibid., 57–58.

21. DIDMCA; P.L. 96-221.

22. Mayer, *The Greatest Ever Bank Robbery;* Pizzo, Fricker, and Muolo, *Inside Job,* 11; Waldman, *Who Robbed America?*

23. NCFIRRE, *Origins and Causes of the S&L Debacle,* 44.

24. House Committee on Banking, Finance, and Urban Affairs, *The Savings and Loan Crisis,* Hearings before the Committee, 101st Cong., 1st sess., 12–13 January 1989; GAO, "Thrift Failures: Costly Failures Resulted from Regulatory Violations."

25. Referring to the ideology of deregulation in the early 1980s, one senior regulator told the authors, "I always describe it as a freight train. I mean it was just the direction and everybody got on board" (personal interview).

26. House Committee on Banking, Finance, and Urban Affairs, *Savings and Loan Policies in the Late 1970s and 1980s,* Hearings before the Committee,

101st Cong., 2d sess., 1 and 3 October 1990, 79–80 (emphasis added).

27.   Quoted in Pizzo, Fricker, and Muolo, *Inside Job*, 32.

28.   While FSLIC insurance was capped at $100,000 per deposit, many brokers placed multiple jumbo deposits of $100,000 apiece, all of which were fully insured.

29.   Merrill Lynch had $248 million in customers' insured brokered deposits in one institution alone—First National Bank of Midland, Texas, which was insolvent and offering the highest interest rates in the country for jumbo deposits in a frenetic effort to attract ever more cash (Mayer, *The Greatest Ever Bank Robbery*.

30.   Quoted in Pizzo, Fricker, and Muolo, *Inside Job*, 106.

31.   William K. Black, "Why (Some) Regulators Don't Think Regulation Works," paper prepared for the annual meeting of the Allied Social Science Association, Boston, 3–5 January 1994, 9.

32.   Quoted in Michael Binstein, "They Were Calling Me the Gestapo: A Conversation with Ed Gray," *Regardie's*, October 1988, 93–94.

33.   Black, "Why (Some) Regulators Don't Think Regulation Works"; Pizzo, Fricker, and Muolo, *Inside Job*, 104–111; Mayer, *The Greatest Ever Bank Robbery*, 116–164; NCFIRRE, *Origins and Causes of the S&L Debacle*, 56–57.

34.   Reprinted in House Committee on Banking, Finance, and Urban Affairs, *The Savings and Loan Crisis*, 670. Despite the impersonal language ("the current chief regulator . . . "), Taggart and Gray had been friends and close associates in San Diego, where Taggart was vice president of Great American First Savings Bank when Gray was its public relations officer. It was on Gray's recommendation that Gov. George Deukmejian had made Taggart commissioner of California S&Ls in 1983, a position he held until January 1985. When Taggart left the California Department of Savings and Loans, he worked as consultant to Charles Keating and, later, Don Dixon and Charles Knapp, all three of whom were subsequently convicted of criminal fraud.

35.   Black, "Why (Some) Regulators Don't Think Regulation Works," 5 (emphasis in original).

36.   Michael Binstein, "In the Belly of the Beast: Renegade vs. Regulator," *Regardie's*, July 1987, 48.

37.   The brokered deposits limitation was soon voided in federal court

(*FAIC Securities, Inc. v. United States,* 595 F. Supp. 73 [D.D.C. 1984], aff'd without op. 752 F.2nd 166 [D.C. Cir. 1985]).

38.   The OMB had turned down repeated requests by the FHLBB for budget increases commensurate with the growth of the thrift industry. Citing OMB's "disdain for the examination process," the former deputy director of the FSLIC told Congress that OMB budgetary policies were directly responsible for the lack of supervision in the thrift industry (House Committee on Government Operations, Subcommittee on Commerce, Consumer, and Monetary Affairs, *Adequacy of Federal Efforts to Combat Fraud*).

39.   Black, "Why (Some) Regulators Don't Think Regulation Works"; NCFIRRE, *Origins and Causes of the S&L Debacle,* 55–57; House Committee on Government Operations, *Combatting Fraud,* 15.

40.   Black, "Why (Some) Regulators Don't Think Regulation Works," 8.

41.   NCFIRRE, *Origins and Causes of the S&L Debacle,* 57.

42.   U.S. GAO, "Thrift Industry Problems: Potential Demands on the FSLIC Insurance Fund" (GAO/GGD-86-48BR), 12 February 1986.

43.   For a full discussion of the sequence of events surrounding the recapitalization bill, see House Committee on Standards of Official Conduct, *Report of the Special Outside Counsel in the Matter of Speaker James C. Wright, Jr.,* Report to the Committee by Special Outside Counsel, Richard J. Phelan, 101st Cong., 1st sess., 21 February 1989 (hereafter *Phelan Report*); NCFIRRE, *Origins and Causes of the S&L Debacle.*

44.   Black, "Substantive Positions of S&L Trade Associations, 1979–1989"; Pizzo, Fricker, and Muolo, *Inside Job*; House Committee on Standards of Official Conduct, *Phelan Report.*

45.   There seems to have been some disagreement among healthy thrifts, initially anyway. Some solvent thrifts were in favor of recapitalizing the FSLIC so that moribund, and often fraudulent, thrifts could be closed down. This, it was reasoned, would reduce competition with zombie institutions, which generally offered higher than average interest rates in a desperate effort to attract funds. This ratcheting up of the deposit interest rate was known as the "Texas premium." In any case, generally it was the more insolvent institutions that had the most political clout as the crisis wore on; Black, "Substantive Positions of S&L Trade Associations."

46.   Quoted in House Committee on Banking, Finance, and Urban Af-

fairs, *The Savings and Loan Crisis*, 114. League president William O'Connell wrote a letter to the *New York Times* contesting Gray's testimony, calling his allegation that the League wanted the crisis to get so big it required a taxpayer bailout "slander" and "fantasy" (William O'Connell, letter to the *New York Times*, 24 June 1987, 2).

47. Quoted in William Greider, *Who Will Tell the People? The Betrayal of American Democracy* (New York: Simon and Schuster, 1992), 72.

48. Quoted in Brooks Jackson, *Honest Graft: Big Money and the American Political Process* (New York: Alfred A. Knopf, 1988), 282.

49. Reprinted in House Committee on Banking, Finance, and Urban Affairs, *The Savings and Loan Crisis*, 670, 674; emphasis added.

50. In congressional hearings in 1989 Taggart was questioned about this letter. Following Taggart's denials of any impropriety, Congressman Jim Leach—consistently an aggressive critic of policy makers' contribution to the S&L crisis—blasted him, saying, "I am really hard pressed not to jump out of my seat, Mr. Taggart . . . . [W]e have an industry of 'cooked' books with regulators serving as master chefs and legislators stirring the pot." Later in the same hearing, Leach told Taggart he was "part and parcel of" a movement that turned thrifts into "private piggy bank[s] for the private speculator" (House Committee on Banking, Finance, and Urban Affairs, *The Savings and Loan Crisis*, 162, 165).

51. Quoted in Waldman, *Who Robbed America?* 75.

52. Ibid., 76.

53. Personal interviews; Mayer, *The Greatest Ever Bank Robbery*, 241.

54. Letter quoted in Mayer, *The Greatest Ever Bank Robbery*, 241.

55. Black, "Substantive Positions of S&L Trade Associations," 70.

56. O'Shea, *Daisy Chain*, 257.

57. Nathaniel C. Nash, "House Vote Authorizes $5 Billion for FSLIC," *New York Times*, 6 May 1987, D1.

58. Letter quoted in Black, "Substantive Positions of S&L Trade Associations," 72.

59. Ibid.

60. Letter quoted in Black, "Substantive Positions of S&L Trade Associations," 34; Senator Pryor subsequently sat on the Ethics Committee that heard the Keating 5 case.

61. As Gray testified, "[Wright] asked me if there wasn't anything I could do about this." While Gray did not report being coerced at this time, he did feel the pressure: "Anybody who has worked in government for very long knows that when the Speaker—soon to be Speaker of the House of Representatives—is asking you to look into it, it's not just anybody" (House Committee on Standards of Official Conduct, *Phelan Report*, 225).

62. Ibid., 21.

63. Quoted in Binstein, "Confederacy of Greed," 28.

64. Jackson, *Honest Graft*, 98.

65. Ibid., 104, 105.

66. Pizzo, Fricker, and Muolo, *Inside Job*, 286–287; Charles R. Babcock, "Banking on Politics: A Texas Tale; How S&Ls with Troubles Made Friends in High Places," *Washington Post*, 8 May 1988, B1.

67. Babcock, "Banking on Politics," B1.

68. Jackson, *Honest Graft*, 266.

69. Pizzo, Fricker, and Muolo, *Inside Job*, 287.

70. Brooks Jackson, "House Speaker's Ally Is Indicted in Texas Land Deal," *Wall Street Journal*, 16 March 1988, A10.

71. John E. Yang, "S&L Owner Suing to Get Back Assets from Bank Board," *Wall Street Journal*, 22 June 1987, 43.

72. House Committee on Standards of Official Conduct, *Phelan Report*; Black, "Substantive Positions of S&L Trade Associations."

73. Personal interview.

74. Quoted in House Committee on Standards of Official Conduct, *Phelan Report*, 239. It was subsequently determined that the operators of Credit-Banc Savings had engaged in serious misconduct and that the institution was insolvent (ibid.).

75. Texas Examination Report, quoted in House Committee on Standards of Official Conduct, *Phelan Report*, 260–262.

76. House Committee on Standards of Official Conduct, *Phelan Report*, 268–269.

77. So frequent were his interventions on behalf of the thrift industry and the industry's continued demands on him, that Wright himself on at least one occasion lost his patience with League lobbyists. As the recap bill

was being finalized in House chambers, Wright met the League lobbyist and League chair in the hallway, in an episode captured by John Barry, a reporter who Wright had allowed to accompany him to private meetings and around the Hill. After thanking Wright for his help, the lobbyist then pressed him on the issue of the reevaluation of property values. Wright erupted, *"Listen! My back got tired of carrying all you people.* When those bastards were writing all those stories about me, I was alone. Where were you then? This is a two-way street. That's the way things work up here" (quoted in John M. Barry, *The Ambition and the Power* [New York: Viking Penguin, 1989], 240; emphasis in original).

78.   Ed Gray, quoted in House Committee on Standards of Official Conduct, *Phelan Report,* 256.

79.   Ibid., 258. Selby was eventually fired by Danny Wall during Wall's first year as FHLBB chair.

80.   Personal interview.

81.   Mayer, *The Greatest Ever Bank Robbery,* 166.

82.   Waldman, *Who Robbed America?* 95.

83.   At the same time Keating offered Gray a job to get him off the Bank Board. In late 1985 Keating invited the Bank Board chairman to a breakfast meeting to discuss the possibility of working for Lincoln. Considering such a meeting improper, Gray sent his chief of staff, Shannon Fairbanks. Fairbanks wrote Sen. William Proxmire, chair of the Senate Banking Committee, "Mr. Keating told me that he wanted Mr. Gray to come with his organization in a job capacity which he described as 'using Mr. Gray's contacts and skills to further the corporate interests and activities of Lincoln Savings' " (quoted in Binstein, "In the Belly of the Beast," 49). Keating explained to Fairbanks that this arrangement would help circumvent "existing regulatory roadblocks" (ibid.).

84.   Reprinted in Mayer, *The Greatest Ever Bank Robbery,* 26.

85.   Ibid., 140.

86.   Through a procedure understandably disliked by Congress, the president can make appointments during the frequent congressional recesses, and these appointees can serve without Senate confirmation for up to one year. In this case, two of the three Bank Board positions were filled through recess appointments. Besides Henkel, Keating tried to have Regan

nominate George Benston, a finance professor at the University of Roches-
ter who had been commissioned by Gray to study the benefits of direct
investments. Because of strong opposition in Congress, Benston was not
appointed (Black, "Why [Some] Regulators Don't Think Regulation
Works," 8; Binstein, "In the Belly of the Beast," 50). Instead, Lawrence
White, another academic economist, was appointed and proved to be
relatively uncontroversial.

87.   James Ring Adams, *The Big Fix: Inside the Savings and Loan Scandal* (New
York: John Wiley and Sons, 1990), 243; Waldman, *Who Robbed America?*;
Kim I. Eisler, "Business Ties Mar Bank Board Member's Debut," *Legal Times*,
9 March 1987, 2–3; Black, "Why (Some) Regulators Don't Think Regulation Works," 8.

88.   Pizzo, Fricker, and Muolo, *Inside Job*, 379.

89.   Binstein, "In the Belly of the Beast," 50; Black, "Why (Some) Regulators Don't Think Regulation Works."

90.   Pizzo, Fricker, and Muolo, *Inside Job*, 379.

91.   Waldman, *Who Robbed America?* 96.

92.   Field notes of meeting, taken by William Black, San Francisco FHLB
representative in attendance, reproduced in Pizzo, Fricker, and Muolo,
Inside Job, 513–525.

93.   Quoted in Waldman, *Who Robbed America?* 97.

94.   House Committee on Standards of Official Conduct, *Phelan Report*.

95.   House Committee on Standards of Official Conduct, *Statement of the
Committee in the Matter of Representative James C. Wright, Jr.*, 101st Cong., 1st sess.,
13 April 1989, 84.

96.   Waldman, *Who Robbed America?* 72.

97.   NCFIRRE, *Origins and Causes of the S&L Debacle*.

98.   Mayer, *The Greatest Ever Bank Robbery*, 260–261; Paul Zane Pilzer, *Other
People's Money: The Inside Story of the S&L Mess* (New York: Simon and Schuster,
1989), 208–209; Waldman, *Who Robbed America?* 90.

99.   Lowy, *High Rollers*, 216.

100. Neil Bush, thirty years old at the time, was asked to be on the board
of directors of Silverado Savings and Loan in Denver in 1985. He served in
that capacity for three years at the same time that he was engaged in a
lucrative partnership with the developers Bill Walters and Kenneth Good.

The two businessmen set Bush up in his own oil exploration firm, with Bush contributing $100 and Good and Walters putting up $10,000 and $150,000, respectively. Walters established a credit line of $1.75 million at his Cherry Creek National Bank in Denver for Bush, from which the young entrepreneur took his $75,000 a year salary. Later Good loaned Bush $100,000 to invest in high-risk commodities, with the condition that if the investment failed—which it did—Bush was under no obligation to repay the loan. Bush admitted sheepishly to Congress during hearings on the Silverado case, "I know it [the 'loan'] sounds a little fishy" (House Committee on Banking, Finance, and Urban Affairs, *Silverado Banking, Savings and Loan Association,* Hearings before the Committee, 101st Cong., 2d sess., pt. 1, 22 and 23 May 1990, 107). As a board member, Neil Bush approved $106 million worth of transactions between Silverado and Walters without revealing his unique business partnership with the developer. In 1986 Bush got the Silverado board to agree to a $900,000 credit line for one of Good's oil ventures in Argentina; what he failed to mention was that he himself was a partner in the venture. When Silverado was declared insolvent in 1988, losses reached $1 billion (ibid., 96–137; Pizzo, Fricker, and Muolo, *Inside Job,* 435–441).

101. William K. Black, "The Southwest Plan and the 1988 'Resolutions,' " Unpublished Staff Report no. 3 (1993), NCFIRRE, 16.

102. Lowy, *High Rollers,* 214.

103. Quoted in Greider, *Who Will Tell the People?* 73.

104. Black, "The Southwest Plan and the 1988 'Resolutions,' " 16.

105. Quoted in Senate Committee on Banking, Housing, and Urban Affairs, *Nomination of M. Danny Wall,* Hearing before the Committee, 100th Cong., 1st sess., 18 June 1987, 12.

106. Ibid., 16.

107. Black, "The Southwest Plan and the 1988 'Resolutions,' " 1; Lowy, *High Rollers,* 199.

108. *Savings and Loan Reporter,* 22 January 1988.

109. Quoted in Pilzer, *Other People's Money,* 214.

110. Robert A. Rosenblatt, "Lawmaker Says S&L Buyer Got 78-to-1 Return," *Los Angeles Times,* 29 August 1990, D2.

111. Quoted in Senate Committee on Banking, Housing, and Urban

Affairs, *Problems of the Federal Savings and Loan Insurance Corporation* (FSLIC), Hearings before the Committee, 101st Cong., 1st sess., pt. 1, 31 January and 2, 7, and 9 February 1989, 23.

112. Lowy, *High Rollers*; Black, "The Southwest Plan and the 1988 'Resolutions' "; Mayer, *The Greatest Ever Bank Robbery*; Waldman, *Who Robbed America?*

113. Mayer, *The Greatest Ever Bank Robbery*, 250.

114. U.S. GAO, "Failed Thrifts: GAO's Analysis of Bank Board 1988 Deals," Statement of Charles A. Bowsher, Comptroller General, before the Senate Committee on Banking, Housing, and Urban Affairs (GAO/T-GGD-89-11), 14 March 1989, 9.

115. Mayer, *The Greatest Ever Bank Robbery*, 215.

116. Ibid., 253.

117. Black, "The Southwest Plan and the 1988 'Resolutions,' " 6.

118. Waldman, *Who Robbed America?* 86.

119. Pilzer, *Other People's Money*, 214.

120. For example, a Dallas developer has successfully sued Sunbelt Savings (a conglomerate created from Ed McBirney's infamous Sunbelt S&L, Tom Gaubert's Independent American Savings, and a few other insolvent thrifts) for $62.9 million in a lender-liability suit. Unless the judgment is reversed on appeal, the FSLIC will be liable under the thrift's purchase agreement (Pilzer, *Other People's Money*, 220).

121. Black, "The Southwest Plan and the 1988 'Resolutions,' " 10.

122. Ibid., 8.

123. Lowy, *High Rollers*, 204.

124. O'Shea, *Daisy Chain*, 286.

125. Quoted in Paulette Thomas and Paul Duke, "Taxpayer Sinkhole: Federal Rescue Efforts for Failed Thrifts Are a Crisis in Themselves," *Wall Street Journal*, 13 January 1989, A6.

126. Quoted in Senate Committee on Banking, Housing, and Urban Affairs, *Problems of the Federal Savings and Loan Insurance Corporation* (FSLIC), 23.

127. Ibid., 71–72.

128. Black, "The Southwest Plan and the 1988 'Resolutions.' "

129. *Economist*, "America's Thrift Crisis: From Drama to Farce," 21 January 1989, 80.

130. Ibid., 80; GAO, "Failed Thrifts: GAO's Analysis of Bank Board 1988

Deals," Statement of Charles A. Bowsher, 13; Black, "The Southwest Plan and the 1988 'Resolutions,' " 12.

131. *Economist*, "America's Thrift Crisis," 80.

132. Black, "The Southwest Plan and the 1988 'Resolutions,' " 11.

133. Ibid., 12; Douglas Frantz and Douglas Jehl, "Favoritism Claims in Texas S&L Probe Stirs Up Washington," *Los Angeles Times*, 16 August 1990, D1, D5; John R. Cranford, "Fail, Thompson Defend Roles in Purchasing Failed S&Ls," *Congressional Quarterly Weekly Report*, 11 August 1990, 2586; Jeff Gerth, "Investigators for Congress Say Unfit Buyer Slipped through to Federal Bonanza," *New York Times*, 8 July 1990, A1; *Los Angeles Times*, "FBI Probing Favoritism in Sales of S&Ls," 2 August 1990, A1, A27.

134. Black, "The Southwest Plan and the 1988 'Resolutions,' " 11.

135. Pilzer, *Other People's Money*, 221.

136. Ibid.

137. Ibid., 225.

138. Quoted in Mayer, *The Greatest Ever Bank Robbery*, 254.

139. As Pizzo, Fricker, and Muolo (*Inside Job*, 447) note, the federal government had bailed out the Hunt brothers in the early 1980s when the bottom fell out of the silver market.

140. Pilzer, *Other People's Money*, 227.

141. Quoted in Jeff Gerth, "Insolvent Bank Bought Cheaply with Help of Former Bush Aide," *New York Times*, 22 July 1990, A1.

142. Senate Committee on the Judiciary, Subcommittee on Antitrust, Monopolies, and Business Rights, *Impact of Restructuring of the S&L Industry: A Case Study on Bluebonnet Savings Bank*, Hearings before the Subcommittee (hereafter Senate Bluebonnet Hearings), 101st Cong., 2d sess., pt. 1, 9 and 31 July 1990, 8. Fail's insurance company, which was already bankrupt at the time, pleaded guilty to the felony charges, and the individual indictment against Fail was dropped (Senate Bluebonnet Hearings, pt. 2, 136).

143. Senate Bluebonnet Hearings, pt. 1, 493.

144. Ibid., 443–444.

145. Ibid., 443.

146. Ibid., 212.

147. Ibid., 446.

148. Ibid., 34.

149. Gerth, "Investigators for Congress."

150. Leah Nathans Spiro and Ronald Grover, "The Operator: An Inside Look at Ron Perelman's $5 Billion Empire," Business Week, 21 August 1995, 54–60.

151. Mayer, The Greatest Ever Bank Robbery, 256; Black, "The Southwest Plan and the 1988 'Resolutions,' " 14; Brett Duvall Fromson, "The Screwiest S&L Bailout Ever," Fortune Magazine, 19 June 1989, 114.

152. Spiro and Grover, "The Operator," 57.

153. Quoted in Mayer, The Greatest Ever Bank Robbery, 259.

154. Spiro and Grover, "The Operator," 57.

155. U.S. GAO, "Failed Thrifts: Bank Board's 1988 Texas Resolutions," Report to the Chairman, House Committee on Banking, Finance, and Urban Affairs, March 1989 (GAO/GGD-89-59), 1.

156. House Committee on Banking, Finance, and Urban Affairs, The Savings and Loan Crisis, 21.

157. Pilzer, Other People's Money, 203.

158. Fromson, "The Screwiest S&L Bailout Ever," 114.

159. Quoted in Thomas and Duke, "Taxpayer Sinkhole," A1.

160. Greider, Who Will Tell the People? 62, 12.

161. Dan Clawson, Alan Neustadtl, and Denise Scott, Money Talks: Corporate PACs and Political Influence (New York: Basic Books, 1992), 21. As Clawson, Neustadtl, and Scott (p. 21) argue, even "motherhood"—ostensibly the most noncontroversial of all American values—does not enjoy the political legitimacy of business, if the fate of the bill endorsing unpaid maternity leaves is any indication.

162. For example, Reisman, Folded Lies; Jackson, Honest Graft; Clawson, Neustadtl, and Scott, Money Talks; and Greider, Who Will Tell the People?

163. The authors do not subscribe to this rendition of the role of economic collapse in the debacle, with its implication that in the absence of economic crisis the thrift industry would have survived. As we argued in chapter 1, the behavior of thrift executives in Texas was part and parcel of the collapse in real estate there, and in California thrifts failed amid a soaring economy. Nonetheless, the notion that the collapse exposed behavior that ordinarily remains concealed is an important one.

164. Quoted in Waldman, Who Robbed America? 53.

165. Clawson, Neustadtl, and Scott, *Money Talks*, 189.

166. Personal interview.

CHAPTER FOUR: CLEANING UP

1.   Waldman, *Who Robbed America?* 102.

2.   GAO, "Financial Audit."

3.   18 USC 1032, 1517.

4.   Senate Committee on Banking, Housing, and Urban Affairs, Sub-committee on Consumer and Regulatory Affairs, *Efforts to Combat Criminal Financial Institution Fraud*, Hearing before the Subcommittee, 102d Cong., 2d sess., 6 February 1992, 59.

5.   Resolution Trust Corporation, *RTC Review*.

6.   Ibid., 117.

7.   Rosenblatt, "Lawmaker Says S&L Buyer Got 78-to-1 Return," D2.

8.   U.S. Department of Justice, *Attacking Financial Institution Fraud: Department of Justice Report to Congress*, 2d Quarterly Report, 1992, 1.

9.   Ibid.

10.   Quoted in House Committee on Banking, Finance, and Urban Affairs, *Effectiveness of Law Enforcement against Financial Crime*, pt. 1, 128.

11.   Senate Committee on Banking, Housing, and Urban Affairs, Sub-committee on Consumer and Regulatory Affairs, *Efforts to Combat Criminal Financial Institution Fraud*, 45.

12.   House Committee on Banking, Finance, and Urban Affairs, *Effectiveness of Law Enforcement against Financial Crime*, pt. 2, 4–5; Department of Justice, *Attacking Financial Institution Fraud*, 2d Quarterly Report.

13.   See chapter 1, note 40, for the definition of major cases.

14.   Senate Committee on Banking, Housing, and Urban Affairs, Sub-committee on Consumer and Regulatory Affairs, *Efforts to Combat Criminal Financial Institution Fraud*.

15.   The law enforcement response to the S&L crisis was of course not without its critics. The Public Citizen's Congress Watch published a critique of the government's effort, arguing, "There is a growing enforcement gap between galloping S&L fraud, and the government's

slow-starting efforts to catch up with the criminals" (reprinted in House Committee on Banking, Finance, and Urban Affairs, Subcommittee on Financial Institutions Supervision, Regulation and Insurance, *When Are the Savings and Loan Crooks Going to Jail?* 98). The report noted that by 1990 close to seven thousand criminal referrals relating to possible S&L crime were unaddressed by the Justice Department. Although the backlog was reduced with the influx of resources subsequent to FIRREA, unworked referrals continued to be a problem for the FBI (Senate Committee on Banking, Housing, and Urban Affairs, Subcommittee on Commerce and Regulatory Affairs, *Efforts to Combat Criminal Financial Institution Fraud*, 61–63).

16.   Calavita, "Demise of the Occupational Safety and Health Administration," 437–448.

17.   Coleman, *The Criminal Elite*, 44–45.

18.   Senate Committee on Banking, Housing, and Urban Affairs, Subcommittee on Consumer and Regulatory Affairs, *Efforts to Combat Criminal Financial Institution Fraud*, 10–11; emphasis added.

19.   U.S. GAO, quoted in Senate Committee on Banking, Housing, and Urban Affairs, Subcommittee on Consumer and Regulatory Affairs, *Efforts to Combat Criminal Institution Fraud*, 1.

20.   Personal interview.

21.   Personal interviews.

22.   U.S. GAO, reprinted in Senate Committee on Banking, Housing, and Urban Affairs, Subcommittee on Consumer and Regulatory Affairs, *Efforts to Combat Criminal Financial Institution Fraud*, 8.

23.   Quoted in House Committee on Banking, Finance, and Urban Affairs, *Effectiveness of Law Enforcement against Financial Crime*, pt. 1, 121.

24.   House Committee on Banking, Finance, and Urban Affairs, *Effectiveness of Law Enforcement against Financial Crime*, pt. 2, 15.

25.   Senate Committee on Banking, Housing, and Urban Affairs, Subcommittee on Consumer and Regulatory Affairs, *Efforts to Combat Criminal Financial Institution Fraud*, 19.

26.   U.S. Department of Justice, *Attacking Savings and Loan Institution Fraud*, 2.

27.   Personal interview. One official spoke of the "havoc ratio," that is, the amount of havoc that a given thrift crime wreaks on the institution,

the community, and the general economy. The reason these crimes are so serious, she said, is that they have the potential to wreak havoc far beyond the millions that the offender actually steals. She explained, "Using a thrift to go on a shopping spree is a lot like a fellow who wants to rob a teller at a bank. . . . In order to get the twenty-thousand-dollar cash drawer, he blows up the entire building" (personal interview).

28.   Personal interviews.

29.   Susan P. Shapiro, *Wayward Capitalist: Target of the Securities and Exchange Commission* (New Haven: Yale University Press, 1984).

30.   Nancy Reichman, "Regulating Risky Business: Dilemmas in Security Regulation," *Law and Policy* 13, no. 4 (1991): 264.

31.   Mitchell Y. Abolafia, "Structured Anarchy: Formal Organization in the Commodities Futures Markets," in *The Social Dynamics of Financial Markets*, ed. Patricia Adler and Peter Adler (Greenwich, Conn.: JAI Press, 1984), 129–151.

32.   Yeager, *The Limits of Law*, 9.

33.   Laureen Snider, "The Regulatory Dance: Understanding Reform Processes in Corporate Crime," *International Journal of the Sociology of Law* 19 (1991): 224.

34.   Personal interview.

35.   Henry N. Pontell, "Deterrence: Theory versus Practice," *Criminology* 16 (1978): 3–22; Henry N. Pontell, "System Capacity and Criminal Justice," in *Rethinking Criminology*, ed. Harold E. Pepinsky (Beverly Hills, Cal.: Sage Publications, 1982), 131–143; Henry N. Pontell, *A Capacity to Punish: The Ecology of Crime and Punishment* (Bloomington: Indiana University Press, 1984); Daniel Nagin, "Crime Rates, Sanction Levels, and Constraints on Prison Population," *Law and Society Review* 12 (1978): 341–366; Michael Geerken and Walter R. Gove, "Deterrence, Overload, and Incapacitation: An Empirical Evaluation," *Social Forces* 56 (1977): 424–447.

36.   Katz, "Legality and Equality."

37.   Michael L. Benson and Esteban Walker, "Sentencing the White-Collar Offender,"*American Sociological Review* 53, no. 2 (April 1988): 294–302; Michael Benson, Francis T. Cullen, and Gilbert Geis, "Local Prosecutors and Corporate Crime," *Crime and Delinquency* 36 (1990): 356–372; John

Braithwaite, *Corporate Crime in the Pharmaceutical Industry* (London: Routledge and Kegan Paul, 1984); Braithwaite, "White-Collar Crime"; Paul Jesilow, Henry N. Pontell, and Gilbert Geis, *Prescription for Profit: How Doctors Defraud Medicaid* (Berkeley: University of California Press, 1993); Shapiro, *Wayward Capitalist.*

38.   Personal interview. Unless otherwise noted, the remaining quotations in this chapter are from personal interviews.

39.   Most of these frauds were committed in the mid-1980s, so in addition to the statute of limitations problem, in their fight against time investigators face the dampening effects of fading witness memories and spotty documentation.

CHAPTER FIVE: PURSUING WHITE-COLLAR CRIMINALS

1.   Pizzo, Fricker, and Muolo, *Inside Job*; House Committee on Banking, Finance, and Urban Affairs, Subcommittee on Financial Institutions Supervision, Regulation and Insurance, *When Are the Savings and Loan Crooks Going to Jail?*

2.   House Committee on Government Operations, Subcommittee on Commerce, Consumer, and Monetary Affairs, *Adequacy of Federal Efforts to Combat Fraud*, 863.

3.   House Committee on Government Operations, Subcommittee on Commerce, Consumer, and Monetary Affairs, *Federal Efforts to Combat Fraud, Abuse, and Misconduct in the Nation's S&L's and Banks and to Implement the Civil and Criminal Provisions of FIRREA*, Hearings before the Subcommittee, 101st Cong., 2d sess., 14–15 March 1990, 954.

4.   House Committee on Banking, Finance, and Urban Affairs, Subcommittee on Financial Institutions Supervision, Regulation and Insurance, *When Are the Savings and Loan Crooks Going to Jail?* 1.

5.   Peter Brewton, "A Bank's Shadowy Demise," *Houston Post*, 8 February 1990, A1–A4; Kathleen Day, *The S&L Hell: The People and the Politics behind the $1 Trillion Savings and Loan Scandal* (New York: W. W. Norton, 1993).

6.   Dick Thornburgh, "Box Score on the Savings and Loans," Remarks by Attorney General of the United States, to the National Press Club, Washington, D.C., 25 July 1990.

7.   Ira Raphaelson, Special Counsel for Financial Institution Fraud, *Statement before U.S. Congress, Senate, Subcommittee on Consumer and Regulatory Affairs of the Committee on Banking, Housing and Urban Affairs,* 6 February 1992, 41.

8.   Senate Committee on Banking, Housing, and Urban Affairs, Subcommittee on Consumer and Regulatory Affairs, *Efforts to Combat Criminal Financial Institution Fraud,* 8.

9.   Ibid., 23.

10.   Shapiro, "Collaring the Crime, Not the Criminal," 361–362.

11.   Gary Becker, "Crime and Punishment: An Economic Approach," *Journal of Political Economy* 76 (1968): 169–217; Richard A. Posner, "Optimal Sentences for White-Collar Criminals," *American Criminal Law Review* 17 (Winter 1980): 409–418.

12.   Joan Neff Gurney, "Factors Influencing the Decision to Prosecute Economic Crime," *Criminology* 23 (1985): 609–619; Levi, "Crisis? What Crisis?"; Benson and Walker, "Sentencing the White-Collar Offender."

13.   John Hagan and Patricia Parker, "White Collar Crime and Punishment: Class Structure and Legal Sanctioning of Securities Violations," *American Sociological Review* 50 (1985): 313; Stanton Wheeler, David Weisburd, and Nancy Bode, "Sentencing the White-Collar Offender: Rhetoric and Reality," *American Sociological Review* 47 (October 1982): 657; Wayne Baker and Robert Faulkner, "The Social Organization of Conspiracy in the Heavy Electrical Equipment Industry," *American Sociological Review* 58 (1993): 845.

14.   For a discussion of the role of the board of directors at one of Texas's most notorious thrifts, Vernon S&L, see O'Shea, *Daisy Chain,* 113–122.

15.   Personal interviews.

16.   We used logistic regression models to supplement the simple bivariate analysis above, because such bivariate analyses can sometimes be misleading (i.e., an apparent relationship between two variables may be spurious, as both variables may be related to a third factor unaccounted for in the analysis).

17.   In these regression models we also included variables indicating the district in which the individual was referred. OTS divides both states into four separate districts. No statistically significant differences in the likelihood of indictment were observed across the districts, except for one.

Those cited in criminal referrals in the Southern District of Texas, which includes Houston, were less than half as likely as those cited in the Northern District of Texas to be indicted. This finding is consistent with our qualitative data in which several of the law enforcement informants mentioned the reluctance of the U.S. Attorney in the Northern District to pursue S&L crooks.

18.   Stephen Pizzo and Paul Muolo, "Take the Money and Run," *New York Times Magazine*, 9 May 1993, 26.

19.   Judge Fish ordered that Dixon's first sentence, of which he had served less than one year, be considered complete when he was indicted in the second case in February 1992 (Hightower, "S&L Swindlers Get Early Withdrawal from Prison").

20.   Quoted in Hightower, "S&L Swindlers Get Early Withdrawal from Prison."

21.   Senate Committee on Housing, Banking, and Urban Affairs, Subcommittee on Consumer and Regulatory Affairs, *Efforts to Combat Criminal Financial Institution Fraud*, 72.

22.   *Dallas Morning News*, "S&L Fines Reaping Little So Far," 25 February 1993, A1.

23.   GAO, "Financial Audit."

24.   G. S. Maddala, *Introduction to Economics* (New York: Macmillan, 1988), 283–287.

25.   Changes in federal sentencing standards mandated by FIRREA and the Crime Control Act of 1990 represented efforts to increase the penalties imposed on perpetrators of financial institution fraud. As these penalties cannot be applied to offenses committed prior to August 9, 1989, their impact on the offenders who contributed to the S&L crisis will be minimal.

26.   Quoted in Hightower, "S&L Swindlers Get Early Withdrawal from Prison."

27.   Property offenses include "burglary, larceny, motor vehicle theft, arson, transportation of stolen property and other property offenses (destruction of property and trespassing)." Drug offenses include "possessing or trafficking in, distribution [sic], importing and manufacturing of controlled substances. Also furnishing of fraudulent or false information concerning prescription as well as any other unspecified drug-related of-

fenses." (U.S. Department of Justice, Bureau of Justice Statistics, *Compendium of Federal Justice Statistics, 1988* [1991], 114–118.)

CONCLUSION

1.   In a separate criminal trial, Arkansas governor, Jim Guy Tucker, and President Clinton's business partners, James and Susan McDougal, were convicted of felonies connected to the Whitewater investment and Madison Guaranty S&L, including wire fraud, mail fraud, defrauding an S&L, making false statements, and misapplication of funds. Maximum possible penalties range from eighty-four years in prison for James McDougal to a ten-year sentence for Governor Tucker (Sara Fritz, "Arkansas Governor, McDougals Convicted in Whitewater Case," *Los Angeles Times*, 29 May 1996, A1, A6).

2.   As confirmation of this essentially environmental-structural model of the collapse of the U.S. thrift industry, Japanese banks are now following a similar pattern, "as precisely as if [Japanese] executives had studied a how-to manual by Charles Keating Jr." (Edmund L. Andrews, "Japan Catches Up in Bank Failures," *New York Times*, 10 September 1995, E1). In late August 1995 the Japanese Ministry of Finance closed down the country's largest credit union and a large bank that together held $16 billion in bad loans. Experts estimate that Japan's banking industry is holding another $400 billion in bad loans, although some report that the total is much higher. Despite vast cultural differences between Japan and the United States, the combination of insured deposits and deregulation in both environments produced speculative real estate lending, unprecedented growth rates, self-dealing, and catastrophic failures.

3.   Tappan, "Who Is the Criminal?"

4.   Geis, "White Collar Crime: What Is It?" 36.

5.   House Committee on Energy and Commerce, Subcommittee on Oversight and Investigation, *Failed Promises: Insurance Company Insolvencies*, Report by the Subcommittee, 101st Cong., 2d sess., 7 February 1990, iii.

6.   Martin Needleman and Carolyn Needleman, "Organizational Crime: Two Models of Criminogenesis," *Sociological Quarterly* 20 (Autumn 1979): 517–539.

7. Albanese, "What Lockheed and Cosa Nostra Have in Common"; Maltz, "On Defining 'Organized Crime' "; Meeker and Dombrink, "Criminal RICO and Organized Crime"; Meeker, Dombrink, and Pontell, "White-Collar and Organized Crime"; Smith, "Paragons, Pariahs, and Pirates," 358–386.

8. Levi, "Crisis? What Crisis?" 209.

9. Reisman, Folded Lies.

10. Harold C. Barnett, "Corporate Capitalism, Corporate Crime," Crime and Delinquency 27, no. 1 (January 1981): 4; R. Cranston, "Regulation and Deregulation: General Issues," University of New South Wales Law Journal 5 (1982): 1–29; Snider, "The Regulatory Dance"; Robin Stryker, "Government Regulation," in Encyclopedia of Sociology, vol. 2, ed. E. F. Borgatta and M. L. Borgatta (New York: Macmillan, 1992); Yeager, The Limits of Law.

11. Nicos Poulantzas, "The Problem of the Capitalist State," New Left Review 58 (November–December 1969): 67–87. See also Louis Althusser, Lenin and Philosophy and Other Essays (New York: Monthly Review Press, 1971); James O'Connor, The Fiscal Crisis of the State (New York: St. Martin's Press, 1973).

12. G. William Domhoff, Who Rules America? (Englewood Cliffs, N.J.: Prentice Hall, 1967); G. William Domhoff, The Powers That Be (New York: Random House, 1979); Gabriel Kolko, The Triumph of Conservatism (Glencoe, Ill.: Free Press, 1963); Gabriel Kolko, Railroads and Regulations (Princeton: Princeton University Press, 1965); Ralph Miliband, The State in Capitalist Society (New York: Basic Books, 1969).

13. Harold C. Barnett, "Wealth, Crime, and Capital Accumulation," Contemporary Crises 3 (1979): 171–186; Calavita, "The Demise of the Occupational Safety and Health Administration"; Snider, "The Regulatory Dance"; Yeager, The Limits of Law.

14. Barnett, "Wealth, Crime, and Capital Accumulation"; W. G. Carson, "Legal Control of Safety on British Offshore Oil Installations," in White Collar and Economic Crime, ed. P. Wickham and T. Dailey (Lexington: Lexington Books, 1982), 173–196; Kitty Calavita, "Worker Safety, Law, and Social Change: The Italian Case," Law and Society Review 20 (1986): 189–227; Eric Tucker, "Making the Workplace 'Safe' in Capitalism: The En-

forcement of Factory Legislation in Nineteenth-Century Ontario," paper presented at the annual meeting of the Canadian Law and Society Association, Hamilton, Ont. 3–6 June 1987; Yeager, The Limits of Law.

15.   Barnett, "Corporate Capitalism, Corporate Crime"; Snider, "The Regulatory Dance"; Yeager, The Limits of Law.

16.   Peter Yeager, "Managing Obstacles to Studying Corporate Offenses: An Optimistic Assessment," paper presented at the annual meeting of the American Society of Criminology, Atlanta, November 1986; Shapiro, Wayward Capitalist.

17.   Personal interview.

18.   Black, "Why (Some) Regulators Don't Think Regulation Works"; Waldman, Who Robbed America?; House Committee on Standards of Official Conduct, Report of the Special Outside Counsel in the Matter of Speaker James C. Wright, Jr.

19.   Quoted in Patrick Lee, "GOP Unveils Legislation to Overhaul U.S. Securities Laws," Los Angeles Times, 28 July 1995, D3.

20.   Michael Schroeder, "Guess Who's Gunning for the SEC," Business Week, 14 August 1995, 40.

21.   Quoted in Scot J. Paltrow, "How Fields' Dream to Cozy Up to Wall Street Backfired," Los Angeles Times, 14 September 1995, D1.

22.   Ibid., D5.

23.   Schroeder, "Guess Who's Gunning for the SEC," 41.

24.   Los Angeles Times, "Senate Votes to End Interstate Banking Curbs," 14 September 1994, D2, D12; Chris Kraul, "In Their Interest: Competitive Pressures Will Encourage More Bank Linkups," Los Angeles Times, 29 August 1995, D1.

25.   Quoted in Bennett Harrison and Barry Bluestone, The Great U-Turn: Corporate Restructuring and the Polarizing of America (New York: Basic Books, 1988), 159.

26.   Business Week, "Casino Society," 90.

27.   Ibid.

28.   Quoted in Pizzo, Fricker, and Muolo, Inside Job, 28.

29.   Eugene Bardach and Robert A. Kagan, Going By the Book: The Problem of Regulatory Unreasonableness (Philadelphia: Temple University Press, 1982); John Braithwaite, To Punish or Persuade: Enforcement of Coal Mine Safety (Albany:

State University of New York Press, 1985); Ian Ayres and John Braithwaite, *Responsive Regulation: Transcending the Deregulation Debate* (New York: Oxford University Press, 1992).

30. See Laureen Snider, "Cooperative Models and Corporate Crime," 380, for a general critique of the cooperative model of regulation, which she argues "fail[s] to deal with the implications of class-based power" and the "broader socioeconomic realities of life in a capitalist society."

31. Greider, *Who Will Tell the People?* 62, 50.

32. Personal interview.

33. Ron Chernow, *The House of Morgan: An American Banking Dynasty and the Rise of Modern Finance* (New York: Atlantic Monthly Press, 1990), 356.

34. Ibid.

APPENDIX

1. Richard Berk, "An Introduction to Sample Selection Bias in Sociological Data," *American Sociological Review* 48 (1983): 386–398.

2. Ibid., 397.

BIBLIOGRAPHY

Abadinsky, Howard. *Organized Crime*. Boston: Allyn and Bacon, 1981.

Abolafia, Mitchell Y. "Structured Anarchy: Formal Organization in the Commodities Futures Markets." In *The Social Dynamics of Financial Markets*, edited by Patricia Adler and Peter Adler, 129–151. Greenwich, Conn.: JAI Press, 1984.

Adams, James Ring. *The Big Fix: Inside the Savings and Loan Scandal*. New York: John Wiley and Sons, 1990.

Adler, Patricia, and Peter Adler. *The Social Dynamics of Financial Markets*. Greenwich, Conn.: JAI Press, 1984.

Akerlof, George A., and Paul M. Romer. "Looting: The Economic Underworld of Bankruptcy for Profit." Edited by William C. Brainard and George L. Perry. *Brookings Papers on Economic Activity* 2 (1993): 1–73.

Albanese, Jay S. "What Lockheed and La Cosa Nostra Have in Common: The Effect of Ideology on Criminal Justice Policy." *Crime and Delinquency* 28 (1982): 211–232.

Alt, Konrad, and Kristen Siglin. Memorandum on bank and thrift fraud to Senate Banking Committee members and staff, 25 July 1990.

Althusser, Louis. *Lenin and Philosophy and Other Essays*. New York: Monthly Review Press, 1971.

Anderson, Annelise Graebner. *The Business of Organized Crime: A Cosa Nostra Family.* Stanford, Cal.: Hoover Institution Press, 1979.

Andrews, Edmund L. "Japan Catches Up in Bank Failures." *New York Times,* 10 September 1995, E1, E3.

Asch, Peter, and J. J. Seneca. "Is Collusion Profitable?" *Review of Economics and Statistics* 58 (1969): 1–12.

Ayres, Ian, and John Braithwaite. *Responsive Regulation: Transcending the Deregulation Debate.* New York: Oxford University Press, 1992.

Babcock, Charles R. "Banking on Politics: A Texas Tale; How S&Ls with Troubles Made Friends in High Places." *Washington Post,* 8 May 1988, B1.

Baker, Wayne, and Robert Faulkner. "The Social Organization of Conspiracy in the Heavy Electrical Equipment Industry." *American Sociological Review* 58 (1993): 837–860.

Bardach, Eugene, and Robert A. Kagan. *Going By the Book: The Problem of Regulatory Unreasonableness.* Philadelphia: Temple University Press, 1982.

Barnett, Harold C. "Corporate Capitalism, Corporate Crime." *Crime and Delinquency* 27, no. 1 (January 1981): 4–23.

———. *Toxic Debts and the Superfund Dilemma.* Chapel Hill: University of North Carolina Press, 1994.

———. "Wealth, Crime, and Capital Accumulation." *Contemporary Crises* 3 (1979): 171–186.

Barry, John M. *The Ambition and the Power.* New York: Viking Penguin, 1989.

Barth, James R. *The Great Savings and Loan Debacle.* Washington, D.C.: AEI Press, 1991.

Bates, James. "Columbia S&L Puts Its Loss at $226.3 Million." *Los Angeles Times,* 26 October 1989, D1–D2.

Becker, Gary. 1968. "Crime and Punishment: An Economic Approach." *Journal of Political Economy* 76 (1968): 169–217.

Benson, Michael, Frances T. Cullen, and Gilbert Geis. "Local Prosecutors and Corporate Crime." *Crime and Delinquency* 36 (1990): 356–372.

Benson, Michael L., and Esteban Walker. "Sentencing the White-Collar Offender." *American Sociological Review* 53, no. 2 (April 1988): 294–302.

Berk, Richard. "An Introduction to Sample Selection Bias in Sociological Data." *American Sociological Review* 48 (1983): 386–398.

Berman, Daniel M. *Death on the Job: Occupational Health and Safety Struggles in the United States.* New York: Monthly Review Press, 1978.

Binstein, Michael. "A Confederacy of Greed." *Regardie's,* July 1989, 26–34.

———. "In the Belly of the Beast: Renegade vs. Regulator." *Regardie's,* July 1987, 45–55.

———. "They Were Calling Me the Gestapo: A Conversation with Ed Gray." *Regardie's,* October 1988, 91–96.

Black, William K. "ADC Lending." Unpublished staff report no. 2, 1993, National Commission on Financial Institution Reform, Recovery and Enforcement.

———. " 'Cash Cow' Examples." Unpublished staff report no. 6, 1993, National Commission on Financial Institution Reform, Recovery and Enforcement.

———. "The Incidence and Cost of Fraud and Insider Abuse." Unpublished staff report no. 13, 1993, National Commission on Financial Institution Reform, Recovery and Enforcement.

———. "The Southwest Plan and the 1988 'Resolutions.' " Unpublished staff report no. 3, 1993, National Commission on Financial Institution Reform, Recovery and Enforcement.

———. "Substantive Positions of S&L Trade Associations, 1979–1989." Unpublished staff report no. 1, 1993, National Commission on Financial Institution Reform, Recovery and Enforcement.

———. 1993. "Thrift Accounting Principles and Practices." Unpublished staff report no. 20, 1993, National Commission on Financial Institution Reform, Recovery and Enforcement.

————. "Why (Some) Regulators Don't Think Regulation Works." Paper prepared for the annual meeting of the Allied Social Science Association, Boston, 3–5 January 1994.

Black, William K., Kitty Calavita, and Henry N. Pontell. "The Savings and Loan Debacle of the 1980s: White-Collar Crime or Risky Business?" *Law and Policy* 17 (1995): 23–55.

Block, Alan A. *East Side, West Side: Organized Crime in New York, 1930–1950.* Cardiff, Wales: University College Cardiff Press, 1980.

————. "History and the Study of Organized Crime." *Urban Life* 6 (1978): 455–474.

Block, Fred. *Revising State Theory: Essays in Politics and Post-Industrialism.* Philadelphia: Temple University Press, 1987.

Braithwaite, John. *Corporate Crime in the Pharmaceutical Industry.* London: Routledge and Kegan Paul, 1984.

————. *To Punish or Persuade: Enforcement of Coal Mine Safety.* Albany: State University of New York Press, 1985.

————. "White-Collar Crime." *Annual Review of Sociology* 11 (1985): 1–25.

Braithwaite, John, and Brent Fisse. "Asbestos and Health: A Case of Informal Social Control." *Australian–New Zealand Journal of Criminology* 16 (1983): 67–80.

Brenner, Joel Glenn. "S&L Bailout: How Delays Drove Up Cost." *Washington Post*, 11 March 1990, H1, H4–H5.

Brewton, Peter. "A Bank's Shadowy Demise." *Houston Post*, 8 February 1990, A1–A4.

Burgess, Ernest W. "Comment." *American Journal of Sociology* 56 (1950): 32–33.

Business Week. "The Casino Society." 16 September 1985, 78–90.

Calavita, Kitty. "The Demise of the Occupational Safety and Health Administration: A Case Study in Symbolic Action." *Social Problems* 30 (1983): 437–448.

————. "Worker Safety, Law, and Social Change: The Italian Case." *Law and Society Review* 20 (1986): 189–227.

Calavita, Kitty, and Henry N. Pontell. " 'Heads I Win, Tails You Lose': Deregulation, Crime and Crisis in the Savings and Loan Industry." *Crime and Delinquency* 36 (1990): 309–341.

———. " 'Other People's Money' Revisited: Collective Embezzlement in the Savings and Loan and Insurance Industries." *Social Problems* 38 (1991): 94–112.

———. "Savings and Loan Fraud as Organized Crime: Toward a Conceptual Typology of Corporate Illegality." *Criminology* 31 (1993): 519–548.

———. "The State and White-Collar Crime: Saving the Savings and Loans." *Law and Society Review* 28 (1994): 297–324.

Carson, W. G. "Legal Control of Safety on British Offshore Oil Installations." In *White Collar and Economic Crime*, edited by P. Wickam and T. Dailey, 173–196. Lexington: Lexington Books, 1982.

Chernow, Ron. *The House of Morgan: An American Banking Dynasty and the Rise of Modern Finance.* New York: Atlantic Monthly Press, 1990.

Clawson, Dan, Alan Neustadtl, and Denise Scott. *Money Talks: Corporate PACs and Political Influence.* New York: Basic Books, 1992.

Clinard, Marshall B., and Richard Quinney, eds. *Criminal Behavior Systems: A Typology.* 2d edition. New York: St. Martin's Press, 1973.

Clinard, Marshall B., and Peter Yeager. *Corporate Crime.* New York: Free Press, 1980.

Clinard, Marshall B., Peter C. Yeager, Jeanne Brissette, David Petrashek, and Elizabeth Harries. *Illegal Corporate Behavior.* Washington, D.C.: Government Printing Office, 1979.

Coleman, James W. *The Criminal Elite: The Sociology of White Collar Crime.* New York: St. Martin's Press, 1985.

———. "Toward an Integrated Theory of White Collar Crime." *American Journal of Sociology* 93 (1987): 406–439.

Collins, Marvin, U.S. District Attorney, Northern District of Texas. Interview in *Corporate Crime Reporter* 6, no. 4 (27 January 1992): 15–19.

Cranford, John R. 1990. "Fail, Thompson Defend Roles in Purchasing Failed S&Ls." *Congressional Quarterly Weekly Report*, 11 August 1990, 2586.

Cranston, R. 1982. "Regulation and Deregulation: General Issues." *University of New South Wales Law Journal* 5 (1982): 1–29.

Cressey, Donald R. *Other People's Money: A Study of the Social Psychology of Embezzlement.* Glencoe, Ill.: Free Press, 1953.

————. *Theft of the Nation: The Structure and Operations of Organized Crime in America.* New York: Harper and Row, 1969.

Crouch, Gregory. "McKinzie Guilty of Looting Savings and Loan." *Los Angeles Times*, 30 March 1990, D1.

Cullen, Francis T., William J. Maakestad, and Gray Cavender. *Corporate Crime under Attack: The Ford Pinto Case and Beyond.* Cincinnati: Anderson Press, 1987.

Dallas Morning News. "S&L Fines Reaping Little So Far." 25 February 1993, A1, A11.

Day, Kathleen. *The S&L Hell: The People and the Politics behind the $1 Trillion Savings and Loan Scandal.* New York: W. W. Norton, 1993.

Deardorff, Charles A. "The Relationships between the Incidence and Cost of Abuse and Fraud by Insiders and the Concentration of Thrift Ownership." Office of Thrift Supervision, San Francisco, 30 April 1991. Unpublished manuscript.

Domhoff, G. William. *The Powers That Be.* New York: Random House, 1979.

————. *Who Rules America?* Englewood Cliffs, N.J.: Prentice Hall, 1967.

Donnelly, Patrick. "The Origins of the Occupational Safety and Health Act of 1970." *Social Problems* 30 (1982): 13–25.

Dowie, Mark. "Pinto Madness." In *Crisis in American Institutions*, edited by Jerome Skolnick and Elliot Currie, 26–34. 4th ed. Boston: Little, Brown, 1979.

Economist. "America's Thrift Crisis: From Drama to Farce." 21 January 1989, 80.

Eisler, Kim I. "Business Ties Mar Bank Board Member's Debut." *Legal Times*, 9 March 1987, 2–3.

Ely, Bert. "Crime Accounts for Only 3% of the Cost of the S&L Mess." Alexandria, Va.: Ely & Co. Unpublished report, 19 July 1990.

―――. "FSLIC's Losses—When and How They Accumulated." Alexandria, Va.: Ely & Co. Unpublished report, 16 October 1990.

Etzioni, Amitai. "Keating Six?" *The Response Community* 1 (1990– 1991): 6–9.

Farberman, Harvey A. "A Criminogenic Market Structure: The Automobile Industry." *Sociological Quarterly* 16 (1975): 438– 457.

Federal Home Loan Bank System. *A Guide to the Federal Home Loan Bank System*. Washington, D.C.: Federal Home Loan Bank System Publishing, 1987.

Frantz, Douglas, and Douglas Jehl. "Favoritism Claims in Texas S&L Probe Stirs Up Washington." *Los Angeles Times*, 16 August 1990, D1, D5.

Fritz, Sara. 1996. "Arkansas Governor, McDougals Convicted in Whitewater Case." *Los Angeles Times*, 29 May 1996, A1, A6.

―――. "Whitewater's Undercurrent of Cash Flows." *Los Angeles Times*, 27 March 1994, A1, A16.

Fromson, Brett Duvall. "The Screwiest S&L Bailout Ever." *Fortune Magazine*, 19 June 1989, 114–119.

Geerken, Michael, and Walter R. Gove. "Deterrence, Overload, and Incapacitation: An Empirical Evaluation." *Social Forces* 56 (1977): 424–447.

Geis, Gilbert. "White Collar Crime: The Heavy Electrical Equipment Antitrust Cases of 1961." In *Criminal Behavior Systems: A Typology*, edited by Marshall B. Clinard and Richard Quinney, 140–151. New York: Holt, Rinehart and Winston, 1967.

―――. "White Collar Crime: What Is It?" In *White Collar Crime*

Reconsidered, edited by Kip Schlegel and David Weisburd, 31–52. Boston: Northeastern University Press, 1992.

Gerth, Jeff. "Insolvent Bank Bought Cheaply with Help of Former Bush Aide." New York Times, 22 July 1990, A1, A15.

———. "Investigators for Congress Say Unfit Buyer Slipped through to Federal Bonanza." New York Times, 8 July 1990, A1.

Graham, Fred, and James Horner. "Bank Failures: An Evaluation of Factors Contributing to the Failure of National Banks." In The Financial Services Industry in the Year 2000: Risks and Efficiency, 405–435. Chicago: Federal Reserve Bank of Chicago, 1989.

Granelli, James S. "Keating Indicted for Fraud, Jailed." Los Angeles Times, 20 September 1990, A1.

———. "Supreme Court Gives Protection to Third Parties in S&L Cases." Los Angeles Times, 14 June 1994, D1, D3.

Grant, James. "Michael Milken, Meet Sewell Avery." Forbes 400, 23 October 1989, 60–64.

Gray, Edwin J. "Warnings Ignored: The Politics of the Crisis." Stanford Law and Policy Review 2 (Spring 1990): 138–146.

Greider, William. Who Will Tell the People? The Betrayal of American Democracy. New York: Simon and Schuster, 1992.

Grover, W. Byron, and Graeme Newman. Punishment and Privilege. Albany, N.Y.: Harrow and Heston, 1986.

Grundfest, Joseph A. "Son of S&L—The Sequel: The Conditions That Caused the Crisis Are Still with Us." Washington Post, 3 June 1990, D1.

Gurney, Joan Neff. "Factors Influencing the Decision to Prosecute Economic Crime." Criminology 23 (1985): 609–619.

Hagan, John, and Patricia Parker. "White Collar Crime and Punishment: Class Structure and Legal Sanctioning of Securities Violations." American Sociological Review 50 (1985): 302–316.

Harrison, Bennett, and Barry Bluestone. The Great U-Turn: Corporate Restructuring and the Polarizing of America. New York: Basic Books, 1988.

Haskell, M. R., and Lewis Yablonsky. Criminology: Crime and Causality. Boston: Houghton Mifflin, 1983.

Hawkins, Gordon. "Organized Crime and God." In The Honest Politician's Guide to Crime Control, edited by N. Morris and G. Hawkins, 203–235. Chicago: University of Chicago Press, 1969.

Hay, George, and Daniel Kelly. "An Empirical Survey of Price-Fixing Conspiracies." Journal of Law and Economics 17 (1974): 13–39.

Hector, Gary. "S&L's: Where Did All Those Billions Go?" Fortune Magazine, 10 September 1990, 84–88.

Hightower, Susan. "S&L Swindlers Get Early Withdrawal from Prison." San Diego Union-Tribune, 31 July 1994, I1.

Hook, Janet. "Investigations Cast Shadows Beyond 7 Senators' Fates." Congressional Quarterly Weekly Report, 27 January 1990, 211–216.

Jackson, Brooks. Honest Graft: Big Money and the American Political Process. New York: Alfred A. Knopf, 1988.

————. "House Speaker's Ally Is Indicted in Texas Land Deal." Wall Street Journal, 16 March 1988, A10.

Jackson, Brooks, and Paulette Thomas. "Waning Power: As S&L Crisis Grows, U.S. Savings League Loses Lobbying Clout." Wall Street Journal, 7 March 1989, A1.

Jesilow, Paul, Henry N. Pontell, and Gilbert Geis. Prescription for Profit: How Doctors Defraud Medicaid. Berkeley: University of California Press, 1993.

Johnston, Oswald. "GAO Says S&L Cost Could Rise to $500 Billion." Los Angeles Times, 7 April 1990, A1.

Katz, Jack "Legality and Equality: Plea Bargaining in the Prosecution of White-Collar and Common Crimes." Law and Society Review 13 (1979): 431–459.

————. "The Social Movement against White-Collar Crime." In Criminology Review Yearbook, edited by Egon Bittner and Sheldon Messinger, 161–184. Beverly Hills, Cal.: Sage Publications, 1980.

Kefauver, Estes. Crime in America. New York: Greenwood Press, 1968.

Knight, Jerry. "Deloitte & Touche Agrees to Pay $312 Million in S&L Settlement." *Los Angeles Times*, 15 March 1994, D2.

Kolko, Gabriel. *Railroads and Regulations*. Princeton: Princeton University Press, 1965.

————. *The Triumph of Conservatism*. Glencoe, Ill.: Free Press, 1963.

Krasner, Stephen D. "Approaches to the State: Alternative Conceptions and Historical Dynamics." *Comparative Politics* 16 (1984): 223.

Kraul, Chris. "In Their Interest: Competitive Pressures Will Encourage More Bank Linkups." *Los Angeles Times*, 29 August 1995, D1, D3.

Kriesberg, Louis. "National Security and Conduct in the Steel Industry." *Social Forces* 34 (1956): 268–277.

Lee, Patrick. "GOP Unveils Legislation to Overhaul U.S. Securities Laws." *Los Angeles Times*, 28 July 1995, D1, D3.

Levi, Michael. "Crisis? What Crisis? Reactions to Commercial Fraud in the United Kingdom." *Contemporary Crises* 11 (1987): 207–221.

Litan, Robert E. "Deposit Insurance, Gas on S&L Fire." *Wall Street Journal*, 29 July 1993, A10.

Los Angeles Times. "Attorney to Testify against S&L Client." 8 November 1993, D6.

————. "CenTrust Chairman Sentenced to 11 Years." 2 December 1994, D2.

————. "FBI Probing Favoritism in Sales of S&Ls." 2 August 1990, A1, A27.

————. "Senate Votes to End Interstate Banking Curbs." 14 September 1994, D2, D12.

Lowi, Theodore. *The End of Liberalism*. New York: W. W. Norton, 1969.

Lowy, Martin. *High Rollers: Inside the Savings and Loan Debacle*. New York: Praeger, 1991.

Macey, Jonathan R., and Geoffrey P. Miller. "Why Bank Regulation Failed: Designing a Bank Regulatory Strategy for 1990's." *Stanford Law Review* 45 (1992): 289–309.

Maddala, G. S. *Introduction to Economics.* New York: Macmillan, 1988.

Mahar, Maggie. "The Great Collapse: Commercial Real Estate Is on the Skids across the Nation." *Barron's,* 22 July 1991, 10–26.

Maltz, Michael D. "On Defining 'Organized Crime': The Development of a Definition and a Typology." *Crime and Delinquency* 22 (1976): 338–346.

———. "Towards Defining Organized Crime." In *The Politics and Economics of Organized Crime,* edited by Herbert E. Alexander and Gerald E. Caiden, 21–35. Lexington, Mass.: D. C. Heath, 1985.

Mayer, Martin. *The Greatest Ever Bank Robbery: The Collapse of the Savings and Loan Industry.* New York: Charles Scribner's Sons, 1990.

Meeker, James W., and John Dombrink. "Criminal RICO and Organized Crime: An Analysis of Appellate Litigation." *Criminal Law Bulletin* 20 (July–August 1984): 309–320.

Meeker, James W., John Dombrink, and Henry N. Pontell. "White-Collar and Organized Crime: Questions of Seriousness and Policy." *Justice Quarterly* 4 (March 1987): 73–98.

Miliband, Ralph. *The State in Capitalist Society.* New York: Basic Books, 1969.

Mills, C. Wright. *The Power Elite.* New York: Oxford University Press, 1956.

Myers, David W. "Accounting Firm to Pay $186.5 Million to Settle Claims." *Los Angeles Times,* 10 August 1994, D1.

Nagin, Daniel. "Crime Rates, Sanction Levels, and Constraints on Prison Population." *Law and Society Review* 12 (1978): 341–366.

Nash, Nathaniel C. "House Vote Authorizes $5 Billion for FSLIC." *New York Times,* 6 May 1987, D1.

National Commission on Financial Institution Reform, Recovery and Enforcement (NCFIRRE). *Origins and Causes of the S&L Debacle: A Blueprint for Reform.* A Report to the President and Congress of the United States. Washington, D.C.: Government Printing Office, July 1993.

Needleman, Martin, and Carolyn Needleman. "Organizational

Crime: Two Models of Criminogenesis." *Sociological Quarterly* 20 (Autumn 1979): 517–539.

O'Connell, William. *America's Money Trauma: How Washington Blunders Crippled the U.S. Financial System.* Winnetka, Ill.: Conversation Press, 1992.

———. Letter to the *New York Times*, 24 June 1987, 2.

O'Connor, James. *The Fiscal Crisis of the State.* New York: St. Martin's Press, 1973.

Office of Thrift Supervision. "United States of America before the Office of Thrift Supervision: In the Matter of Thomas Speigel, Former Director and Chief Executive Officer, Columbia Savings and Loans Association; Re: Order No. 90-1619." Notice of Charges against Thomas Speigel. 4 September 1990.

Orland, Leonard. "Reflections on Corporate Crime: Law in Search of Theory and Scholarship." *American Criminal Law Review* 17 (1979–1980): 501–520.

O'Rourke, P. J. "Piggy Banks." *Rolling Stone Magazine*, 24 August 1989, 43.

O'Shea, James. *Daisy Chain: How Borrowed Billions Sank a Texas S&L.* New York: Pocket Books, 1991.

Paltrow, Scot J. "How Fields' Dream to Cozy Up to Wall Street Backfired." *Los Angeles Times*, 14 September 1995, D1, D5.

Pilzer, Paul Zane. *Other People's Money: The Inside Story of the S&L Mess.* New York: Simon and Schuster, 1989.

Pizzo, Stephen, Mary Fricker, and Paul Muolo. *Inside Job: The Looting of America's Savings and Loans.* 2d ed. New York: HarperCollins, 1991.

Pizzo, Stephen, and Paul Muolo. "Take the Money and Run." *New York Times Magazine*, 9 May 1993, 26.

Plotkin, Sidney, and William E. Scheuerman. *Private Interests, Public Spending: Balanced-Budget Conservatism and the Fiscal Crisis.* Boston: South End Press, 1994.

Pontell, Henry N. *A Capacity to Punish: The Ecology of Crime and Punishment.* Bloomington: Indiana University Press, 1984.

————. "Deterrence: Theory versus Practice." *Criminology* 16 (1978): 3–22.

————. "System Capacity and Criminal Justice." In *Rethinking Criminology*, edited by Harold E. Pepinsky, 131–143. Beverly Hills, Cal.: Sage Publications, 1982.

Pontell, Henry N., Kitty Calavita, and Robert Tillman. *Fraud in the Savings and Loan Industry: White-Collar Crime and Government Response.* Executive Summary of the Final Report to the National Institute of Justice. 1994.

Posner, Richard A. "Optimal Sentences for White-Collar Criminals." *American Criminal Law Review* 17 (Winter 1980): 409–418.

————. "A Statistical Study of Antitrust Enforcement." *Journal of Law Enforcement and Economics* 13 (1970): 365–420.

Poulantzas, Nicos. "The Problem of the Capitalist State." *New Left Review* 58 (November–December 1969): 67–87.

President's Commission on Law Enforcement and Administration of Justice Task Force Report: Organized Crime. Washington, D.C.: Government Printing Office, 1967.

Raphaelson, Ira, Special Counsel for Financial Institution Fraud. *Statement before U.S. Congress. Senate. Subcommittee on Consumer and Regulatory Affairs of the Committee on Banking, Housing, and Urban Affairs,* 6 February 1992.

Reichman, Nancy. "Regulating Risky Business: Dilemmas in Security Regulation." *Law and Policy* 13, no. 4 (October 1991): 263–295.

Reisman, W. Michael. *Folded Lies: Bribery, Crusades, and Reforms.* New York: Free Press, 1979.

Rempel, William C. "2 Whitewater Partners, Gov. Tucker Indicted." *Los Angeles Times,* 18 August 1995, A1, A32.

Resolution Trust Corporation. *Annual Report.* Washington, D.C.: Resolution Trust Corporation, 1989.

————. *RTC Review.* Washington, D.C.: Government Printing Office, August 1992.

Riedel, Marc. "Corporate Crime and Interfirm Organization: A Study of Penalized Sherman Act Violations." *Graduate Sociology Club Journal* 8 (1968): 74–97.

Risen, James, and John M. Broder. "U.S. Regulators Clear Hubbel in S&L Probe." *Los Angeles Times*, 18 February 1994, A16.

Rosenblatt, Robert A. "GAO Estimates Final Cost of S&L Bailout at $480.9 Billion." *Los Angeles Times*, 13 July 1996, D1, D6.

————. "Insurers Vow to Fight Plan to Let Banks on Their Turf." *Los Angeles Times*, 10 July 1995, D1, D6.

————. "Lawmaker Says S&L Buyers Got 78-to-1 Return." *Los Angeles Times*, 29 August 1990, D2.

Salerno, Ralph, and John S. Tompkins. *The Crime Confederation: Cosa Nostra and Allied Operations in Organized Crime*. Garden City, N.Y.: Doubleday, 1969.

Samuelson, Robert J. "S&Ls: Much More than Sleaze." *Washington Post*, 7 July 1993, A21.

Savage, David G. "High Court to Rule on Lawyer Liability in S&L Failures." *Los Angeles Times*, 30 November 1993, D1, D7.

————. "Replay of '80s Not Flattering to Clintons." *Los Angeles Times*, 13 August 1995, A16–A17.

————. "Rose Firm Tied to Deals That Led to S&L Failure." *Los Angeles Times*, 11 August 1995, A4.

Savage, David G., and Edwin Chen. "S&L Examiner Says Officials Impeded Probe." *Los Angeles Times*, 9 August 1995, A1, A24.

Savings and Loan Reporter. 22 January 1988.

Schroeder, Michael. "Guess Who's Gunning for the SEC." *Business Week*, 14 August 1995, 40–41.

Seidman, L. William. "Seidman Lectures." In *Focus on the 90s: Economics at Home, Turmoil Abroad*, edited by Mel G. Grinspan, 32–50. Memphis, Tenn.: Rhodes College, 1992.

Shapiro, Susan P. "Collaring the Crime, Not the Criminal: Reconsidering the Concept of White-Collar Crime." *American Sociological Review* 55 (June 1990): 346–365.

————. Thinking about White Collar Crime: Matters of Conceptualization and Research. Washington, D.C.: National Institute of Justice, 1980.

————. Wayward Capitalist: Target of the Securities and Exchange Commission. New Haven: Yale University Press, 1984.

Skocpol, Theda, and Kenneth Finegold. "State Capacity and Economic Intervention in the Early New Deal." Political Science Quarterly 97 (1982): 255–278.

Smith, Dwight C., Jr. The Mafia Mystique. New York: Basic Books, 1975.

————. "Paragons, Pariahs, and Pirates: A Spectrum-Based Theory of Enterprise." Crime and Delinquency 26 (July 1980): 358–386.

Snider, Laureen. "Cooperative Models and Corporate Crime: Panacea or Cop-out?" Crime and Delinquency 36 (1990): 373–390.

————. "The Regulatory Dance: Understanding Reform Processes in Corporate Crime." International Journal of the Sociology of Law 19 (1991): 209–236.

Spiro, Leah Nathans, and Ronald Grover. "The Operator: An Inside Look at Ron Perelman's $5 Billion Empire." Business Week, 21 August 1995, 54–60.

Staw, Barry M., and Eugene Szwajkowski. "The Scarcity-Munificence Component of Organizational Environments and the Commission of Illegal Acts." Administrative Science Quarterly 20 (1975): 345–354.

Stearns, Lisa. "Fact and Fiction of a Model Enforcement Bureaucracy: The Labor Inspectorate of Sweden." British Journal of Law and Society 6 (1979): 1–23.

Stolberg, Sheryl. "Keating Trades His Business Suit for Prison Blues." Los Angeles Times, 21 September 1990, D1.

Strunk, Norman, and Fred Case. Where Deregulation Went Wrong: A Look at the Causes behind Savings and Loan Failures in the 1980s. Chicago: U.S. League of Savings Institutions, 1988.

Sutherland, Edwin H. "Is 'White Collar Crime' Crime?" American Sociological Review 10 (1945): 132–139.

————. *White Collar Crime.* New York: Dryden, 1949.

————. *White Collar Crime: The Uncut Version.* New Haven: Yale University Press, 1983.

————. "White-Collar Criminality." *American Sociological Review* 5 (1940): 1–12.

Tappan, Paul W. "Who Is the Criminal?" *American Sociological Review* 12 (1947): 96–102.

Thomas, Michael M. "The Greatest American Shambles." *New York Review of Books,* 31 January 1991, 30–35.

Thomas, Paulette, and Paul Duke. "Taxpayer Sinkhole: Federal Rescue Efforts for Failed Thrifts Are a Crisis in Themselves." *Wall Street Journal,* 13 January 1989, A1–A6.

Thornburgh, Dick. "Box Score on the Savings and Loans." Remarks by Attorney General of the United States, to the National Press Club, Washington, D.C., 25 July 1990.

Trillin, Calvin. "Zsa Zsa's Crowd Knows Why the Rich and Famous Deserve a Capital-Gains Cut." *Los Angeles Times,* 4 October 1989, B7.

Tucker, Eric. "Making the Workplace 'Safe' in Capitalism: The Enforcement of Factory Legislation in Nineteenth-Century Ontario." Paper presented at the annual meeting of the Canadian Law and Society Association, Hamilton, Ontario, 3–6 June 1987.

U.S. Congress. House. Committee on Banking, Finance, and Urban Affairs. *Effectiveness of Law Enforcement against Financial Crime.* Hearings before the Committee, Dallas, Texas. 101st Cong., 2d sess., 11 April 1990. Pt. 1.

————. *Effectiveness of Law Enforcement against Financial Crime.* Hearings before the Committee, Dallas, Texas. 101st Cong., 2d sess., 12 April 1990. Pt. 2.

————. *Investigation of Lincoln Savings and Loan Association.* Hearings before the Committee. 101st Cong., 1st sess., 1989. Pt. 2.

————. *The Savings and Loan Crisis.* Hearings before the Committee. 101st Cong., 1st sess., 12–13 January 1989.

————. *Savings and Loan Policies in the Late 1970s and 1980s*. Hearings before the Committee. 101st Cong., 2d sess., 1 and 3 October 1990.

————. *Silverado Banking, Savings and Loan Association*. Hearings before the Committee. 101st Cong., 2d sess., 22–23 May 1990. Pt. 1.

U.S. Congress. House. Committee on Banking, Finance, and Urban Affairs. Subcommittee on Financial Institutions Supervision, Regulation and Insurance. *Financial Institutions Reform, Recovery and Enforcement Act of 1989* (H.R. 1278). Hearings before the Subcommittee. 101st Cong., 1st sess., 1989. Pt. 1.

————. *When Are the Savings and Loan Crooks Going to Jail?* Hearings before the Subcommittee. 101st Cong., 2d sess., 28 June 1990.

U.S. Congress. House. Committee on Banking, Finance and Urban Affairs. Subcommittee on General Oversight and Investigation. *Findings of Booz Allen and Hamilton Study of FHLBB*. Hearings before the Subcommittee. 100th Cong., 1st sess., 14 May 1987.

U.S. Congress. House. Committee on Banking, Currency, and Housing. Subcommittee on Financial Institutions Supervision, Regulation and Insurance. *Failure of Citizens State Bank of Carrizo Springs, Texas, and Related Financial Problems*. Hearings before the Subcommittee. 94th Cong., 2d sess., 30 November–1 December 1976. Pt. 1.

U.S. Congress. House. Committee on Energy and Commerce. Subcommittee on Oversight and Investigations. *Failed Promises: Insurance Company Insolvencies*. A Report by the Subcommittee. 101st Cong., 2d sess., 7 February 1990.

U.S. Congress. House. Committee on Government Operations. *Combatting Fraud, Abuse, and Misconduct in the Nation's Financial Institutions: Current Federal Efforts Are Inadequate*. Report by the Committee. 100th Cong., 2d sess., 1988. H. Rept. 100–1088.

U.S. Congress. House. Committee on Government Operations. Subcommittee on Commerce, Consumer, and Monetary Affairs. *Adequacy of Federal Efforts to Combat Fraud, Abuse, and Misconduct in Federally*

Insured Financial Institutions. Hearings before the Subcommittee. 100th Cong., 1st sess., 19 November 1987.

—————. *Federal Efforts to Combat Fraud, Abuse, and Misconduct in the Nation's S&L's and Banks and to Implement the Civil and Criminal Provisions of FIRREA.* Hearings before the Subcommittee. 101st Cong., 2d sess., 14–15 March 1990.

—————. *Fraud and Abuse by Insiders, Borrowers, and Appraisers in the California Thrift Industry.* Hearings before the Subcommittee. 100th Cong., 1st sess., 13 June 1987.

U.S. Congress. House. Committee on Standards of Official Conduct. *Report of the Special Outside Counsel in the Matter of Speaker James C. Wright, Jr.* Report to the Committee by Special Outside Counsel, Richard J. Phelan. 101st Cong., 1st sess., 21 February 1989.

—————. *Statement of the Committee on Standards of Official Conduct in the Matter of Representative James C. Wright, Jr.* 101st Cong., 1st sess., 13 April 1989.

U.S. Congress. Senate. Committee on Banking, Housing, and Urban Affairs. *Nomination of M. Danny Wall.* Hearing before the Committee. 100th Cong., 1st sess., 18 June 1987.

—————. *Problems of the Federal Savings and Loan Insurance Corporation (FSLIC).* Hearings before the Committee. 101st Cong., 1st sess., 31 January and 2, 7, 9 February 1989. Pt. 1.

U.S. Congress. Senate. Committee on Banking, Housing, and Urban Affairs. Subcommittee on Consumer and Regulatory Affairs. *Efforts to Combat Criminal Financial Institution Fraud.* Hearing before the Subcommittee. 102d Cong., 2d sess., 6 February 1992.

U.S. Congress. Senate. Committee on the Judiciary. Subcommittee on Antitrust, Monopolies and Business Rights. *Impact of Restructuring of the S&L Industry: A Case Study on Bluebonnet Savings Bank.* Hearings before the Subcommittee. 101st Cong., 2d sess., 9 and 31 July 1990. Pt. 1.

—————. *Impact of Restructuring of the S&L Industry: A Case Study on Bluebonnet*

Savings Bank. Hearings before the Subcommittee. 101st Cong., 2d
sess., 6 August 1990. Pt. 2.

———. *Impact of Restructuring of the S&L Industry: A Case Study on Bluebonnet
Savings Bank*. Hearings before the Subcommittee. 101st Cong., 2d
sess., 11 September 1990. Pt. 3.

U.S. Department of Justice. Office of the Attorney General. *Attacking
Financial Institution Fraud. Fiscal Year 1992. (First Quarterly Report to Congress.)*

———. *Attacking Financial Institution Fraud. Fiscal Year 1992. (Second Quarterly Report to Congress.)*

U.S. Department of Justice. Bureau of Justice Statistics. *Compendium of
Federal Justice Statistics, 1988*. Washington, D.C.: U.S. Department of
Justice, Bureau of Justice Statistics, 1991.

U.S. General Accounting Office. "Bank Insider Activities: Insider
Problems and Violations Indicate Broader Management Deficiencies." Report to the Congress. GAO/GGD-94-88. March
1994.

———. "CPA Audit Quality: Failures of CPA Audits to Identify and
Report Significant Savings and Loan Problems." Report to the
Chairman, House Committee on Banking, Finance, and Urban
Affairs. GAO/AFMD-89-45. 2 February 1989.

———. "Failed Thrifts: Bank Board's 1988 Texas Resolutions."
Report to the Chairman, House Committee on Banking, Finance,
and Urban Affairs. GAO/GGD-89-59. 11 March 1989.

———. "Failed Thrifts: GAO's Analysis of Bank Board 1988 Deals."
Statement of Charles A. Bowsher, Comptroller General, before
the Senate Committee on Banking, Housing, and Urban Affairs.
GAO/T-GGD-89-11. 14 March 1989.

———. "Failed Thrifts: Internal Control Weaknesses Create an Environment Conducive to Fraud, Insider Abuse, and Related Unsafe Practices." Statement of Frederick D. Wolf, Assistant Comptroller General, before the Subcommittee on Criminal Justice,

House Committee on the Judiciary. GAO/T-AFMD-89-4. 22 March 1989.

————. "Financial Audit: Resolution Trust Corporation's 1995 and 1994 Financial Statements." Letter report. GAO/AIMD-96-123. 2 July 1996.

————. "Thrift Failures: Costly Failures Resulted from Regulatory Violations and Unsafe Practices." Report to the Congress. GAO/ AFMD-89-62. 16 June 1989.

————. "Thrift Industry Problems: Potential Demands on the FSLIC Insurance Fund." Report to the Congress. GAO/GGD-86-48BR. 12 February 1986.

————. "Thrift Industry Restructuring and the Net Worth Certificate Program." Report to the Congress. GAO/GGD-85-79. 24 September 1985.

Vaughan, Diane. "The Macro-Micro Connection in White-Collar Crime Theory." In *White-Collar Crime Reconsidered*, edited by Kip Schegel and David Weisburd, 124–145. Boston: Northeastern University Press, 1992.

Waldman, Michael. *Who Robbed America? A Citizen's Guide to the Savings & Loan Scandal.* New York: Random House, 1990.

Weisburd, David, Stanton Wheeler, Elin Waring, and Nancy Bode. *Crimes of the Middle Classes: White-Collar Offenders in the Federal Courts.* New Haven: Yale University Press, 1991.

Wheeler, Stanton, and Mitchell Lewis Rothman. "The Organization as Weapon in White Collar Crime." *Michigan Law Review* 80, no. 7 (1982): 1403–1426.

Wheeler, Stanton, David Weisburd, and Nancy Bode. "Sentencing the White-Collar Offender: Rhetoric and Reality." *American Sociological Review* 47 (October 1982): 641–659.

White, Lawrence J. *The S&L Debacle: Public Policy Lessons for Bank and Thrift Regulation.* New York: Oxford University Press, 1991.

Wiebe, Robert H. *The Search for Order, 1877–1920.* New York: Hill and Wang, 1967.

Yang, John E. "S&L Owner Suing to Get Back Assets from Bank Board." *Wall Street Journal*, 22 June 1987, 43.

Yeager, Peter. *The Limits of Law: The Public Regulation of Private Pollution*. Cambridge: Cambridge University Press, 1991.

————. "Managing Obstacles to Studying Corporate Offenses: An Optimistic Assessment. Paper presented at the annual meeting of the American Society of Criminology, Atlanta, November 1986.

INDEX

Index:	Carol Roberts
Compositor:	Maple-Vail Book Manufacturing Group
Text:	11.5/14 Joanna
Display:	Franklin Gothic
Printer and Binder:	Maple-Vail Book Manufacturing Group